FOREX TRADING
QuickStart Guide®

FOREX TRADING

QuickStart Guide®

The Simplified Beginner's Guide to
Successfully Swing and Day Trading the
Global Foreign Exchange Market Using
Proven Currency Trading Techniques

Troy Noonan

Editors: Bryan Basamanowicz, Marilyn Burkley
Cover Illustration and Design: Katie Donnachie, Copyright © 2022 by ClydeBank Media LLC
Interior Design & Illustrations: Katie Donnachie & Brittney Duquette, Copyright © 2022 by ClydeBank Media LLC

First Edition - Last Updated: July 4, 2023

ISBN: 9781636100128 (paperback) | 9781636100135 (hardcover) | 9781636100142 (ebook) | 9781636100159 (audiobook) | 9781636100265 (spiral bound)

Publisher's Cataloging-In-Publication Data
(Prepared by The Donohue Group, Inc.)

Names: Noonan, Troy, author.
Title: Forex trading QuickStart guide : the simplified beginner's guide to successfully swing and day trading the global foreign exchange market using proven currency trading techniques / Troy Noonan.
Other Titles: Forex trading Quick Start guide
Description: [Albany, New York] : ClydeBank Finance, [2022] | Series: QuickStart Guide | Includes bibliographical references and index.
Identifiers: ISBN 9781636100128 (paperback) | ISBN 9781636100135 (hardcover) | ISBN 9781636100265 (spiral bound) | ISBN 9781636100142 (ebook)
Subjects: LCSH: Foreign exchange. | Foreign exchange market. | Day trading (Securities)
Classification: LCC HG3851 .N66 2022 (print) | LCC HG3851 (ebook) | DDC 332.4/5--dc23

Library of Congress Control Number: 2021953473

Author ISNI: 0000 0004 8306 9010

For bulk sales inquiries, please visit www.go.quickstartguides.com/wholesale, email us at orders@clydebankmedia.com, or call 800-340-3069. Special discounts are available on quantity purchases by corporations, associations, and others.

OVER 850,000

READERS **LOVE** *QuickStart Guides.*

Really well written with lots of practical information. These books have a very concise way of presenting each topic and everything inside is very actionable!

— ALAN F.

The book was a great resource, every page is packed with information, but [the book] never felt overly-wordy or repetitive. Every chapter was filled with very useful information.

— CURTIS W.

I appreciated how accessible and how insightful the material was and look forward to sharing the knowledge that I've learned [from this book].

— SCOTT B.

After reading this book, I must say that it has been one of the best decisions of my life!

— ROHIT R.

This book is one-thousand percent worth every single dollar!

— HUGO C.

The read itself was worth the cost of the book, but the additional tools and materials make this purchase a better value than most books.

— JAMES D.

I finally understand this topic ... this book has really opened doors for me!

— MISTY A.

Contents

PART II – TOOLS OF THE TRADE

BEFORE YOU START READING, DOWNLOAD YOUR FREE DIGITAL ASSETS!

 **Ultimate Trade Analyzer**

 Broker Evaluation Checklist

 Trade Chart Visualization Tool

 HTChop Histogram Indicator

TWO WAYS TO ACCESS YOUR FREE DIGITAL ASSETS

Use the camera app on your mobile phone to scan the QR code or visit the link below and instantly access your digital assets.

or

go.quickstartguides.com/forex

 SCAN ME

 VISIT URL

Introduction

Foreign exchange is one of the most exciting markets for traders. It is open nearly 24 hours a day during the week and is far more liquid than other financial markets. Every day, the world's governments, banks, businesses, and traders buy and sell currencies. Some are simply looking to buy or sell goods in other countries. Others are hedging risks or speculating on major changes in the market. To me, it doesn't matter why they're placing trades, only that they are trading. Their activities create opportunities for me—and for you, if you learn the techniques of how to effectively trade in this lively market.

In fact, the activity in the forex markets presents profitable opportunities for the smallest of traders. The long open hours make it accessible to those who need flexibility. New traders can get started with relatively small amounts of initial capital and use leverage to build their accounts over time.

I've been trading for close to 30 years. I've seen technologies change, currencies consolidate, and new assets emerge. The fundamentals don't change, though. The best traders pay attention to the basics and take the time to do the work before they start to trade. I've learned from them, and I want to pass that discipline on to you.

My approach to trading is based on a straightforward idea: we need to win more than we lose; otherwise, we just lose. As traders, we win by implementing techniques, or trading methodologies, combined with "tradeplans" using clear parameters that we have backtested, forward tested, and practiced. It is this rigorous testing that allows us to prove to ourselves that our tradeplans will win more than 50% of the time. From there, we supplement our winning tradeplans with smart money management techniques—methods for determining how much we risk and when we risk it. Beyond that, we do nothing, absolutely nothing other than allow the trade to play out as it will. Believe it or not, that last part is the hardest to master. When I say we do nothing, I mean we don't get in our own way. Sounds easy enough, right? It's not. To be successful, you have to shut out the noise, abandon the emotion, and just execute. The reason for trading is to make money, that's it. If you can begin to accept that now, then your chances for success will grow. Again, it sounds easy. It's not.

I know you're ready to get started, but I hope you'll take the time to read through this book before you turn your hard-earned money over to a broker. Too many traders rush in without doing the work, and they do so to their detriment. The up-front work of reading books like this cover to cover, learning how to trade using a simulated account (not real money), and committing to the rigorous testing of your tradeplans before you deploy them is what will create your edge in the market. Most traders don't take the time to study, practice, and test. Consequently, they never learn how to properly trade. They jump in unprepared and without a plan. One of the main reasons I'm writing this book is to prevent you from making that mistake. I want you to be prepared, ready and determined to succeed.

Who I Am

I'm a California dude, through and through. I grew up here and love the climate, the beaches, and the mountains. I've taken to the culture, the laid-back hustle that goes on. People here work hard, but they also know how to have fun. Before I took up trading, I was ensconced in the music business. I played drums in a few rock bands, and I did event production on the jazz scene. As a musician, I understood that making music becomes more fun the better you are at it, and the only way to get better is to practice.

As with drumming, the path to becoming a real winning trader is long and arduous, but for me, the payoff that makes it all worthwhile is that it has given me the means and the flexibility to enjoy the rest of my life. While I continue to trade, teach trading, and write books about trading like this one, I also continue to play drums and hang out with my friends and family, all while enjoying the financial fruits of my labors.

My proficiencies in trading span the gamut from swing trades to day trades, from commodities futures to spot market trades in dented pizza sauce cans that fell off the forklift. I've done a lot of different things in life, but, for better or for worse, I can confidently say that there's nothing out there quite like forex. It's the largest financial market, open nearly 24 hours a day during the week (its hours are almost as nonstop as mine were when I was a professional musician). Forex is active, attracting banks, corporations, and individual traders. Great trading opportunities are simply among the by-products of the forex market's massive, nonstop activity. I've always loved this market. In fact, it was my experience in the forex market that altered my personal life forever—in a good way!

The Great Pound Short (and How It Changed My Life)

The story starts in 1991. That year, the British government joined the

European Exchange Rate Mechanism (ERM). This was the predecessor to the European Union's single currency, the euro. Under the ERM, the central banks of the European nations agreed to keep their exchange rates in tight ranges relative to the other European currencies. This reduction of exchange-rate risk would make it easier for businesses to buy and sell goods across the continent. The Bank of England needed to keep interest rates high in order to maintain the agreed-upon exchange rate against the German mark.

In 1992, George Soros, a hedge fund manager with a penchant for currency trading, noticed that this arrangement had created a problem for the British pound. It was overvalued relative to where it should have been based on the British economy. Soros started betting that the pound would fall in value, a process known as *short selling* in trader language. Over the summer of 1992, he built up a short position that was reported to be worth $10 billion.

On September 16, 1992, the British government realized that it could not meet the standards it had agreed to. The Bank of England announced that it would be leaving the ERM. The next day, the pound fell by 15% against the German mark, and Soros made an estimated $1 billion in profit, a trade that would infamously become known as the "trade that broke the Bank of England."

Almost 30 years later, this Soros trade remains a legend in the currency markets. Soros's firm had an army of analysts who were able to look at the political and economic situation in Europe and then draw up a trade with little downside risk. Had Soros been wrong, the pound's exchange rate would have been almost exactly the same as it was when he opened the short position. In the worst case, then, he would have broken even.

I was just beginning to trade forex myself at the time of Soros's famous short, and, by coincidence, my best reading of the charts at that time led me to place a similar trade, shorting the British pound against the US dollar. Because the world's financial markets are intertwined, the fall of the pound against the mark also led to its fall against the dollar. I was hoping to make a profit, but I wasn't expecting that particular trade to be the catalyst for a sequence of events that would change my life forever.

I made enough money on that trade to put my financial concerns aside for a while. I decided to hit the road. I took an extended sabbatical and backpacked my way through Europe. I couldn't bring my drums along, so one of my first purchases after the plane touched down was a set of bongos. As I traversed the Old Continent, I sat in with street musicians, joined open mic sessions in nightclubs, and even did a little bit of work in recording studios.

One summer evening in August, I was jamming with some musicians on the Ponte Vecchio in Florence, Italy. I struck up a friendship with a musician from Venezuela. We started playing around the local bars and taverns, offering our musical services in exchange for free beer. Imagine a Venezuelan mandolin player who barely spoke English, phonetically sounding out the lyrics to Beatles songs, accompanied by my pulsing bongo rhythms, while drunk travelers and locals alike danced on the tables. It was amazing. The travel bug sank its teeth into me. I had an exhilarating sense of total freedom. I loved that I could explore the world and meet new people, all because of that one forex trade I made.

Months later, back home in San Francisco, I received a fax (remember those?) from my Venezuelan musician friend. He was inviting me to come for an extended visit to Venezuela. The plan was to hang out with his band, practice Venezuelan rhythms, and explore his beautiful country.

This inspired me to later coin the "Backpack Trader" brand, which emphasized freedom and mobility (this was a few years after my Venezuela trip, during the age of the internet café). I became accustomed to traveling at my own discretion, while leaving a trail of (hopefully) winning trades.

I soon found myself touching down at Maiquetia Airport outside Caracas, along the beautiful Venezuelan Caribbean coast. Within 24 hours of my arrival, I met the woman I would marry, just eight months later. As I write this book, we are looking forward to celebrating our 26th anniversary.

This story offers three lessons. First, forex trading can be profitable. Second, trading can give you a level of freedom limited only by your own imagination. Third, you can never know for certain how a trade is going to end. George Soros made the same bet on the British pound that I did. He made billions of dollars. While I didn't come close to a Soros-level payday (I made only thousands, not billions), I did make enough to do some serious traveling and experience my first true taste of absolute freedom. In the end, he got billions, and I got a beautiful wife and two amazing kids!

Trading, Teaching, and Learning Forex

When I'm trading forex, I am in my home office with 12 computer monitors. Several have forex price charts going, and others show some of the other markets I trade, futures and equities. I have dedicated monitors just for entering trades and others for doing trade analysis. I am often calling trades in a live trading room; anyone who is in the room can see what I'm doing and follow along. This is one of the ways that I teach people how to trade my strategies.

This book is another.

Trading has been fantastic for me. I've made a great career that allows me to support my family and gives me the flexibility to enjoy family life. Heck, you could even go so far as to say that trading gave me my family. I enjoy the challenge of figuring out new trade methodologies, and I delight in helping all kinds of traders, beginner and experienced alike, find success.

Although I do trade other assets (and have written about them in *Day Trading QuickStart Guide*), forex is one of my favorites to this day. The market is so large, active, and liquid that it offers many opportunities to find trades that work. Trading in the forex market is an essential component of my trading career. I am so excited to introduce you to the challenges, joys, and pitfalls of this lively and gargantuan marketplace.

Trading Is War. Don't Be a Casualty.

Trading isn't for everyone. It requires mastery of psychology, risk, and methodology. Learning to trade is challenging. It will test your nerves and your patience. If you are to succeed, then you have to put in a good amount of work up front, robust preliminary study and analysis. It's what I often refer to as the "ditch digging" of good trading. You have to build the foundation before you can lay the pipe, and you have to lay the pipe before you can build the road. And you have to build the road if you want to go anywhere. The more care and effort you put into your preproduction work, the more fruitful your result will be when you go into full production. When you remember that "full production" in trading means risking your hard-earned cash in the live markets, then the importance of learning to trade the right way becomes clear.

Many active forex traders (and potential forex traders) want to understand the role that the forex market plays, not just in the world of trading, but in the global economy. I know many of you are anxious to set foot in the arena and place your first real-money trade, and while I appreciate your enthusiasm, I do want to issue a very serious caveat:

Because it is easy to enter the forex market, a lot of people do. The problem is that the majority of them do not take the time to learn how to trade successfully. To produce good trading results, you have to do the preproduction work. A lot of people don't want to hear that. They rush in with no foundation and little knowledge. These folks then find out that it is just as easy to crash out of the forex market as it was to enter it. I'd rather see you invest the time than lose the money.

Meet Two Traders

Harvey is an engineer. He's really smart. But because he knows so much about engineering, he thinks he knows a lot about everything. As much as he hates to admit it, he has a big ego, which results in his trying to control everything. It's difficult to tell him things because, as he will say, "I already know that." He also thinks all problems can be solved by thinking them through and engineering an answer, even things that can't be controlled or solved.

Trish is a long-haul trucker. She dropped out of high school due to life circumstances, but now she's studying to pass her GED. She enjoys the road and considers truck driving a good way to see the country. Trucking has taught her a lot, and one main thing in particular: the importance of patience. Without it, she would never survive as a trucker. She's able to pay attention for long periods of time, waiting until the roads or traffic call for a quick reaction. She also knows how to go with the flow. She knows that if she is stuck in gridlock, her only choice is to wait it out, or to be flexible enough to change her route on those rare occasions when that is possible. She can't change the weather or the road or traffic conditions, but she can adapt her driving so that she and her cargo arrive safely.

Guess what? Trish will be the better trader. Harvey believes he is always in full control and therefore thinks he can control the markets. In fact, he believes he is smarter than the market. He doesn't see the need to learn how to trade properly or limit his risks because he "already knows how"—or so he believes. Trish, on the other hand, knows that the only thing she can control is herself. She wants to learn how to trade safely and what to do when things go wrong, because she knows they *will* go wrong sometimes.

I'll come back to Harvey and Trish a lot in the book. It's important to learn how to trade, but it is also important to understand how best to approach the markets. Harvey wants to be in control. Trish understands that the name of the game is response. Trish's commitment to preproduction work provides her with valuable experience. By taking time up front to learn how to plan, place, and analyze trades, she will end up keeping her wits about her when the market is in turmoil. We don't have to control the markets to be successful. In fact, it is this irrational quest for control that is the folly and downfall of many would-be traders. Engineers, in my experience, often struggle to find trading success.

Traders need to learn how to respond to changes in the market. The way to learn is through practice, commitment, and experience. If you're an engineer, like Harvey, or you just think like one, I can teach you to trade as long as you accept that you need to learn, and as long as you have enough humility to realize there are things that cannot be controlled. Don't be discouraged, just maintain perspective.

Let's Get Started

The purpose of this book is to teach you how to trade successfully. Unlike the countless companies online that falsely promise "quick-and-easy" trading systems, I'm going to spare no effort in teaching you how to do the essential preproduction work that will form the bedrock of your rewarding trading career.

NOTE

Please don't misunderstand me. I don't mean to broadly disparage online trading services. Some are indeed good companies. There are some that truly will put your best interests first, but unfortunately, they are few and far between. Many are just out to make a quick buck, selling you a dream that is unrealistic and will always remain just a dream. It is my intention to help you take a realistic and responsible approach to trading. Nothing against dreaming (or dreamers), but success is sweeter.

Here's the game plan. This book will help you understand the forex market, then choose a broker and a trading platform. Next, we will spend some time learning how to read price charts, use indicators, and develop tradeplans. Only then do I want you to enter the market, using simulated trading at first to practice placing trades. As you do this, you will collect data so you can refine and prove your tradeplan.

NOTE

In several places throughout the book, I include an "In the Trading Room" walk-through to show you how I apply the material you're learning to actual trades.

It may be a while before you start trading with real money. That's okay. I want you to be a successful long-term trader. I have used these techniques to train hundreds, if not thousands, of other traders over the years, all over the world. I have found that success comes by taking the time to learn the basics, doing thorough preproduction, and simply repeating what works. Trading can give you great freedom in life, but you are also committing money up front. That's why you should work to get it right from the very first step. It's far easier to develop good habits and best practices from the start than to find out the expensive way that you have to unlearn bad habits. Just ask Harvey!

Are you ready?

Chapter by Chapter

» **Part I: Exploring the Forex Market**

» Chapter 1, "The Great Big World of Financial Markets," provides a broad survey of modern global finance. We'll explore the spectrum of popular financial instruments and the markets they populate, concluding with a formal introduction to the largest of all financial markets, the foreign exchange (forex) market.

» Chapter 2, "Understanding How the Forex Market Works," covers the history of foreign exchange from precious metals to digital currencies. We'll also introduce you to the roles played by participants in this massive global enterprise, from the central banks to the retail traders, people like me who study and capitalize on price action trends.

» Chapter 3, "Currencies and Lot Sizes," gets right to the point by covering the nature of currency pairs. Currencies always trade in pairs, because traders have to sell one in order to buy another. The most liquid pairs are the major pairs, representing the free-floating currencies from the largest economies, such as the United States, the European Union, and Japan. Some traders find opportunities in pairs from smaller and developing nations. Others choose pairs that are active when they are trading, which is easy in this global market. For example, someone trading when it's evening in the United States may be more interested in trading pairs that involve Asian currencies, because that is when the Tokyo market is active.

» Chapter 4, "Factors that Affect Currencies," looks at the forces that change forex prices. Supply and demand for currency is driven by supply and demand for goods and services, government policies, political decisions, and even natural disasters. All the events in the world play out in the forex market, and that creates opportunities for traders. Although successful traders do not need to understand and analyze geopolitics and macroeconomics, it helps to be aware of factors that can cause trades to be in your favor or swing away from you.

» Chapter 5, "Determining If Forex Trading Is Right for You," introduces the practicalities of being a trader. Whether you do it full time or part time, trading is a business activity and should be approached as such. Trading is great for people who are independent and want flexibility. It also requires discipline and mastery. As much as I love trading, I know it's not for everyone.

» **Part II: Tools of the Trade**

» Chapter 6, "Choosing a Broker and a Trading Platform," delves further into the practicalities of trading. Individual traders need to have an account with a forex brokerage firm, and they need a software platform to analyze and enter trades. There are a lot of great companies out there, and there are a lot of scams. Forex is a decentralized market, meaning each broker "makes" its own market. They set their own prices. In most cases, the broker is not your friend. The information in this chapter will help you make smart choices.

» Chapter 7, "Using Technical Analysis When Buying and Selling Pairs," is an introduction to one of the primary research systems used by forex traders. Technical analysis involves looking at how information about the supply and demand for currency pairs plays out in the price charts, which are nothing more than a reflection of price action. These charts help traders identify where to place trades, where to close them out, and where to set stop losses and profit targets. Traders study charts. Here, you will learn the basic vocabulary of technical analysis and the theories that govern it.

» Chapter 8, "Understanding Chart Patterns," gets into technical analysis in more depth. It introduces basic chart patterns that show, with a certain degree of accuracy, what might happen next. This helps traders identify profitable trades and avoid unprofitable ones. With the information in this chapter, new traders can start watching charts and looking for entry and exit points, a key step in learning to be a successful forex trader.

» Chapter 9, "Understanding Indicators," is an even deeper look at technical analysis. Indicators are calculations and overlays on price charts that give traders more information. They are like salt; a little bit of work with indicators makes trading more productive, but too many indicators ruin the recipe. This chapter introduces indicators, discusses some that I find to be especially useful in forex, and gives advice on how to use them effectively.

» Chapter 10, "Applying the SMA Indicators In the Trading Room," features two detailed walk-throughs of trades where I utilize a 20 SMA on a five-minute and a 15-minute chart.

» Chapter 11, "Using Trading Systems," works on putting the components of a trade together and evaluating its performance. Some traders find that subscription services and trade room memberships help. Others prefer to develop and refine their own systems. This chapter has information to help both types of traders improve their trading in the face of ever-changing financial markets.

» Chapter 12, "Using Dynamic Systems In the Trading Room," features detailed explanations and walk-throughs of two trading techniques I use frequently, the *Snapshot Trading Technique* and the *1-2-3 Setup.*

» **Part III: Increasing Your Chances for Success**

» Chapter 13, "Putting Risk and Money Management to Work for You," talks about setting loss limits and determining position sizes, among other things. These factors will do more to improve trading results than anything. It is imperative that you understand how to properly manage your risk if you want to be a long-term trader. In trading, a relatively small edge will become exponentially powerful if it is allowed to work over lots of trades, but only if your risk and money management is properly included. Cutting losers before they do significant damage to your account will let the winners do their magic. And yes, losing trades are inevitable, but good risk and money management can curtail the harm and keep you moving in the right direction.

» Chapter 14, "Managing Trades In the Trading Room," offers a protracted study of "exhaustion levels" and the way we can use them to our benefit when managing our trades.

» Chapter 15, "Trading and Digging Ditches," emphasizes the three components of successful long-term trading. These are psychology, risk and money management, and trade methodology. Of the three, psychology is the most important. Doubt, fear, and greed have brought down more traders than a bad decision on the direction of the euro. The processes in this chapter will teach you how to master your trade psychology by teaching you how to trade. Your understanding will turn your psychology into a source of strength, rather than the detriment that it is for most traders. Once you have a foundation in place, you can build on it to turn your trading activities into a true business venture.

EXPLORING THE FOREX MARKET

| 1 |

The Great Big World of Financial Markets

Chapter Overview
» The role of the markets
» Beyond stocks and bonds
» How markets work
» From small to huge

An investment in knowledge pays the best interest.
— BENJAMIN FRANKLIN

Some of you may be eager to jump headfirst into the trenches of actual forex trading. I understand. I'm the same way. That said, I think it's important that I at least offer a summary-level survey of the underlying asset you will be using to make money as a trader. For this reason, I've included two chapters here at the beginning of the book that will explore the anatomy, utility, and history of global finance. If you are absolutely determined to move straight into the nuts and bolts of placing trades in the forex market, then I advise you to skip ahead now to chapter 3.

Financial markets make the world go round, and foreign exchange is their fuel. We know there is a strong link between financial market development and economic growth. There are some exceptions, but when a country's financial markets are doing well, its economy tends to also do well. That's because financial markets and financial institutions, when working properly, are effective in channeling money to where it's needed, whether to a business that needs money in order to expand production or to a community that needs to build a new fire station. Those infusions of cash—which, of course, come at a cost to the borrowers—help to keep the economy moving and communities growing and operating effectively.

When financial markets and institutions fail, it comes at a cost to entire countries and, in some cases, impacts the economy worldwide. An economic crash can occur for a variety of reasons; you'll read more about that later. But when the crash is serious enough and lasts long enough, as was the case after the stunning collapse of the U.S. stock market in October 1929 that resulted in the Great Depression, it can take many years for an economy to recover. As a result, individuals, communities, businesses, financial institutions, and societies as a whole suffer.

With stakes that high, it makes good sense for individuals to understand how financial markets work and why they're important in keeping a society functioning and healthy. So, before we dive into forex trading, let's dig a little deeper into the role of the financial markets, take a look at some different types of investment vehicles, and get an understanding of how the markets work.

What Are Financial Markets, and Why Do We Need Them?

Markets are places where we buy and sell things, but different types of markets are organized differently and have different functions. So let's first take a look at two types of markets that you may be familiar with: supermarkets and flea markets.

A supermarket is a place where people come together to buy and sell food. The sellers are all of the different food manufacturers and distributors who work with the store to put their items on the shelves, set prices, and run special promotions. The buyers are the customers who come into the store to compare the different brands and prices, make their choices and purchases, and then leave. The store operator provides the space to bring the buyers and sellers together and manages the prices and inventories.

A flea market is a place where people come together to buy and sell just about anything (although most items are miscellaneous personal belongings). The flea market operator charges individual vendors for space at the market and may charge shoppers for admission. But beyond that, the buyers and sellers negotiate their own deals.

Bank CEOs like to talk about financial supermarkets, but the truth is, most financial markets resemble flea markets. A financial market is a place where firms and individuals enter into contracts to sell or buy a specific product such as a stock, bond, or futures contract. People who want to sell list their offerings, and people who want to buy check what's available. Regardless of what is being exchanged, or traded, buyers look to buy at the lowest price they can, and sellers want to sell at the highest price they can.

Financial markets come in many flavors, including the *stock market*, *bond market*, *money market*, *commodities market*, *derivatives market*, and *forex market*. Then there are related markets, such as those for real estate and collectibles. You'll learn a little bit about each of them later in this chapter. For now, let's have a closer look at what financial markets do and why they are important.

Main Functions of Financial Markets

If you research the primary function of financial markets, you'll find a lot of different opinions. Generally speaking, the markets are credited with enabling buyers and sellers to easily trade financial holdings. This makes them important to the economies of the countries in which they are located because they facilitate the flow of assets and ensure that resources get allocated properly.

Within that broader purpose, there are several main functions.

The first is price determination. Financial markets help to determine the *market price* of various financial instruments. The market price is the most recent price at which a good or service has been bought or sold. It can remain steady for long periods of time or can fluctuate frequently and rapidly due to various factors. Market price is largely determined by supply and demand within the market. There is an economic theory that asserts that market price occurs when the supply of a product or service meets the demand for it. If the supply increases and demand decreases, the market price for the product or service will decline. On the other hand, if demand increases and there's not enough supply to meet that demand, buyers tend to be willing to pay more.

fig. 1

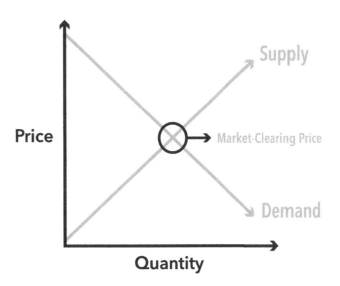

If you took economics, you're all too familiar with the graph in figure 1. If you didn't, here's an explanation: The supply line shows how much of a good someone is willing to sell at a given price. The higher the price, the more of a product people are willing to supply. The demand line is the opposite. Buyers prefer low prices, so the higher the price, the less they are willing to buy. The point where the lines cross is known as the market-clearing price. That's the price where the buyers receive the quantity they want for the price they are willing to pay, and the sellers receive the price they want for the amount of the thing they are willing to supply.

The *law of supply and demand* is not only an economic theory, but also just the way things work.

We saw an example of supply and demand in action when US oil prices turned negative during the worldwide coronavirus outbreak. Starting in March and extending into April 2020, the price of US oil went on a steady decline as travel restrictions were put in place and people sheltered at home to help avoid the spread of COVID-19. That was amid fears that the worldwide economy would see its greatest decline since the Great Depression as production slowed or halted, companies closed, and millions and millions of people lost their jobs. Producers continued to turn out near-record levels of crude oil, despite warnings from analysts who predicted the coronavirus would result in a screeching halt in demand. The analysts were right. Air travel had come to an almost complete halt and, despite low gas prices, consumers weren't buying. And some oil producers ran out of space to store their excess supplies. As a result, they had to pay buyers to take the excess oil, resulting in a negative price for the commodity. Oil prices on April 20 fell as low as minus $37.63 a barrel, according to a report in *The Guardian*. The price of crude oil bounced back for the June contract, selling for more than $30 a barrel as energy firms cut production and travel picked up after restrictions were modified.

Another pivotal function of financial markets (and a key to economic success) is *mobilization of funds*. Money within the economy needs to be mobile, so it can reach the areas where it is most beneficial. To have money sitting idle is the equivalent of putting all your savings under the mattress. You'll know the money is there, but you'll have no opportunity to increase its value via smart investing. Through mobilization of funds, financial markets help to direct the flow of savings and investment in the economy, to the advantage of both borrowers and lenders. Money gets to where it needs to be, whether that's an individual borrowing money to buy a house, a business borrowing to open a new production plant, or a school district that needs more money than local taxes provide to build a new school. That's good for the borrower and the overall economy.

Jessie, who borrowed money to buy the house, not only acquires a piece of property but needs to buy furniture, carpets, and other items to make it into a home. A couple of years after she moves in, she decides to hire someone to build a deck in the backyard. She also contracts with a landscaping firm to do yard work. She's pumping money into the economy, which helps to keep it strong.

The school district that borrowed money to build the new school experiences an influx of new families as a result. Those families not only start paying taxes to the school district, but they buy a home there, shop for food and clothing, and patronize local restaurants. The business that borrowed money to build the new production plant hires 60 additional workers, who then have money to spend on cars, houses, and college tuition.

Meanwhile, the lenders of all that money are rewarded because they charge interest on the money they loan and end up getting more back than they loaned out. Effective mobilization of funds is a win-win for the borrower and the lender, and it benefits the overall economy.

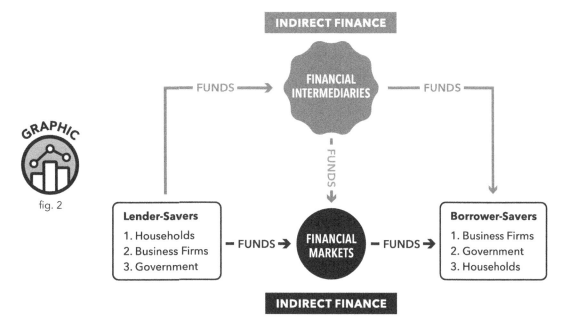

fig. 2

Figure 2 shows how funds flow through the financial system. The financial intermediaries at the top are the organizations that manage funds for people, such as banks, hedge funds, and mutual funds. At the bottom left corner are the people who have money to save, invest, and lend out to others, such as households, businesses, and governments in this country and around the world. These funds flow to intermediaries (indirect finance) or directly through the financial markets (direct finance) so that other households, businesses, and governments have the funds they need for whatever projects they choose to pursue.

Liquidity is another key market function and refers to the ease with which an asset can be bought or sold in the market at a price that reflects its real value. The most liquid asset is cash, which can easily be converted into other assets. So if you want to buy something, say a new racing bike, the easiest way to do so is to pay for it with cash.

In financial markets, a high level of liquidity occurs when there is a substantial level of trading activity and high supply and demand for an asset. That makes it easier for assets to be traded, as there is a large number of buyers and sellers. A slow-trading market with just a few traders is considered to have low liquidity.

The liquidity of the market is important because it affects how quickly you can open and close positions. Generally, a more liquid market carries less risk because it is likely that someone will be willing to take the other side of a given position. That makes the market attractive to investors and speculators and improves market conditions. And, when assets are being quickly bought and sold, a seller is likely to find a buyer without having to reduce the price of the asset, and a buyer won't have to pay an inflated price to obtain an asset.

In financial terms, someone who owns an asset is "long" it and someone who sells an asset is "short" it. For example, in the commodities market, someone who sells cattle futures is "short cattle futures" and someone who buys cattle futures is "long cattle futures." In many markets, it's possible to sell an asset short by borrowing it and selling it in the hope that you'll be able to buy it back at a lower price to pay back the loan. Other assets have built-in long and short positions. If you take out a mortgage to buy a house, you are long real estate and short cash.

Liquidity makes it easy to turn assets into cash and vice versa. The easier, faster, and cheaper it is to conduct a transaction, the more liquid its financial market is. Figure 3 summarizes it all.

fig. 3

One reason the markets work is that they are accessible. Without financial markets, it would be difficult for traders to do what they do, which is trade. Someone wanting to sell an asset would not easily be able to do so, and the same would apply to someone wanting to buy an asset. The way our financial markets work is that everyone with some basic knowledge, good common sense, the right mindset, and some money they can afford to invest can be engaged in the markets. Brokers do basic screening before you open an account to ensure that you are who you say you are (a process known as Know Your Customer) and that you have the funds to cover the cost of any trades that you place. After that, the markets are all yours.

In fact, the markets work so well that we say that they are "efficient." For a financial market to be efficient, its current asset prices must be based on all available information. And that information must be available to everyone at the same time. The *efficient market hypothesis* (EMH), sometimes called the efficient market theory, states that assets bought and sold on exchanges always trade at their fair values. That's important because it means investors cannot buy assets that are undervalued or sell assets for prices higher than what they're worth. If that's the case, then investors cannot beat the market (which means earning returns that are higher than what the market as a whole achieves).

There are certainly debates over exactly how efficient the markets are. The consensus is that in the long run, efficiency rules. In the short run, there are pockets of profitable inefficiency for traders to find. By finding and exploiting these inefficiencies, traders force the market back into efficiency.

In the long run, we are all dead.

— JOHN MAYNARD KEYNES

All these factors keep money moving through the economy in ways that encourage the accumulation of *capital*. That means capital is available for businesses and other entities to borrow and use to grow. When capital is effectively allocated and put to work, it contributes to increased production and an improved overall economy.

How Financial Markets Help Ensure the Smooth Operation of Capitalist Economies

Financial markets that are healthy and operating efficiently make it easy for buyers and sellers to trade assets. They also encourage the accumulation of capital, which ensures that money will be available to businesses and entrepreneurs looking to expand or start a new venture. Governments, individuals, local groups, and others also have access to capital through the financial markets. They can find funds to back the purchases and investments they make.

Well-regulated, transparent, accessible, efficient markets benefit businesses, workers, investors, and society at large. The targeted, flexible, and efficient deployment of capital helps to keep an economy healthy and operating smoothly. It ensures that the forces of supply and demand are in order so that prices remain steady and consumers can get the goods and services they need.

One thing that's changed in the past few decades is the ease with which people can participate in the financial markets that affect them. The cost of investing has decreased significantly, largely due to advances in technology that make it possible for increasing numbers of people to access financial markets. Lower costs lead to higher levels of market participation, which in turn make the markets fairer and ensure that investors get the best possible prices when buying and selling assets. And, with an array of diversified, low-cost investment choices at their disposal, opportunities for investors abound.

Types of Financial Markets

There are several types of markets within the broad category of "the financial market." And while we tend to think of financial markets as modern innovations, the truth is that they have been around for a long time. Almost as soon as people began to do business, they organized markets; archeologists have found evidence that there were markets in Mesopotamia more than 6,000 years ago. Commodities markets flourished in China and Japan more than 2,000 years ago. The first known securities market systems were put in place in Venice in the 1300s and progressed throughout the centuries that followed. The New York Stock Exchange, known as the NYSE or "Big Board," was founded in 1792 and is the oldest stock exchange in the United States.

Over time, other types of markets have emerged, creating diverse means for investors. Let's have a brief look at some of these markets and how they work.

Stock Market

The stock market is a group of organized markets and exchanges where traders buy and sell *stock*, which is shares of publicly held companies. Companies issue stock to raise money that allows them to grow and become more profitable. When you buy a company's stock, you actually are buying a piece of the company. If the company is wildly successful and profitable, you get to share in that success because you are a shareholder. On the other hand, if the company fails, you are a partner in the failure.

The two main types of stock are *common stock* and *preferred stock*. There are other categories of stock within common and preferred, but we will focus on just those two main types. If you own common stock, you own a share in the company's profit (or loss) and, as a shareholder, you have the right to vote on matters of corporate policy.

Owners of preferred stock typically receive a fixed dividend. A *dividend* is a payment companies make on a regular basis to owners of their stock as a way of distributing profits to investors. Owners of common stock may or may not receive dividends. If you own preferred stock, you are not entitled to voting rights.

There are advantages and disadvantages to owning common and preferred stock, and investors should consider factors such as their age and investing goals when deciding which to buy.

GRAPHIC

fig. 4

	COMMON STOCK	PREFERRED STOCK
PROS	• Potential for higher long-term return • Voting rights	• Dividends are typically higher, fixed, and guaranteed • Share price experiences less volatility • Preferred shareholders are more likely to recover at least part of their investment in case of bankruptcy
CONS	• Dividends, if available, are often lower, variable, and not guaranteed • Stock price and dividend may experience more volatility • More likely to recover at least part of their investment in case of bankruptcy	• Lower long-term growth potential • No voting rights in most cases
BEST FOR	Investors looking for long-term growth	Investors looking for income

Stock is generally bought and sold on a ***stock exchange***. Over the years, there has been an enormous amount of consolidation among the stock exchanges as well as the development of completely new ones. Most trading now takes place outside of the two remaining traditional exchanges, the New York Stock Exchange (NYSE) and the National Association of Securities Dealers Automated Quotation System (Nasdaq). The NYSE and the Nasdaq remain formidable players, however.

Stock exchanges host markets within which stocks and other securities can be traded. The exchanges are essentially businesses and they make money in various ways, including by charging initial and annual fees to the companies listed on them.

Stock market indexes, also known as indices, are used to measure the performance of the stock market on any given day. An index is a group of securities that is collectively used as an indicator of performance. That group of securities can represent the entire stock market or just a segment of it. There are about 5,000 US indexes, but the three that are most broadly followed are the Standard & Poor's 500 (S&P 500), the Dow Jones Industrial Average, and the Nasdaq Composite. Other countries have their own indexes to track their markets, and some indexes combine the market performance of several different countries.

A ***broad-based index*** represents the performance of the entire market, while an ***industry index*** concentrates on one segment of the stock market, such as technology stocks. It's a good idea to look at several indexes to get a more accurate reading of market performance. It's also smart to keep your eye on international indexes such as the Financial Times Stock Exchange 100 Index (FTSE 100) or the Nikkei 225, because you can learn a lot about markets in other countries by watching the indexes. That, of course, is especially important in forex trading.

Market indexes give you a way to compare how your collection of stocks, or ***stock portfolio***, is performing in relationship to the performance of the market. The S&P 500 is a good standard for investors in US stocks. If you hold a diversified portfolio of shares in large US companies, your performance should be similar or, hopefully, even better than that of the S&P 500. Index mutual funds and exchange-traded funds will match the index performance almost exactly. If your performance beats the index, you may have bragging rights—or you may have invested in stocks that have greater risk or are otherwise different from the stocks in the index.

Bond Market

The **bond market** is a marketplace on which investors can buy **debt securities**, which are securities that represent borrowed funds that must be repaid. The bond market is also known as the debt market, fixed-income market, or credit market.

Bonds are the most commonly used type of **lending investment**, a type of investment in which you loan your money with the understanding that you'll get back your principal, along with interest, in a specified amount of time. There are numerous types of bonds, including municipal bonds, corporate bonds, revenue bonds, general obligation bonds, savings bonds, and others.

The thing to understand about bonds is that when interest rates go up, the value of your bond goes down, and when interest rates go down, the value of your bond goes up.

Let's say you're holding a 10-year government bond with a face value of $1,000 that pays 4% interest. When the bond matures, you will get the $1,000 back. In the meantime, you will receive interest payments of $20 every six months ($40, or 4% of $1,000, each year). If the interest rates goes up to 6% and you sell that bond, investors will want to pay less than $1,000 for it because it pays only $40 in annual interest, and they could spend $1,000 on a new bond paying $60 per year. If the interest rate drops to 2%, however, you'll still earn 4% interest on the bond. That will make it more valuable than the new bonds coming on the market, so a buyer would pay more than $1,000. The point to understand is that there is an inverse relationship between the price of a bond and the yield it pays. As the yield goes up, the value of the bond goes down, and vice versa.

Governments generally issue bonds to raise money either to pay for infrastructure projects or to pay down debt. Publicly traded companies typically issue bonds to finance expansion of facilities or products or to be able to continue operating. New debt is issued on the **primary market**, while existing debt is sold on the **secondary market** through brokers or other third parties. For example, if you bought the government bond in the example above direct from the US Treasury (www.treasurydirect.gov), you would be buying from the primary market. If you then sold it to another investor, that would take place through your brokerage firm and would be on the secondary market.

Just as the S&P 500 tracks the performance of stocks, indexes such as the S&P 500 Bond Index or the Bloomberg Barclays US Aggregate Bond Index track how bonds perform over a given period of time.

With the possible exception of the US government bond market, the bond market is less liquid than the stock market, because many bond investors buy and hold their bonds to collect the interest payments.

Money Market

When you hear about the *money market*, chances are you think of a *money market account* or *money market funds*. And you would be correct, because those are retail versions of the larger money market. At the wholesale level, the money market is a huge network of lending and borrowing cash in a variety of currencies. Borrowing and lending generally occurs among financial institutions such as banks, governments, manufacturers, and other large entities. These are obligations that come due in a short amount of time, as little as overnight and generally less than thirty days.

Money market securities include commercial paper, which are overnight loans to major corporations; jumbo CDs, bank certificates of deposit that are too large to qualify for deposit insurance and so have higher interest rates; bonds that are going to mature in the next thirty days; and inter-bank loans.

Having these short-term funds available is critical to the efficient operation of large organizations. For example, a major multinational company needs to have enough money in its accounts to meet payroll each payday. With all of its money flowing all over the world, it might not know for sure that it will have the precise amount needed. Borrowing money for a day or two in the commercial paper market can eliminate that risk. On the retail side, investors buy money markets as a form of savings account. They lack federal insurance but often pay higher interest. The short time frame means that traders have a pretty good idea of what is going to happen. For example, global war might break out in the next 30 years. Will it break out this week? Probably not.

When traders in the money market are caught unaware, though, the reverberations are scary. In the financial crisis of 2008, the money market collapsed so thoroughly that General Electric nearly missed making payroll. It suddenly seemed too risky to lend money to one of the largest companies in the world for two days.

Money market *funds* are mutual funds that are invested in money market securities and **Treasury bills**. A goal of money market funds is to never lose money and to maintain a **net asset value** (NAV) of $1. The NAV of a fund is the value reached when the fund's liabilities are deducted from its assets. In exchange for this safety, the rate of return is usually lower than on other types of investments. If the NAV of a money market fund falls below $1, the investor will lose some money, but that rarely happens. The last time there was risk of that level was in the 2008 financial crisis.

Interest rates on individual money market accounts and money market funds vary, but they tend to be lower than on other types of investments but higher than on insured bank accounts. Think of money markets as savings accounts. You deposit your money in the account and earn interest on it. Some money market accounts even allow you to use debit cards or checks to access your funds.

Some money market accounts based in banks are insured by the **Federal Deposit Insurance Corporation** (FDIC), an entity that provides insurance to depositors in US banks. Money market accounts based in credit unions are insured by the **National Credit Union Administration**, the FDIC's counterpart. Insured money market accounts pay lower interest rates than uninsured ones. Uninsured money market funds are generally considered to be safe investments, but there is no government backing should something go wrong.

The best traders have a walking-away fund, so that they can take a break from the markets when their head is not in the game or the markets are moving against them. A money market account is a decent place to keep this money so that it is accessible. The return might not be great, but neither is the risk. You can set up a "sweep" with your broker, which will automatically move some profits from your trading account into a money market account. That way, you build some savings without even thinking about it.

Derivatives Market

The derivatives market is where **derivatives** are traded. There is a lot of argument about the size of the market, but to be sure, it is huge. Some analysts estimate the value of the derivatives market at more than $1 quadrillion on the high end. Other analysts claim that it's nowhere near that large.

So what are derivatives? Simply put, derivatives are financial contracts that are dependent on an underlying asset or group of assets to determine their value. Typically, the assets that determine the value of derivatives are stocks, bonds, currencies (including cryptocurrencies), commodities, or market indexes. Traders enter the derivatives market hoping to earn profits by speculating on the future values of the underlying assets.

There are several common types of derivatives:

» **Options** give you the right, but not the obligation, to do something. The most common options that traders come across are options on common stock. A **call option** gives you the right to buy an asset on a date in the future at a price determined today. For example, you buy a call option to buy shares of XYZ stock at $45 in three months. In three months, say the stock is at $55; you can exercise the call to buy the stock at $45 and then turn around and sell it at $55 for a quick profit. Many options can be exercised before the expiration date, giving option holders even more flexibility. If the stock goes down to $40, you can just let the option expire unexercised because it has no value to you. The opposite of a call is a **put option**, which gives you the right but not the obligation to sell an asset in the future at a price determined today. Put options are profitable when the price of the stock falls. Many traders use call options as a way to play the stock market without committing as much cash. Others write options, taking the other side in exchange for the premium. Options go up and down in value and can be traded like one would trade shares of stock. You can control the asset in a way that gives you unlimited upside potential while limiting your risk to the cost of the option. When an option is losing value because the security it represents is also declining in value, then you can sell your option and recapture some of its value. In other words, you are not required to hold the option until it expires.

» **Futures contracts** come with the obligation to buy or sell an asset in the future. A long futures position requires you to buy the asset, and a short futures position requires you to sell it. Most futures traders close their position out before the expiration date. Futures contracts are standardized and traded on organized exchanges.

> » **_Forward contracts_** lock in a future price on an asset. Unlike futures contracts, these are negotiated contracts. Banks are the big players in the forward market, setting these up for clients and facilitating trading by investment funds. Individual traders rarely work with forwards.

> » **_Swaps_** are trades that allow one party to change the form of a payment due. For example, the holder of a bond denominated in yen may prefer to make payments in euros. Like forwards, these contracts are usually negotiated by banks for their customers.

A benefit of derivatives is that they can hedge, or reduce, risk exposure. Because the value of the derivative contract is linked to the value of an underlying asset, contracts are largely used to hedge the risk of adverse price movements in the underlying asset. A farmer might want to lock in the price of a wheat harvest when the planting season starts; an airline might want to avoid a surprise increase in fuel costs. Traders who are interested in this use of derivatives are known as hedgers.

The opposite of a hedger is a speculator, someone who trades in derivatives to make a profit. Hedgers and speculators working together keep the market efficient and liquid. Speculating in the derivatives market can be extremely lucrative, but it carries a high degree of risk due to high volatility and leverage. It is not advisable for beginners without proper training.

Commodity Markets

Commodity markets are marketplaces where **_commodities_** are traded. Commodities are basic assets, such as agricultural products, metals, oil, gold, and beef. They have been traded for millennia. They are often traded using futures contracts, because that's easier than lugging around barrels of oil or herding live hogs.

There are about 50 major commodity markets around the world, trading basic categories of commodities.

» Energy
» Metals
» Livestock and meat
» Agriculture

Energy commodities include unleaded gasoline, natural gas, crude oil, propane, and heating oil. Metals, which are sometimes categorized as precious and non-precious, include aluminum, copper, tin, gold, silver, palladium, platinum, and others. Livestock and meat, of course, are items such as lean hogs, live cattle, feeder cattle, and pork bellies. And agricultural commodities include products such as coffee, sugar, soybeans, corn, wheat, milk, and cocoa. As with all markets, the commodity market is primarily driven by supply and demand, and that is subject to disruptions by natural disasters, disease, and other factors.

There are several ways to invest in commodities. The most common is through a futures contract. Most of the better-known commodity markets, like the Chicago Mercantile Exchange (CME), the New York Mercantile Exchange (NYMEX), and the London Metal Exchange, are actually futures markets.

Another way to invest in commodities is to buy stocks of companies that are linked to a particular commodity. If you are interested in the energy sector, for instance, you could consider buying stock in oil refineries or oil drilling companies. You can play in agriculture with investments in big growing conglomerates or food production companies.

You can also buy mutual funds invested in stocks of companies that deal in commodity-related industries. Commodity *exchange-traded funds* (ETFs) and *exchange-traded notes* (ETNs) are additional options for investing in the commodities market. ETFs are similar to mutual funds, as they are collections of stocks and bonds in a single fund. However, they trade like shares of stock. An ETN is a debt security issued by a financial institution. These funds invest in securities that are designed to mimic the price trends of a given market sector.

Futures contracts on stock market indices, interest rates, and currencies are also traded on commodity markets. These are known as financial commodities.

Collectibles Market

The *collectibles market* includes art, antiques, jewelry, stamps, and coins. These are physical assets that are traded, although not on organized markets. Auctions and price guides give people some guidance on the value of these items, but, to a great extent, value is in the eye of the beholder.

Some investment companies have put together funds to buy high-value pieces of art and then sell shares to individual investors. As of this writing, some of these types of funds are offering exceptional returns for their investors.

Collectibles have two sources of value, *extrinsic value* and *intrinsic value*. Extrinsic value is that which originates in the eye of the beholder, qualities like the artistic merit of a painting or the condition of a coin. Intrinsic value is the value of the metal or other materials that make up an object, including the provenance that documents the authenticity of a piece of art or an antique. (A badly worn but verified Louis XIV chair will be worth more than a beautiful copy that your amateur-woodworker cousin made.)

These assets help people diversify their portfolios. Coins, jewelry, and other collectibles also have worth in extreme political and economic situations. In this sense, they are related to the forex market. Jewelry can be melted down for the metals and stones in it, and even antique stamps are valid as postage. People who live in places with high inflation or unstable currencies often keep some of their wealth in coins, jewelry, and other collectibles because they will retain value.

Frauds and forgeries abound in art and collectibles markets. And the supply and demand is often determined by changing fads, not long-term investment quality. Buy these items because you like them, not necessarily to make money. Remember that Beanie Baby collection you had back in the day? How much is it worth now?

Real Estate

Real estate is an interesting market because each investment is a package of different components. The land itself is a store of value. It tends to be worth what you paid for it, adjusted for inflation. Buildings are depreciating assets because they need constant upkeep. But they generate economic value through rent payments. (In the case of your own house, the rental value is in the form of the money you won't have to pay each month to live in it once the mortgage is paid off.) Farmland and forests generate marketable commodities. Real estate is usually purchased and improved with leverage. This can allow people to build big profits on a (relatively) stable investment, owning a small piece but benefiting from the growth of the entire value. Banks invest in real estate when they extend loans to their customers.

Buying land, homes, or buildings outright is only one way to buy real estate. Another way is to invest in a fund known as a *real estate investment trust*, or REIT, which owns various types of real estate. Some REITS specialize in apartment buildings, others may hold such things as nursing homes or commercial office space. Investors can buy shares in some REITS in order to play in these real estate sectors. One can also invest in the stocks of businesses that have exposure to real estate, such as construction companies or furniture stores.

Many types of bonds are used to finance real estate. These are known as *mortgage-backed securities*. The bond issuer buys a large package of mortgages from banks and mortgage companies. These are pooled together, and investors buy a share in the pool. The investors then receive a portion of the principal and the interest from the pool until all the mortgages are paid off (or go into default).

Forex Market

And now we get to the market that is the topic of this book: *foreign exchange*, also known as *forex*. Every day, individuals, businesses, and governments have to make transactions in different currencies. An American buying mail-order drugs from Canada, a Mexican bookstore importing titles from Spain, or the Chinese government buying bonds from the British government all need to change their home currency into another to make the transaction.

Currencies are all the many forms of money. Most are issued by national governments. Some are issued by groups of governments, like the European Union's euro or the Central African CFA franc, and others, like bitcoin and other cryptocurrencies, have been invented by people wanting to create alternatives to traditional currencies. The basics of trading are the same for each: people sell the currency they have, or that they think will go down in value, in order to buy the currency they need or that they think will increase in value.

Foreign exchange is quoted in pairs, with each currency being priced in terms of the other. And because you are selling one currency and buying the other, there are built-in long and short trades. This makes currency slightly more complex than some other financial assets.

The currency market takes place *over the counter* (OTC). It is a decentralized market, with banks and dedicated currency trading companies making up the markets rather than organized exchanges like the CME or the NYSE. Trading can take place in the spot market—the cash price quoted in the market right now—or in the forward market, with a rate quoted today for an obligation to trade currency in the future. Because it is a market for money, leverage is also involved. Traders often rely on borrowed funds to establish their positions. Money is a commodity with price risk. Think about a Canadian company that is making a big purchase in Japan. If the Japanese yen strengthens against the Canadian dollar, the price has just gone up. The Canadian company can use derivatives to manage this risk, which is why many parts of the forex market take place in the derivatives markets.

Forex is the largest of the financial markets, and it connects to all the others. In other words, it would be important even if it were not the focus of this book.

How Financial Markets Work

As the summation of all the supply and all the demand in our economy, the financial markets end up influencing how things happen in our businesses, politics, and culture. They do it by harnessing the pure self-interest of buyers and sellers. This section covers some of the distinctions within the markets to give you more detail about how they work.

Motivation of the Participants

In addition to bringing buyers and sellers together, the financial markets bring together people with differing motivations. Speculators are taking risks in order to make a profit. Hedgers are buying insurance against a loss. Investors plan on holding a position for a long period of time, and traders are looking to make a quick profit.

Some financial markets are known as *zero-sum games*. This means that for every winner, there is a loser. Not all of these losers are unhappy about it. Those who are hedging are actually willing to pay a price for protection against a larger loss, the same way that you are willing to pay for car insurance in order to avoid a greater cost in the event of an accident.

In the financial markets, people discuss their positions as being *long* or *short*. If you own something, you are "long" it. You benefit from a long position when the price goes up. To go short, you borrow the asset, sell it, and hope to repurchase it at a lower price.

Bringing Parties Together

All financial markets serve as a place to bring buyers and sellers together. Market participants know where to go to conduct their transactions, and they have met certain requirements (identity, or *Know Your Customer*, regulations; financial wherewithal to complete the transaction; backing to ensure that the trade clears). This keeps the markets liquid and efficient. Within the financial markets are distinct market structures; just as supermarkets and flea markets work differently, so do primary and secondary markets, OTC markets and exchanges, and physical and virtual markets.

The *primary market* is where a security is sold for the first time, say through an initial public offering of common stock by a corporation or a bond auction by a government's central bank. The *secondary market* is where the trading takes place after that primary transaction. This even holds for art and collectibles; the gallery is the primary market for an artist's work, and the auction house is the secondary market.

Brokers and Dealers

To trade in the financial markets, you generally need to open an account with a *broker*. A broker is an agent that brings buyers and sellers together in exchange for a commission on the trade or for other compensation, like the bid-ask spread. When you open your account, the broker will ask for paperwork to ensure that you are who you say you are (and not someone committing fraud, aiding terrorism, or laundering money). The broker will also ask for assurance that you can meet the obligations that arise in your trading.

A *dealer* buys and sells with other traders. Unlike brokers, dealers are willing to buy and sell securities for their own accounts. They can make profits from bringing buyers and sellers together or from their own trading. Their profit is the change in value of their inventory as well as any commission they might receive. Legally, a dealer is different from a broker.

In the financial markets, most brokers are also dealers. As you pay the market price, the legal structure of the agent facilitating the trade should not matter. Just remember that the broker/dealer has many sources of profit as well as certain conflicts of interest.

Developing New Products

Because of the power of financial markets to set efficient pricing, new types of investment and trading products can be created to meet various needs, finding prices that attract buyers and please sellers. Buyers and sellers do their research and come to the markets to discover the price that makes everyone better off. *Cryptocurrencies* were recently invented to test a theory, to see what would happen when people tried out this new type of currency. The exchange-traded fund (ETF) is another fairly new financial product that was developed to help investors get low-cost exposure to specific markets and give traders another way to work with market indexes.

The financial markets are also seriously powerful. The people who participate in them believe in their ability to improve the economy. Robust financial markets help businesses grow, make it easier for families to buy houses, and allow farmers to manage risk. Whether the product is common stock, mortgage-backed securities, or commodity futures, new types of securities and derivatives have made the economy work better for more people.

The financial markets help investors and traders make money. This seems obvious, but it also has a broader function: as investors make more money, colleges can give more scholarships, more workers can retire comfortably, and foundations can better support charities.

Categories of Markets

The stock market and the bond market are *auction markets*, in which buyers determine the highest price they are willing to pay and sellers determine the lowest price they are willing to accept. Buyers and sellers enter competitive bids at the same time, acting through brokers. Trading is conducted on a stock exchange such as the NYSE or the London Stock Exchange, and traders typically do not negotiate directly with one another. Such markets are more akin to supermarkets, where the sellers and buyers transact but don't interact directly.

Things work differently in an *over-the-counter* (OTC) market, a decentralized market in which two parties trade directly, going through their banks or brokers and without the involvement of a central exchange. The Nasdaq is the largest of the OTC stock exchanges. Forex is another OTC market. Trading takes place through a network of banks rather than on a centralized currency exchange. In a sense, OTC markets are more like flea markets.

While stock exchanges have physical locations, all trading on OTC markets is conducted electronically. Of course, most stock exchanges use electronic trading too, so the difference between the two types of exchanges is much less significant than it once was.

Forex: The Largest Market of Them All

One of the reasons I like forex so much as a trader is that it is the largest and most liquid of the financial markets. This means that there are opportunities for traders of all levels to participate.

How Big Is the Forex Market?

Statistics on the foreign exchange market are kept by the **Bank for International Settlements** (BIS), a global organization owned by 62 of the world's central banks. It was founded in 1930 because central bankers realized that it would greatly simplify foreign trade if one organization managed the clearing of transactions on a global level. For example, if the Bank of Japan wants to buy euros to manage Japanese trade balances, it could have trouble finding enough traders in the market looking to sell. So instead, it can buy its euros from the Bank for International Settlements. This allows central banks to do the work they need to do without creating massive disruption in the forex market.

A *counterparty*, by the way, is the entity that takes the other side of a trade. Certain traders, like the European Central Bank or the Federal Reserve Bank, are so large that they need a designated counterparty.

According to the *2019 BIS Triennial Central Bank Survey of Foreign Exchange and Over-the-counter (OTC) Derivatives Markets*, the daily trading volume in foreign exchange was $6.6 trillion, up from $5.1 trillion three years before. In terms of tech company market capitalizations or government debt, maybe that seems like a reasonable number. But actually, a trillion is a really big number. Here are a few ways to think about it:

Ten percent of a trillion is 100 billion. Ten percent of 100 billion is 10 billion. Ten percent of 10 billion is 1 billion.

When I was in second grade, our teacher told us to bring in bottle caps; the goal was to see if the class could collect 1 million bottle caps. By the end of the year, we had brought in 18,000—less than 2% of our goal. The teacher's goal was met, though: we had a greater understanding of just how big a million was. Those 18,000 bottle caps represented 0.000018% of a trillion. If you stacked up a million dollars in single dollar bills, it would be 417 feet high, the same as a 40-story building. A stack of a trillion dollars in singles would be 79,000 miles high.

The point is that there is lots of opportunity in the forex market, even excluding securities related to forex, such as oil company stocks. (Most of the world's wholesale oil market trading is conducted in US dollars, so oil prices are a measure of the dollar's value relative to other currencies. When the dollar is stronger, oil is cheaper for Americans—and more expensive for everyone else.)

By the way, you can invest in forex through ETFs, bank accounts, or just by holding on to the cash. Somewhere in my desk, I have an envelope of pesos from my last trip to Mexico. That is a form of forex investment.

Advantages of Trading in the Forex Market

The forex market is a great one for traders. It is liquid—large and active—creating opportunities for making winning trades almost all the time. With forex, it's easier to establish and close a position than in most other markets.

One reason that the forex market is so liquid is that it is (almost) always open. It closes each weekend based on London time, meaning that in the US there is trading from 5:00 p.m. eastern time on Sunday until 5:00 p.m. eastern time on Friday. This is a huge advantage if you want to trade early in the morning or late at night when other financial markets are closed. The stock exchange closes at 4:00 p.m. eastern time, but the forex market continues.

The forex market also accommodates a range of order sizes, making it efficient for the world's largest central banks as well as individual traders. The varying prices of currency mean that you can more efficiently place trades that match your account size.

The forex market has low barriers to entry for new traders. Many brokers are open to small accounts, and there is less paperwork needed to establish an account than in some other markets. The basic trading platform is free, and participants can be located anywhere in the world with internet access. Transaction costs are low, especially relative to derivatives markets.

In addition to the factors just mentioned, I like forex because of the good trending activity. Forex prices reflect the big macro cycles and changing circumstances in the world. The charts often reflect long trends as currencies readjust to the ever-changing conditions caused by world events, presenting very profitable trading opportunities.

Chapter Recap

» Financial markets are the places where buyers and sellers come together to trade stocks, bonds, and other types of securities. They may be physical or virtual. By vetting the players, they ensure that a transaction can take place.

» The financial markets are distinct. Different financial products trade in different markets, and the rules for participation are different for each. Each financial product has a different form of risk-and-return trade-off.

» Financial markets work by supply and demand. Buyers and sellers come together and list the prices and quantities they need to get a deal done.

» Foreign exchange, or forex, is the largest of the financial markets.

| 2 |

Understanding the Forex Market

Chapter Overview
> » The evolution of forex
> » Knowing the players
> » Open day and night
> » Some trading times are better than others

When humans started trading with strangers for goods and services, they used small, portable items of value to complete the trade. The adoption and use of currency accelerated commerce by clearing common obstacles. The earliest currencies were shells, followed by coins. With currency, people had access to more than they could receive by exchanging gifts and favors within a close circle. Currency was also more convenient than direct barter. It was easier to carry to market than household goods, and it ensured that you would be able to make a trade for something you wanted. For example, a grape grower no longer had to find people willing to receive grapes in exchange for fabric or pottery. The grape grower could sell grapes for currency, then use that currency to buy other things. And now, thousands of years later, here we are sending around electronic signals to pay our mortgages, cover the costs of a gym membership, and buy groceries.

The forms of money have changed, but the need for it has not. We need a medium for trade no matter where we are in the world or what we want to purchase.

Foreign exchange is only one piece of the financial markets, but because of its size and its connection to the others, it has outsized importance in the world economy. This is one of the reasons it's so attractive to traders. The next section will cover the history and evolution of foreign exchange while introducing you to some important concepts about forex trading. It will help you decide whether and how to trade forex. Knowing more about the specifics of this market will help you make important decisions about how to trade in it.

A Brief History of Forex Trading

Once upon a time, currencies were standardized on the weight of gold. It remained the standard as trade expanded because gold was recognized as a metal that was valuable, relatively lightweight, and easy to mold into new shapes. It's pretty, too. When gold was the only currency for international trade, forex trading wasn't really an issue; the goal was to accumulate more gold. As trade expanded further and the limitations of gold as a primary currency became clear, the world's merchants and nations demanded something else. Now we have a system that is almost entirely virtual. The world's major currencies are spent electronically, traded electronically, and backed by the full faith and credit of the issuing nations.

Gold and Silver

It would seem that gold and silver, sometimes known along with other metallic money as *specie*, would be perfect for currency. In fact, there are many political movements aimed at returning world currencies to a gold standard. But there are a few big problems with tying currency directly to an underlying metal: an economy can only grow as fast as the amount of specie that it has. Poor countries were poor because they didn't have treasuries full of gold and jewels. To get around this problem, Europe's kings and queens sent their navies to find more specie. That's why the European nations that had the largest navies became colonial powers. England, France, and Spain wanted to trade, but they could not grow their economies without more gold. North America, South America, and Africa offered tantalizing possibilities of precious metals for the conquering. This conquering also created hardship, enslavement, and ill will that continue to plague global politics and life as we know it.

During this era, governments minted metal coins (usually gold), and exchange rates were based on the actual weight of gold. Coins could be cut into smaller pieces to make change. Unscrupulous traders would shave off the edges of coins, which led to the practice of putting ridged edges on coins to make shaving apparent.

Countries trying to expand their economies by taking over regions with gold proved to be a short-term solution to the trade problem. It gave the world's trading powers a one-time bump in economic growth, but the dilemma of how to grow economies with the world's fixed amount of gold remained. In fact, it got worse. Colonialism created more groups that wanted in on foreign trade, as well as the need for the colonizers to raise money to fight revolutions. England and Spain didn't realize that they would have to deal with wars and new trading partners when they claimed the United States and Mexico for themselves.

The Gold Standard of 1876

By 1876, it was clear that there was a huge problem. Once again, the world did not have enough gold and silver to use it for direct trading, but nations needed currency to trade with each other. Representatives of the major industrial nations met and established what we think of as the classic *gold standard*. Exchange rates for the world's trading currencies were fixed relative to each other, and London was designated as the central currency market.

When World War I broke out in 1914, all bets were off. Besides the fact that the parties to the gold standard were now at war with each other, they also needed to spend money on soldiers and weapons. The nations that were at war printed money to cover expenses, with no regard for how much gold they had. England was weakened and not able to defend its currency as it once had. Its leaders were not interested in going out and finding gold to back the pound, so the pound stopped being the world's de facto currency. The United States was not ready to take over. The result was chaos, including *hyperinflation* in Germany following the war. This contributed to the outbreak of World War II.

The lesson is that foreign exchange plays a big role in global politics, and that's one reason that the market is so active.

The Bretton Woods System

In 1944, a new currency treaty was negotiated by 730 people representing 44 countries. They met in Bretton Woods, New Hampshire, and agreed on a new system, one with the US dollar at its center. The Bretton Woods Agreement maintained gold's role as the basis for USD and tied in other currencies to the value of the dollar. It set exchange rates and adjustment practices based on the world as it was. The price of gold was fixed at $35 per ounce.

Under the Bretton Woods Agreement, the *International Monetary Fund* (IMF) was created to manage the system. The IMF now has 189 member nations, and it provides loans to nations that need help managing their balance of payments. It also provides technical assistance to member banks, writes policy guidelines, and is a fantastic source of data on the forex market. A related organization, the **World Bank**, provides economic development assistance and loans to help countries expand their infrastructure and create more opportunities for economic activity.

The Bretton Woods system held until 1971, when the United States government realized that it could not manage its economy (including the cost of the Vietnam War) under that system. President Richard Nixon announced that the US would leave the gold standard. Most of the rest of the world followed, leading to the system that we have today, which is based on floating rates of exchange.

Floating Foreign Exchange Rates

The current *floating rate system* works by the concept of supply and demand. It is pure capitalism. The currency price for one country is set in the forex market and is based on its supply and demand relative to other currencies. As with the gold standard, the forex market is still centered in London (although people can trade from everywhere). As with the Bretton Woods system, the US dollar is the world's central currency. Everything else has changed.

Floating exchange rates are not the only way to determine a currency's value. Under a system of a *fixed exchange rate*, also known as a *pegged exchange rate*, a nation decides to set its currency's value relative to that of another currency. China is the largest economy with a pegged currency, the yuan. The Bank of China allows occasional adjustments, but at the time of this writing, one dollar equals 6.85 yuan. It will stay at that level until the Chinese government decides to change it.

Some nations simply abandon their currency in favor of another one, almost always the US dollar. This is known as *dollarization*. The dollar may be used widely in nations with large tourist economies, and Canadian coins, for example, are accepted in place of US currency in border communities, but an economy where people use other currencies on occasion is not the same as a dollarized economy. As of this writing, Panama and Liberia are the world's two dollarized nations.

The nations that allow their currencies to float rarely allow pure market forces to reign. Their central banks often intervene in the market to manage the exchange rate; this is known as a *managed float* or a *dirty float*.

NOTE

There's also a black market in currency, in which unofficial and sometimes illegal trading occurs. It is widespread in countries with economic problems. If the people don't trust the official exchange rate, they will be willing to exchange currencies at rates that better reflect perceived values. In other words, the market prevails even when governments try to stop it.

Cryptocurrency

Cryptocurrency is a relatively new form of money. It emerged in 2008 after someone using the name Satoshi Nakamoto released a white paper setting forth the argument for a new digital currency known as bitcoin. People can earn bitcoin by solving a series of computer problems, and the ownership of bitcoin is tracked through a *blockchain*, which is a technology that can, among other things, track the buyers and sellers of each specific bitcoin transaction. This type of blockchain-based currency became known as cryptocurrency, and bitcoin is one of an almost countless number of them on the market now. Cryptocurrency is popular with a lot of traders. Sometimes it can be used to buy and sell things too.

Crypto rates are quoted along with other exchange rates, and they sometimes trade on the same platforms. We do not cover crypto specifically in this book, but the basic principles that apply to other currencies apply to crypto as well.

Now, some of you crypto skeptics out there may be thinking that it will all disappear one day. That is entirely possible, because countless real-world currencies have disappeared. French francs and German marks have value only to collectors, as both disappeared from the market with the introduction of the euro. Meanwhile, hyperinflation—extremely high rates of inflation usually caused by governments printing money in order to spend—destroyed the Zimbabwean dollar and the Venezuelan bolivar. Nothing lasts forever. Traders can find opportunities to make money in the meantime, and crypto may be one way to do it.

Who Trades in the Forex Market?

As a market that connects all the others, the forex market has a lot of players, ranging from the largest *central banks* to a vacationer withdrawing currency from a cash machine. The current market for currency is also known as the *spot market*, and it is incredibly active.

fig. 5

Central banks are at the center of it all. They make the biggest trades, and their trades are vital to the functioning of the global economy. They trade with the major banks and the Bank for International Settlements, and the major banks trade with investment funds and corporations. At a lower level are the market makers and brokers that work with retail traders.

A retail trader is too small to affect market dynamics, but it can take advantage of all the activity created by the other players.

Central Banks

Central banks are predominant players in the global financial system. These are the government agencies that support a nation's financial system, such as the Federal Reserve Bank in the United States, the European Central Bank in the European Union, and the Bank of Japan.

In some countries, the central banks provide direct regulation of local banks. In others, the central banks influence their practices by setting *reserve requirements*, which refer to the percentage of total customer account balances that a bank must keep on hand in cash. Banks with balances greater than the reserve requirement can deposit the extra money with the central bank to earn interest, which in the United States is paid at a rate known as the *federal funds rate*. If banks lack the cash to meet their reserve requirements, they can borrow money from the central bank. In the United States, the rate that the Federal Reserve Bank charges for overnight loans to banks is known as the *federal discount rate*.

The powers of the central bank include acting as a lender of last resort in times of serious crisis, such as the 2008 financial crisis in the United States. Central banks can also manage the money supply to provide price stability and control inflation, and they can intervene in currency markets to help manage exchange rates in accordance with national economic policies.

Banks

While central banks are the biggest players in the forex market, they are not the most active. That honor goes to the world's commercial and investment banks. Every day, these banks trade foreign currencies with each other to settle credit card transactions, help customers with import and export financing, and hedge the currency risks in their operations. They are also trading for their own accounts, which is why forex is known as a dealer market.

A dealer buys and sells with other traders for its own account. This means that dealers are managing their own trading profits while also helping others to complete trades. A dealer is different from a broker, which brings buyers and sellers together but does not buy or sell on its own. Most brokers are also dealers, so no distinctions are made when you are trading.

fig. 6

SHARE OF FOREX MARKET ACTIVITY IN 2020			
Rank 2020	Rank 2019	Counterparty	Market Share % 2020
1	1	JPMorgan	10.78%
2	5	UBS	8.13%
3	4	XTX Markets	7.58%
4	2	Deutsche Bank	7.38%
5	3	Citi	5.50%
6	8	HSBC	5.33%
7	11	Jump Trading	5.23%
8	10	Goldman Sachs	4.62%
9	6	State Street	4.61%
10	9	Bank of America	4.50%

Source: Euromoney

Please note that these numbers are adjusted for swap agreements.

The world's banks are behind most activity in the forex market. The greatest volume of trade occurs in the inter-bank market, which is made up of banks trading with each other. Banks also act as dealers to conduct currency transactions for their clients.

And, no surprise, the world's largest banks are among the world's largest forex traders (figure 6).

Corporations

Trade is global. Companies based in one country sell all over the place. McDonald's, Coca-Cola, Honda, Unilever, Bayer, Aldi: in our everyday lives, we are surrounded by goods and services from all over the world. When you get in your Honda to drive to Aldi for groceries, swing by McDonald's for a cold drink, and stop at BP to top off the gas tank, you set off a series of chain reactions involving foreign exchange. You may be paying in dollars, but not everything that you purchased was originally purchased in dollars, and the profits from your transactions may be calculated in a different currency altogether. Honda makes and sells cars in the US (and China, and Brazil, and India), but its profits are recorded in yen back in Japan. Aldi may purchase tomatoes grown in Mexico to sell in the United States, but its profits are recorded in euros.

And you know what? You could do almost the same shopping trip in England, Australia, or China, where Honda, Aldi, McDonald's, Coca-Cola, and BP have customers. The products and brands may be the same, but the currency implications are different.

It's no surprise, then, that multinational corporations are major players in the forex markets.

Businesses often use the forex market to hedge transactions, although many speculate a little, too. To manage risk they often use swap contracts, which allow them to trade a stream of payments in one currency for a stream in another. The other side of the trade could be a corporation with a mirror image of the problem, the bank that set up the swap, or an investment fund.

Investment Funds

Banks often trade with investment funds that are looking for exposure to different financial markets. These organizations are in the business of making money from money, and they do this by accepting various forms of risk. These funds fall into many categories. Some represent large foundations, endowments, or trusts and are looking for a way to increase return on the money that has been allotted to cash. Some are hedge funds or major speculators wanting to either offset risk or take on a huge amount of it. Collectively, investment funds are second only to commercial banks and central banks as players in forex market.

Retail Speculators

Retail speculators make up a small but growing segment of the forex market. These participants are folks like me and maybe you. We do a far smaller share of forex trading than do central banks, commercial banks, forex brokers, multinational corporations, or investment funds. And that's okay. Although retail traders don't make the market, there is plenty of room for us to ride in the wake of the whales.

Forex Market Hierarchies

Forex is traded both over the counter and electronically. Instead of an organized exchange, there is a network of banks making trades for their customers and managing their own risk levels. Smaller traders use a market maker or broker to give them access to this network.

The decentralized nature of the forex market means that banks, market makers, and brokers are competing for customers—which helps keep the markets as efficient as possible. Because they are constantly looking for the best price for themselves and others, all the market participants, in theory, collectively ensure that prices reflect the current state of supply and demand—but at the same time, that state is in constant flux, changing in response to all the countless other influences coming from the dynamic world we live in. Political upheaval, changing economic tides, and global environmental developments are all factors that can contribute to the state of the forex market.

The Hierarchy of Forex Traders

The central banks are at the top of the forex market. Although they are not always active traders, they make an impact whenever they enter the market.

Next in the ranking are the commercial banks. The global household-name banks like J.P. Morgan Chase are the largest of the commercial banks in the forex market, followed by medium-sized and even small commercial banks. After all, companies of all sizes are active in import and export markets, so they are looking to their bankers for help. Some of the smaller banks work with a broker to place their trades.

GRAPHIC

fig. 7

After the banks come the traders. These include **market makers** and **electronic communication networks** (ECNs) that work with brokerage firms, hedge funds and other investment companies, and multinational corporations that use the forex market to manage their currency exposure.

Retail forex traders are at the bottom of the hierarchy. Although they do not have the power to change the prices of currency pairs, they can profit by surfing the trends created by everyone else. George Soros, with his big hedge fund, helped to bring down the price of the pound when he shorted it in 1992. I went along for that ride.

How Big and Small Players Affect One Another

Some of the bigger traders in the hierarchy, such as the market makers and ECNs, represent retail traders. They become major players by aggregating the activity of many smaller traders. Beyond that, retail traders do not have much influence on currency price movements.

In trader lingo, the largest market participants are known as **whales**. These are the players in the top layers of the hierarchy that have the ability to move the markets and affect price action and liquidity. Farther down the list are participants who are doing research, mostly to manage their own risk. As a result, they are informed traders who may capitalize on trends and other price patterns as they emerge. Unlike the whales, they do not themselves exert any significant influence on price action.

The activity of the whales, whether they be mighty orcas or baby belugas, shows up in forex prices. The price changes show their current supply and demand, and the volume and urgency behind that supply and demand show up in price trends. We cover *price charts* in great detail elsewhere in this book. The point to remember is that the big players create price trends that the small players can follow.

How the Internet Opened the Forex Market to Retail Traders

Until the United States went off the gold standard in 1971, trading currency made no sense. Currency prices were fixed. Banks needed to exchange currencies to meet customer needs, but they were doing it as a service rather than as a source of profit.

When the world's major currencies started trading freely, there were opportunities to make money by speculating on currency prices. The whales jumped in the pool and played around. Still, it was not practical for small traders to work in the forex markets. Doing so required access to expensive telecommunications lines and subscription trading terminals.

In the mid-1990s, the commercialization of the internet increased price transparency in the forex market, and it gave small traders a way to place trades. The internet opened up trading in other financial markets too, and new traders flocked to the stock markets first. These beginner traders knew more about the stock market than other financial markets, and the rise of the technology industry created hot stocks for them to follow.

Traders started becoming more interested in other markets after the tech stock bubble burst in 2000, and by the time of the financial crisis in 2008, forex was in vogue with small traders. The ease of access and increased transparency offered on electronic trading platforms made it easy for them to approach the market, follow trends, and evaluate performance.

And now you have this book to tell you all you need to know to get started in forex trading.

Chapter Recap

» The foreign exchange market as we know it developed in the 1970s. It expanded when internet trading was introduced, and new forms of currency continue to be developed, such as the euro (1999) and bitcoin (2009).

» Forex traders include government central banks, commercial and investment banks, brokers, corporations, and individuals. Different participants have different needs, but the big ones create trends that small traders can play with.

» Internet trading made the forex market accessible to individual traders. While they may be the smallest segment, there are opportunities to make money and take advantage of the market's high liquidity and low barriers to entry.

| 3 |

Currencies and Lot Sizes

Chapter Overview
» The currencies we trade
» Understanding currency pairs and quotes
» Varying lot sizes accommodate traders of all levels

A *currency* is something that is traded for items of value. In a grade-school lunchroom, the most popular currency might be candy; in prison, inmates use cigarettes or packets of ramen noodles.

Some currencies are items of value themselves. You can always have ramen noodles for lunch or melt coins down for their metal. Some are backed by items of value, as most of the world's currencies were before 1972. Others have value only because we perceive them to. These are known as *fiat currencies*. They are not backed by gold or anything else of value, and they account for most of the world's money right now.

Currencies do not have to be physical items, and, in fact, most of us use something in addition to actual currency to make transactions. Once upon a time, we might have written checks. Now we send money by Venmo, use credit cards, and pay for travel with frequent flier miles. When we log into our bank account, we see a number on the screen that shows how much "money" we have.

In other words, currency is not necessarily a physical object. It is something that is recognized for its ability to hold and transfer value. As long as someone else sees the value, then a trade can take place. We say that national currencies are backed by the "full faith and credit" of the governments that issue them. How valuable is that? It depends. The full faith and credit of the Canadian government is more valuable than the full faith and credit of the Venezuelan government, and that's why the Canadian loonie is worth a lot more than the Venezuelan bolivar. Although the Venezuelan government tried to keep the bolivar pegged to the US dollar, businesses and consumers in Venezuela knew that it was worth far less than what the government pegged it at, thus inadvertently creating a very active black market where dollars were traded for bolivars at a more realistic exchange rate, often several times more than the official government rate.

Currencies Traded on the Forex Market

Most countries have their own currencies, but there are a few notable exceptions. The European Union's currency, the euro, is used by 19 countries, and another currency, the Central African CFA franc, is used by multiple nations in both Central and West Africa, and is tied in value to the euro.

For currency to trade on the forex market, it must have a free float. This means that the issuing government is willing to allow the currency's value to change with market conditions. Not all governments agree to this, most notably India and the People's Republic of China. Those nations have large economies, but traders rarely speculate in their currencies—at least not on the open market. You can bet there's activity on the black market as the true value finds its way out into the open.

Of course, governments that allow their currencies to float intervene in the market to help nudge the exchange rate in order to support their economic policy objectives. The currency's resulting market valuation is known as a "dirty float." The Bank of Japan is notorious for intervening in the market, which is why many traders shy away from the USD/JPY.

The Bretton Woods agreement of 1944 set the US dollar as the world's *numeraire* currency. It became the basis for all other transactions, a position it continues to hold. This is a function of the size of the US economy, the relative stability of the US government, and the general willingness of the Federal Reserve Bank to allow the dollar to float freely. Before World War II, the numeraire was the British pound.

Most of the world's transactions are denominated in US dollars due to the size of the US economy and the role of the dollar in the global monetary system. Besides trade that involves the United States, trade between many developing nations is denominated in dollars. This allows participants to manage risk better than they could in their local currencies. The dollars used in trade can be more easily used in future trade, too.

An Indian oil company ships refined petroleum to Eritrea. It accepts payment in US dollars not only because oil trades in dollars, but also because dollars are more valuable to it than Eritrean nakfas.

There's nothing inevitable about the US dollar's position, but for now, it's the big one in the forex market, a position it is likely to hold for a long time into the future.

When I first backpacked through Europe as a result of my version of the Soros trade, I rode the Eurail trains all over. I had to make sure that I had lira when going into Italy, French francs when in France, Swiss francs in Switzerland, marks in Germany, and crowns in the Czech Republic. The crown was a soft currency, meaning that no one wanted to take it in exchange.

I played with a musician on the Charles Bridge in Prague for about a week. He would draw hundreds of spectators, and at the end of each set he would pass the basket and make hundreds of dollars in Czech crowns. He made more in an hour than Czech doctors did at that time. My musician friend was from Brazil, but, with only crowns at his disposal, he would not be able to get home. His crowns were a soft currency and there was no exchange where he could convert them into a hard currency like the US dollar or the German mark to buy a plane ticket home. Sure, he lived like a king in Prague, but he was stuck. Finally, I convinced him to buy cases of whiskey and other spirits using crowns and then drive it up into Germany and sell it for marks. At last, he had hard currency and a nice profit to take back to Brazil.

Currency Pairs

Currencies always trade in pairs. After all, this is foreign *exchange*. People traded currency even when the price was fixed, because they needed another currency to get things done. Even now, when the market welcomes speculators, traders sell one currency when they buy another.

The pairs that see the most activity are pairs of currencies from countries that trade with each other. Obviously, some countries and regions have bigger economies than others, but these patterns are influenced by geography and historical ties. Different pairs have different active trading times and patterns. Many traders choose a few pairs and stick to them.

The Most Popular Currency Pairs

The most popular currency pairs, also called the ***major pairs***, are those involving the largest economies with free-floating currencies: the US dollar (USD), the euro (EUR), the Japanese yen (JPY), and the British pound (GBP). Also on this list is the Swiss franc (CHF) because of Switzerland's role in the international banking system. Thus the major pairs are EUR/USD, USD/JPY, GBP/USD, and USD/CHF.

All major currency pairs include USD because most world trade is denominated in dollar terms, thanks to the greenback's numeraire status. About two thirds of daily trading involves the major pairs. EUR/USD is the most traded of all the pairs, which makes sense given that it involves the world's two largest free-floating economies.

Minor, Exotic, and Other Pairs

Minor pairs don't involve the US dollar but do involve one of the three other major currencies: the British pound (GBP), the euro (EUR), and the Japanese yen (JPY). In a minor pair, one of these major currencies is paired with the free-floating currency of other developed nations, such as Australia (AUD), Canada (CAD), or New Zealand (NZD). Minor pairs trade less than the major pairs but have decent overall volume. If you do most of your trading during Sydney session hours, you will often see fairly regular activity in the AUD, NZD, and even JPY pairs.

The appendix has a full listing of currency pairs.

Exotic pairs involve free-floating developing nation currencies, such as the Mexican peso (MXN), the South African rand (ZAR), and the Thai baht (THB). These pairs tend to have wider spreads (bidding prices versus asking prices, which will be explained in detail later in this chapter) because they are traded far less often than the major pairs. The trade they do have is mostly regional. For example, MXN pairs will be more active in the New York session than during the London, Tokyo, or Sydney sessions.

When discussing forex, we traders almost always refer to currencies by their initials. It simplifies things in a world where, for example, the US, Canada, Australia, and New Zealand all call their currency the dollar, and both the US and Mexico signify their currencies with $.

Some forex traders prefer to branch out beyond traditional currency pairs. Because gold and crude oil are both priced in US dollars, trading in them is related to forex. There are several bitcoin/forex pairs out there too. European traders engage in something called *spread betting*, in which they bet on price changes in forex. Since they're placing bets rather than trades, less capital is involved. Spread betting also has tax advantages in some countries.

Because forex trading is decentralized, brokers make their own markets, and they introduce pairs that they think their customers might be interested in trading. Some of the more unusual pairs are not available in the United States and Canada due to regulation. Traders working in Europe or Asia may see more variety.

Understanding a Currency Quote

Take a look at this price quote (figure 8) from one of the many forex trading platforms. The top line tells you what pair is being quoted; here it is the EUR/USD. The first currency in the quote, EUR, is the base currency. The note "daily" shows that this chart is based on a daily price bar. Each price bar represents a full day's worth of trading, one bar per day. Some charts track price changes over a shorter period (5 minutes, 15 minutes, 240 minutes, etc.) and others over a longer period, like a week or a month. The chart in figure 8 is a daily chart, based on the eastern time zone (where the NYSE operates). Other charting platforms use different time zones, like, for example, Greenwich mean time (GMT). It depends on the broker. Remember, forex is decentralized and each broker makes his own market; therefore, the time stamp on a price bar will vary as well, depending on what time zone the chart is set to.

fig. 8

EURUSD Daily X								
L: 1.19492 0.00383 0.32% B: 1.19491 A: 1.19493 O: 1.19106 Hi 1.19557 Lo 1.18780 VO BSO	ASO	TSO	TRFOREX

»   *L* shows the price of the last trade. One euro bought USD 1.19492. This is also known as the spot price.

»   0.00383 is the price change for the day. The euro rose .00383 against the dollar.

»   0.32% is the percentage of change for the day.

»   *B* is the bid price. This is the price at which the broker buys the currency pair from a customer.

»   *A* is the ask price, the price at which the broker sells the currency pair to a customer. The difference between the bid and the ask is profit to the broker and is referred to as the "spread."

»   *O* is the price where the trading session opened for the day.

»   Hi is the high price for the day.

»   Lo is the low price for the day.

- » *V* is for volume, *BS* is for bid size, *AS* is for ask size, and *TS* is for trade size. These are irrelevant in forex trading.
  - Because forex is decentralized and each broker makes their own market, there is no standardized information regarding volume.
- » *TR* is a little reminder that you are trading in forex. If you were trading shares of Johnson & Johnson stock, this would read TR NYSE.

When you are new to currency trading, it can be hard to remember which currency is going up and which is going down. The first part of the quote (in this case, EUR) is always the same: it is 1.00. So in figure 8, €1.00 buys 1.19492 dollars now, but it bought slightly fewer, 1.19106, at the open. Thus, the euro has become 0.32% more valuable relative to the dollar, and the dollar has become less valuable.

Commentators often talk about a currency "strengthening" or "weakening." If a currency strengthens, then it will buy more of a foreign currency. If it weakens, it will buy less. Stronger is not necessarily better. Strength and weakness reflect price changes, not underlying economic or political values.

The Bid-Ask Spread

The quote sample in figure 8 has two current prices, the *bid* of 1.19491 and the *ask* (sometimes called the "offer") of 1.19493. The ask is always higher than the bid, and the difference is known as the *bid-ask spread* and is profit to the broker.

In this example, the broker pays a trader looking to sell euros USD 1.19491 for each euro being sold. Another customer looking to buy the pair will pay the ask price, or USD 1.19493, for each euro received. The spread is $1.19493 - $1.19491, or $0.00002. This may not seem like a lot, but multiply it over millions of dollars' worth of trades and it starts to add up.

From the trader's perspective, the spread is the price of every transaction. Pairs that trade less frequently have wider spreads than the major pairs do. The size of the spread matters. Sometimes it is cheaper to pay a commission to trade with a broker that maintains narrow spreads than to trade with a commission-free firm that has wider spreads.

Don't expect a given currency pair to always show the same bid-ask spread. Other factors, such as volatility and perceived risk, can widen the spread. Sometimes the spread will widen just before an important economic report is released. It also tends to widen when markets close in New York (before they open again in Australia) and over the weekends. After Australia opens, however, the spreads tend to go back to normal.

Pips and Ticks

A *pip* is the unit of measurement used to show the change in value between two currencies. It is different for different currencies. It used to be the last decimal place of the price quote, but a few years ago most brokers added an extra digit, one tenth of a pip.

In the EUR/USD example, a pip is 0.0001. That's the typical value of a pip, although it does vary. Among the major currencies, the Japanese yen is the only one with a different pip. For USD/JPY, a pip is 0.01.

Some currencies trade so much that price changes are now recorded in even smaller increments, known as *pipettes*, *baby pips*, or *ticks*. Once a pip was recognized as the smallest increment of change, but there's now an even smaller increment, and a new word to note the difference.

Here's an example that shows the places of the pips. If you saw a quote for the Canadian dollar, USD/CAD 1.32245, you could break it out like this (figure 9):

fig. 9

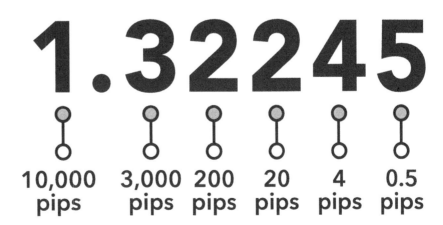

| 10,000 pips | 3,000 pips | 200 pips | 20 pips | 4 pips | 0.5 pips |

Forex Lot Sizes

Forex lot sizes are based on the amount of base currency that you are trading. Remember that the major pairs are based on the US dollar. Figure 10 shows the usual lot sizes and the value of 1 pip for each.

Standard, Mini, Micro, and Nano Lots

The units of currency are the same even when the base currency is not the dollar. If you placed an order to "go long" 1 micro lot of EUR/USD, you would be buying 1,000 EUR. If you placed an order to "short" 1 micro lot of EUR/USD, you would be selling 1,000 EUR.

GRAPHIC

fig. 10

LOT NAME	AMOUNT OF BASE CURRENCY	VALUE OF A PIP AT .0001
Standard	$100,000	$10.00
Mini	$10,000	$1.00
Micro	$1,000	$0.10
Nano	$100	$0.01

NOTE

As in any type of trading or investing, "going long" indicates that you believe the underlying asset will increase in value and "shorting" indicates that you believe the underlying asset will decrease in value.

Factors to Consider When Deciding on Lot Size

In general, each trade should risk about 2% of your total trading capital. I risk between 1% and 5%, depending on the market and the strategy. A $5,000 account would be enough to trade mini lots, especially for a day trader who is making many small trades. A swing trader, making a few large trades, may need more capital or may need to trade smaller positions. If you have a small initial amount of trading capital, you may choose to take more risk in the early days of your trading endeavor. As the money in your account builds, it usually makes sense to take your trade sizes down as a percentage of your total account.

CAUTION

I'm not recommending here that you jump quickly into trading high-risk positions. Learning to trade and win more than you lose takes a lot of time and a serious commitment. Be sure to complete your backtesting and other preproduction work (see part III) before beginning any trading endeavor.

On the flip side, if you're beginning with a significant store of trading capital, let's say $5,000 or more, you may feel inclined to start with nano or micro lots until you feel more comfortable placing 2% or more of your total capital at risk. In fact, using nano or micro lots is a great way to hone your skills and test your trade method with real money while not risking much capital. Real markets are real, and traders react differently in them (usually due to psychology) than they do in demo accounts—which also use simulations that aren't directly based on actual real-time market order executions.

Beyond that, traders may consider deviating from the 2% guideline as they develop more experience. Some traders feel comfortable risking more than 2% (and some are hesitant to risk even that much), but the decision should include an analysis of strategy as much as one's personal attitude toward risk. If you have a strategy that wins 85% of the time, you can take more risk with it than with a strategy that wins only 55% of the time. Always manage your risks, though; a strategy with a 90% win rate loses 10% of the time, and you don't want that 10% to wipe you out.

There are old traders, and there are bold traders, but there are no old, bold traders.

– HEARD AT THE CHICAGO BOARD OF TRADE

Forex traders work with leverage, also known as borrowed money. This comes in the form of margin loans extended by their broker and allows them to buy larger lot sizes than they might otherwise be able to afford. Leverage increases potential return, but it also adds risk. For now, know that you do not need $100,000 to trade $100,000 worth of currency. We'll learn more about leverage in chapters 6 and 13.

Forex: The Market that Never Sleeps

Because forex is a global marketplace, it has continuous trading hours. Its opening and closing times are based on London hours (Greenwich mean time), given that city's historical role in currency markets. Except for Saturday and Sunday in London, someone somewhere is trading forex. The forex market thus provides a huge advantage for anyone whose preferred trading hours are different from local business hours.

The Four Major Trading Sessions

The forex market has four major trading sessions. Relative to eastern time in the United States, the sessions and their hours are as follows:

» Sydney Session: 5:00 p.m. to 2:00 a.m. (the next day)
» Tokyo Session: 7:00 p.m. to 4:00 a.m. (the next day)
» London Session: 3:00 a.m. to noon
» New York Session: 8:00 a.m. to 5:00 p.m.

From the perspective of a North American trader, the Tokyo and Sydney sessions are referred to as "overnight" markets. Sydney is often listed first because it is the first market to open after the Sunday trading break.

Trading hours may change with the daylight saving practices of various countries. The dates of the time change vary from country to country and can change from year to year, so make it a point to check on the hours for your preferred trading session.

Knowing the Best Times to Trade—or Not to Trade

Although the forex market is always on, not all currency pairs are active at the same time. Trades involving the Australian dollar, the New Zealand dollar, and the Japanese yen are often quite active during the Sydney and Tokyo sessions, but still, some of the best day-trading price action takes place during the London and New York morning sessions. In fact, I find the London and New York sessions to be more consistent when it comes to tradeable price action and achieving consistent positive results.

If you have a particular interest in certain currencies or a strategy that works better with some pairs than others, you'll need to carefully consider the most effective times to pursue that interest. I typically go through my specific steps of testing my strategy and proving it will work before attempting to trade it with real money. Considering what will work for me from a lifestyle point of view plays a major role in my decision as well. If my plan works great during the London hours, I need to consider the fact that I live on the West Coast of the United States and that my days of pulling all-nighters, like I did when I was younger, are probably over. Usually, I find that most of my day-trading approaches work equally well during the New York session, which is a better choice for me.

Conversely, if your schedule only permits you to trade during certain times, then you should focus on the currency pairs and strategies that are most correlated with your availability. The markets do what they will do, regardless of your preferences.

Looking at the trading hours, you'll notice that there are times when the markets overlap and times when they do not. The market in Sydney is open for two hours before the Tokyo market opens. There is more activity when both markets are running than when only one is. Likewise, the end of the Tokyo session overlaps with the London session for an hour. London and New York overlap for four hours, for what is normally the busiest period in the forex market. After London closes at noon New York time, trading slows down for several hours. New York closes, Sydney opens, then the Tokyo market wakes up and the activity begins all over again.

Chapter Recap

» The forex market includes the free-floating currencies of the world's developed nations and the largest of the developing countries.

» Currencies are always traded in pairs because a trader must sell one currency in order to buy another. These pairs cover the world's major and minor free-floating currencies.

» A currency quote has two numbers, the bid price (the price to sell a currency) and the ask price (the price to buy the currency). The difference between the bid and the ask is the spread, which is the dealer's profit.

» A standard lot for a forex trade is 100,000 units of the base currency, which means $100,000 dollars in dollar-denominated pairs. Smaller lots are available, including the mini lot (10,000 units), the micro lot (1,000 units), and the nano lot (100 units).

» The value of a pip changes based on the lot size used in a trade; the larger the lot size, the more valuable will be each pip of movement in a given direction.

| 4 |
Factors that Affect Currencies

Chapter Overview

» Economies are always changing
» Fundamental factors that affect currency values
» Recognizing the strength or weakness of an economy
» Watching the headline news

Every day is a new day, with new government decisions, new weather conditions, and new headlines—all of which can influence the forex market, often by impacting supply and demand.

The US government announces a new food aid program for lesser-developed countries. Great quantities of US food exports are delivered, free of cost, to the receiving countries, with the result that downward pressure is exerted on the USD. Why? Because if we assume that there is a demand in these countries for US food supplies, then there would be a concurrent demand for the USD needed to purchase them. Without the aid package, the benefiting countries would need to find a way to pay these US food suppliers with USD. Because of the food aid program, that demand is now quashed, and the result is downward pressure on the USD.

Japan is hit by a costly natural disaster, a tidal wave. This reduces short-term demand for JPY by business and pleasure travelers, who would have needed JPY to cover the costs of their travel.

The Queen of England calls a new election in the United Kingdom, which creates some uncertainty about the future direction of the country and puts downward pressure on the GBP. With the UK's future less certain, businesses, especially bigger ones, are less inclined to want to keep large stores of GBP on hand for use in potential future endeavors.

Every day there are new forces moving prices in the forex market and new opportunities to find profitable trades. The needs of large forex traders are expressed in the global financial market, which creates new patterns for small forex players—traders like us—to search for, analyze, and trade.

Things that affect forex trading do so in a number of ways. To a certain extent, you do not need to know what they are, because they will all show up in price patterns on the charts. Your job as a trader is to pay attention to the price action and the patterns it creates, not to the factors driving them. It is impossible for us as traders to know everything, but everything gets reduced down to real-time price action.

Political, Natural, or Social Circumstances

Forex movement occurs throughout the day and night. It can lull you to sleep and then wake you up with a flurry as some piece of "news," real or merely perceived, impacts the market. Forex prices often reflect the news before the story reaches the public. That said, I encourage traders to concentrate on what is happening to prices, not on what is happening in the news. I know that most trading rooms have CNBC or other news channels on in the background, but that is likely to distract you from what matters.

News events create changes in forex prices, making some traders really happy and others not so much. Because the price changes precede or coincide with the announcements, following the news will not help you be a better trader. It may help you understand where some of your trades went wrong, however.

I use the ForexFactory.com events calendar, which tells me when an economic report is going to be released. The calendar events (report releases) are labeled yellow, orange, and red. Beware of the red reports and sometimes the orange ones. I stand down from trading five minutes in front of an event and wait two to five minutes after the event to begin looking for new trades. It is especially important to pay attention to what your broker is doing to the spread. Spreads tend to widen dramatically during these news events. It is not wise to trade until you see the spreads go back to normal afterward. We always want to remain in control of our trade, and placing trades through major market events is how we might lose that control.

Political Upheaval and Social Unrest

Geopolitics affects currency prices like few other things. On some level, the exchange rate is a measure of how much people want to do business in another country. If there's uncertainty about the direction of a country's gross domestic product (GDP) growth and productivity, it will show up in exchange rate weakness. Upheaval and unrest detract from growth and productivity, as anyone who compulsively checks headlines on a busy news day while trying to get to work can tell you.

NOTE

If you are easily distracted by news sites, social media, or anything else, for that matter, you should block them before you start your daily trading sessions. It will make a huge difference.

Here is an example: the state of the British pound following the United Kingdom's referendum on membership in the European Union. On June 23, 2016, the people of the UK voted to leave the EU, a situation known as Brexit. The exit itself was not finalized until January of 2020, and, as I write this, there are details of trade and immigration that still must be worked out. All this makes it difficult to do business in the UK, as managers cannot make plans when they don't know what the rules will be or what it will cost to comply. Bank of England data shows that the GBP (the British pound, aka the sterling) was worth USD 1.48 the day of the Brexit vote, USD 1.36 the day after, and USD 1.29 in September of 2020. It is currently around USD 1.19.

The forex market does not care whether you agree or disagree with situations going on in the world. The only thing that matters is the supply and demand playing out at any one moment. You may be right about the future and all the world's traders may be wrong, but a lot of money will be made and lost in the meantime. Even if you *are* right, you can still lose, because timing is everything.

Wars

The most drastic outcome of political upheaval and social unrest is war. In the near term, the government will spend heavily on weapons and war fighters, and that helps the economy. In the long run, military spending will cause the government to take on debt and may lead to inflation.

Wars make currencies weaker. The threat of war can do so too. Investors will often move their money from a country at risk to one that is not, a process known as *flight to safety*.

Natural disasters

Fires and floods, droughts and derechos happen. They destroy property and take people's lives. Natural disasters also affect exchange rates. A nation that experiences a disaster will see its currency weaken because of concerns about the disaster's effect on the economy and the inflationary costs that may be involved with rebuilding. For example, Australia experienced wildfires in the early months of 2020, which weakened the currency. Concerns that climate change will make these fires a permanent part of life in Australia is hurting the long-term outlook for the Australian economy.

Pandemics and Other Health Emergencies

Pandemics, like COVID-19, hurt productivity and affect trade across borders. In July of 2020, the Organisation for Economic Co-operation and Development released a study that showed that concerns over the spread of the coronavirus led to a slow-down in cross-border investment. The currencies in developing economies and energy-exporting nations depreciated. Some of the major currencies strengthened as money was moved to safer markets.

Inflation and Interest Rates

An interest rate is the price of money in its own currency. It reflects the supply and demand of money in the economy, known as the *real rate of interest*, and the *inflation rate*, which is the rate by which prices are increasing. The *nominal rate of interest* is what's quoted on bonds and loans. It does not take inflation into account.

In an economy with many opportunities for investment and not a lot of money to go around, the real rate of interest will be high. Think about India. It's an emerging market with a high level of poverty but also a lot of people starting new businesses and buying consumer goods. The demand for money is so great relative to the supply that interest rates are high. Compare that to Japan, which is a mature economy with a high savings rate. The supply of money is greater than the demand, so interest rates are low.

How Inflation and Interest Rates Are Related

If an economy is growing, the money supply will grow too. This leads to increased prices, an effect known as inflation. The inflation rate and the real rate of interest are combined in the interest rate that you see quoted in the market. Moderate inflation is common in a growing economy. But extremes of inflation are destructive to economies.

Deflation is another extreme—a steady decrease in price levels. This seems like a good thing, doesn't it? But it's not. People will keep waiting to spend money in the hope of receiving a lower price. Businesses cannot invest if people are not spending money. Wages and property values decline. The economy gets into a funk that it cannot shake off. It doesn't respond to stimulus because everyone is waiting for prices to get just a little bit lower before they commit to making a purchase.

In the 1980s, Japan had a fast-growing real estate market that turned into a bubble. In 1992 the bubble burst, and the nation began a ten-year period of falling asset values, sometimes referred to as Japan's Lost Decade. The deflation from falling prices made it difficult for the nation to resume economic growth.

The other extreme is *hyperinflation*. This is a steady and dramatic increase in price levels. Economists usually consider inflation over 20% to be hyperinflation. Were it not for the sheer human misery that results, the extremes of hyperinflation would be comical. If prices double over the course of a day, then standing in line hoping to buy groceries will be a better use of your time than going to work. If you go to work, your pay will be based on yesterday's prices, or last year's prices, and you will actually lose money. With hyperinflation, productivity shuts down as everyone tries to lock in necessities before prices go even higher.

Thanks to a combination of high government debt, botched land reform, and a war with Congo, the government of Zimbabwe started printing money. This led to extraordinary inflation. In November of 2008, the annual inflation rate was estimated at 79,600,000,000%.

In general, inflation has negative effects on currency values and on foreign exchange rates. To maintain the same amount of purchasing power in the base currency, you need more and more of the currencies affected—so those currencies become weaker if everything else stays the same. Hyperinflation destroys currencies. In Venezuela, which has had a great deal of social, political, and economic upheaval, the government began printing money to meet its obligations. Then they started printing larger denominations of currency, such as 500-bolivar notes instead of 100-bolivar notes. Inflation continued, and people needed a backpack of money just to buy a loaf of bread. The merchants stopped accepting the money because they had no place to store it and no way to move it to the bank. Moreover, the banks didn't want all those bills either, although they needed them because their customers were withdrawing money. To make things worse, though the government promised to print larger denominations, they didn't even have the paper to print on (or the money to buy the paper), so people were left with money they couldn't spend and that was losing value by the minute. In most cases, nations that experience hyperinflation wipe the slate clean and start over with a new currency.

A nation's central bank influences interest rates because it charges banks interest to borrow money and pays them interest on their deposits. Banks use these rates to set rates with their customers. When interest rates are low, it costs less for consumers to borrow money to buy houses, cars, and furniture. Businesses can afford loans to expand. Cutting interest rates is an easy way to encourage economic growth.

But while low inflation leads to stronger exchange rates, low interest rates do not have the same effect on their own. Investors prefer to move their money to markets offering a higher rate of return. Higher interest rates increase demand for a currency and cause it to strengthen. There are exceptions. In the financial crisis of 2008, the US Federal Reserve Bank cut interest rates to ensure that businesses had sufficient funding. The dollar gained in strength because people in other countries were looking for the safest place to put their money, and at that time, the safest place was US government bonds.

Although interest rates include both the real rate of interest and inflation, the two factors have different effects on exchange rates. The chart in figure 11 summarizes the effects:

fig. 11

WHAT CHANGES	HOW IT CHANGES	EFFECT ON CURRENCY
Real Rate of interest	↑	↑
Real Rate of interest	↓	↓
Inflation	↑	↓
Inflation	↓	↑
Nominal rate of interest	↑	?
Nominal rate of interest	↓	?

The effect of a change in the nominal rate of interest depends on what caused it to change. A change in supply and demand of the currency has a different effect than a change in price levels brought about by inflation or deflation.

National Debt

Just as households and businesses borrow money to pay for things they need, so do governments.

But just as households and businesses sometimes borrow money to buy things they do not need and really cannot afford, so do governments. Just as some households and some businesses take on a reasonable amount of debt but then face changed circumstances, so do governments. The debt itself is not the problem, as long as the borrower has the means to pay it back.

Governments have one advantage over businesses and households: they can print money to pay off debt. In the modern world, nothing backs currency but the "full faith and credit" of the issuing government, and some have better faith and greater credit than others. Most politicians understand that printing money to pay off debt is an extreme decision that leads to high inflation and even hyperinflation, but some are quick to advocate for it if it solves a short-term problem.

Nations do default on their debts, although it is not common. Both printing money and defaulting on debt are destructive to currencies, but sometimes these seem like the more politically acceptable alternatives.

The Relationship Between High Debt and Inflation

Deficit financing is used to pay for public projects and to fund the government. Debt is not bad per se, as long as the money borrowed is put to a productive use. Many people borrow money to buy a house and a car, because they need a place to live and a way to get around. Borrowing money for those things is often a wise financial decision.

In the same way, government borrowing can be good. For example, a nation may borrow money to invest in needed infrastructure and pay contractors a competitive amount for their services. That's different from borrowing money because politicians refuse to make hard choices about taxation and spending, or to sustain an extensive system of corruption and kickbacks.

Some debt can keep an economy growing, especially in times of recession. If the private sector is not able to make investments, then the government can step in. The key is to pay off that debt when the recession ends. Otherwise, nations risk inflation and, in extreme cases, default.

Understanding Debt Rating

You know how you have a credit score that affects your ability to borrow money at a favorable interest rate? Governments have the same ratings, and this ends up being reflected in exchange rates. Several bond rating agencies, such as Fitch and Moody's, rate governments. They refer to governments as *sovereign issuers*. The agency analysts look at the amount of debt that a country has, how it is using that debt, what its tax system looks like, the state of its economy, and the nature of its political system. The assigned ratings are different combinations of letters and numbers, but generally, A is great, D is the worst, and AAA is best of all.

All else being equal, countries with higher credit ratings will have stronger exchange rates. There is less chance of inflation or default that would hurt the currency's value.

Balance of Trade and Current Account Deficits

The *balance of payments* is the system of accounting used for international transactions. It is not well understood by the general public, and it has a huge effect on exchange rates. The balance of payments has three parts:

- » The *current account*, which shows the imports and exports of goods and services;
- » The *capital account*, which records capital transfers such as patents, trademarks, and funds that migrants send back home; and
- » The *investment account*, which includes investments in stocks, bonds, and real estate by private investors, corporations, and governments.

The total amount of money that comes in and the total amount of money that goes out must equal zero for the accounts to balance. Within the three accounts, nations may have deficits or surpluses, and the reasons for these affect both exchange rates and central bank policies toward exchange rate management.

Export Prices vs. Import Prices

The *current account* is a measure of imports and exports in a nation over a given time period. If a nation has a current account surplus, then it is exporting more than it imports. If it has a current account deficit, then it imports more than it exports. Consumers have two main reasons for buying imports. The first is that they want things they can't find in their home country. The second is that sometimes goods made abroad cost less than goods made at home.

From the standpoint of currency, the current account is critical. If people want to buy a nation's goods, then they need to exchange their money for the nation's currency, and that increased demand strengthens the exchange rate. Likewise, a nation that has a lot of imports has to sell its currency to buy others, increasing the supply and thus weakening the exchange rate.

If a government wants to make its goods more attractive to buyers in other countries, it will work to weaken its exchange rate to make its currency relatively cheaper. Moreover, a stronger currency makes its exports more expensive, causing it to lose market share to lower-cost competitors. That will have an adverse effect on its economy by leading to lower sales, which in turn leads to layoffs and other undesirable economic effects.

Governments have other ways to manage imports and exports. They can charge taxes on imports, require importers to have licenses, and even set quotas on the amount of goods that can come in. These practices usually create a lot more political drama than managing the exchange rate.

The Dangers of a Current Account Deficit

Because the balance of payments has to balance, a deficit in the current account has to be made up in the capital and investment accounts. A current account deficit indicates that a country is spending more on foreign trade than it is earning. The next question is, how does it make that up?

In most cases, the money comes from the investment account. Countries that export end up with a lot of foreign currency that they want to put to work. They can do this by buying businesses or real estate, building factories, or buying bonds. Remember that a bond is a loan, so this means foreign investors are loaning money to the country with the deficit. At some point, that loan comes due, and then the supply of currency increases.

If a nation has a persistent current account deficit, then its currency will weaken, all else being equal, because the deficit will lead to an increased supply of its currency on foreign exchange markets.

Time Value of Money

The "time value of money" concept refers to how the value of money changes. Money today is worth more than money in the future, in large part because you can spend or invest it today if you want to, and if you invest it in a relatively conservative fashion, then you can reliably collect returns on it. If you won't receive the money until a later time, then you can't spend it, invest it, or collect returns on it until then. Therefore, money in your hand is always worth more than money you will receive in the future.

In addition, future money is worth less than current money because of the effects of inflation. Not only can't you spend or invest the money now, but it will buy less when you finally receive it. This also means that if you borrow money, you get to spend or invest it now when it's more valuable and pay it back later when it's less valuable. The interest rate that you are charged is based in part on future inflation expectations.

Gauging the Effects of These Factors

fig. 12

WHAT CHANGES	HOW IT CHANGES	EFFECT ON CURRENCY
Amount of National Debt	↑	↓
Amount of National Debt	↓	↑
Sovereign Credit Rating	↑	↑
Sovereign Credit Rating	↓	↓
Current Account Deficit	↑	↓
Current Account Deficit	↓	↑
International Investment	↑	↑
International Investment	↓	↓
Net Effect	?	?

Some of the economic factors that affect exchange rates cancel each other out, and others reinforce each other. There's great danger in focusing on only one. For example, the United States has had a current account deficit since it went off the gold standard in 1933. At times, its currency has been stronger than it is now, and at times it has been weaker. The current account is only one of many factors to consider.

Because all these factors are working at the same time, it's not clear what will be the net effect of a single change. But traders don't need to make a guess, because the market will tell them.

The chart in figure 12 summarizes these factors.

Recognizing Strengths and Weaknesses of Various Economies

Prices change based on fluctuating economic factors, not absolute numbers. Anyone who takes even a cursory look at world trade can see that the US runs a chronic current account deficit. This is not a secret, so it's not in and of itself a reason to bet against the dollar. The question is, what could make the deficit smaller or larger, and how would that affect everything else?

People who analyze currencies and sovereign credit are not looking at something this obvious. They tend to get into the weeds of policies and develop complex probability models. You, as an individual, are not going to be able to get an edge in the analysis of currencies, especially not for short-term trading.

Other people have done extensive work developing and testing indicators. It is easier to learn from them than to try to develop your own system, at least at first. The most powerful indicators are the price patterns in various pairs. The other set of indicators to look at are *currency strength meters*. These are analytics available in most trading platforms that show which currencies tend to be stronger and which tend to be weaker.

You can combine these indicators with information about a currency's correlation with other currencies or with economic factors. For example, the Mexican economy is based on two things: oil and trade with the United States. The currency strengthens when oil prices increase and when Mexico exports more goods to the United States. If you see movements in the US dollar or in other petroleum-centered economies, then you can anticipate whether or not the peso is due for movement.

Applying What You Learn to How You Trade

So many different factors affect exchange rates that it can be difficult to determine which factors will dominate at any one time. Just keep two things in mind: you are not smarter than the market, and what the market knows is in the prices right now. The immediate past predicts the immediate future. Think about identifying price patterns that repeat over and over again, giving us a high degree of probable subsequent outcomes, which in turn present tradeable opportunities.

If you really love the research aspect of forex, then you might be better off investing rather than trading. Investors buy and hold for long periods of time and rely on *fundamental analysis*, which is the process of researching markets and economies to form a long-range forecast. The time it takes to do fundamental analysis, and its long investment time horizon, typically makes it unsuitable for traders. Traders rely on *technical analysis*, which involves looking at the patterns of supply and demand that show up in price action to make forecasts of short-term directional moves.

Chapter Recap

» Currency prices are affected by the willingness of people to buy into a country. Politics, societal cohesion, war, and disaster figure into price movements.

» An exchange rate is the price of a currency relative to another currency. An interest rate is the price of money in its own currency. Interest rates measure both the supply and the demand in the overall economy (the real rate of interest) and changes in price levels (inflation). Thus, interest rates and inflation affect exchange rates.

» When governments need money, they sell bonds to investors, often investors in other countries. Levels of government debt affect the inflation rate, all else being equal.

» The balance of trade shows the sources of foreign exchange relative to trade in goods and services, investment, and national reserves. The changes in these accounts can affect exchange rates.

» All these factors combine to create the price movements that traders seek out. And they are not the only factors, either. The price is always seeking its true value at any moment in time and is extremely sensitive to countless pieces of information.

| 5 |
Determining If Forex Trading Is Right for You

Chapter Overview
» Thinking about goals and how to reach them
» Being realistic about how much you can invest
» Assessing your personality fit with forex
» Picking a trading strategy

The first few chapters of this book covered a lot of background information. We've described the market and the factors that affect it. You should now have an idea of all that you can trade on the forex market, as well as what makes this market particularly interesting.

Trading can be a tough game. People make money and people lose money—lots of it. Some traders find that they become consumed by the market or begin to judge their worth by their trading prowess. Psychology is key, both to trading success and to keeping your trading in perspective.

And that's all well and good, but it won't help you with the big question: Should you, the person reading this book right now, trade forex?

By the way, it's okay if the answer is no. I have enjoyed trading forex and profited from it, but there are plenty of other ways to make money inside and outside of the financial markets.

Assessing Your Goals

A good place to start in determining if forex is right for you is figuring out what your goals are. How do you want to work, and how much money do you want or need to make?

Everybody is different. I never particularly liked working for other people, and trading was not my first business. I came to it with the idea that I wanted to be my own boss, and, in light of my previous business experience, I was confident in my ability to manage profits and losses.

What do you want from trading? Why did you pick up this book?

Freedom

I began trading in the early 1990s, placing orders through a full-service broker by landline telephone. I ended up making enough money from shorting the GBP against the USD (at the same time that George Soros was shorting the pound against the deutsche mark, unbeknownst to me) that I hired a manager for my business so I could take a leave of absence. Then I went on a backpacking trip through Europe and South America. It was a journey that would lead to meeting my wife, a win more significant than anything I ever accomplished in the trading room. During this time, I finally laid to rest the idea of returning to regular employment, realizing once and for all that it was not for me. A few years later, on a subsequent backpacking trip to Europe, I saw internet cafés everywhere and realized that I could trade from almost anywhere in the world. When I returned to the US, I took up trading full time. It was a career that let me do something I was good at and gave me the flexibility to travel and spend time with my family. Hence, my trading business is named Backpack Trader.

I believe that if you do the work, you can form reasonable expectations about the future. You will be wrong sometimes, but you should be right more often than not. Successful trading is a numbers game. We have to be sure we stack the odds in our favor with every trade, and that is what this book is about.

A trading lifestyle has given freedom to me and many other people, but discipline is required to achieve it. If you understand that paradox, you are in a good position to make this work.

Financial Security

Trading is not a way to make money fast. It is a way to make money as a full-time or part-time occupation. If you enjoy it, it can contribute to your retirement savings, serve as a productive side hustle in retirement, or give you money toward a future goal.

Not everyone is cut out to be a trader, and that is perfectly fine. There are other ways to achieve your financial objectives.

For me, trading has been a great way to make a living. It may be for you too.

Assessing Your Current Situation

Taking up trading is a lot like starting a business. It's not something to rush into. The market is a fantastic teacher, and a harsh one; proper preparation will make your early trading experience so much better.

Reading this book is an excellent first step, and I recommend that you read it to the end before you start trading. Right now, make a commitment to use best practices so as not to develop bad habits, which are hard to break and really expensive. Being a beginner is a big advantage because you have the opportunity to learn things the right way right from the start.

Does Forex Trading Make Sense for You?

Let's start with the one thing that none of us has enough of: time. Do you have the time to dedicate to your trading? You need time to learn the markets and research your trading, time to work on your trading plan, time to place your trades and monitor the market, and time to evaluate your trading performance. Most of this is work done before you start trading with real money. Once your systems are in place, you may find that your actual trading takes very little time. For example, swing trading with daily charts takes me about five to ten minutes a day or less. If you do the work before you start trading, you will work more efficiently and more profitably.

Begin by considering your schedule. When will you find the time to learn to trade? Once you determine the time commitment you're willing to make, the next big challenge will be your willingness to be patient. Although trading does at times call for quick action and fast decision making, it also calls for patience. You need to have enough patience to learn about trading, and you need to have patience when activity is slow. Sometimes it takes a long time for a trade to work out or even to set up. If you are not patient by nature, then this is a skill you will need to work on. Patience is critical. The right tools will help, too. You can use strategies that alert you when a trade is setting up. I have spent the last 14 years or so developing trading tools that actually print the entire trade right on the chart, complete with entries, targets, and stops, based on a distinct set of rules, making the trade planning and preproduction process infinitely easier, not to mention the actual trading itself.

Consider your lifestyle too. The Backpack Trading philosophy is about freedom, but some trade strategies require a greater time commitment than others. The four-hour price chart might look like the chart you'd love to trade on; you may be able to vividly see all the great winning trades and clear patterns. But are you able to monitor your charts every four hours, day in and day out? Some people can but most can't. Charts do not teach you what the passing of time actually feels like, or what it means to you in practical terms.

The next big consideration is your available capital. Do you have money put aside for trading that you can afford to lose? If you get into a situation where you need a trade to work out in order to pay for groceries, then you have a real problem. The mistake I see most inexperienced traders make is putting their personal financial needs in front of the needs of their trading. That never works, because they are two completely different things. Your trading activity requires a detached and dedicated capital supply, and that usually means you have another source of income available when you're starting out. The point is, you cannot be attached to the money you use to trade with if you hope to succeed.

One of the hardest things to learn when first starting out is how to take what the market wants to give you, and not what you want or need from the market. We accomplish this with tradeplan rules, smart money management (small risk in relation to our available capital), and dynamic trading goals that can adjust to the market day in and day out. The great irony, of course, is that if you begin your trading endeavor properly, then at some point down the road, at the right time, your income from trading should have grown to the point where it actually *can* take care of your personal needs. It's never the other way around, though. If your motivation is to pay your electric bill or your mortgage today, you will find yourself forcing trades, forcing the market to give you something it just doesn't want to give. That's the beginning of the end for a trading account—and the mortgage will remain unpaid.

Finally, you must be able to honestly assess your risk tolerance. Some people are more comfortable with risk than others. Good traders learn to become comfortable with (and even embrace) risk; however, they also respect it and are committed to controlling it. Trading is not the same as gambling. Trading forex is not like going to the races and choosing a horse because you like the name.

Without adequate risk management skills, a trader will fail. Do you want to achieve your financial goals and realize your dreams, or do you want to end up as a casualty on the battlefield of trading? If you take the time to read this book, I will teach you how to manage risk using stop losses (predetermined exits from a trade), proper position sizing (determining how much of your capital to risk at various points within a trade), and how to create a proven tradeplan designed to stack all the odds on your side and, hopefully, grow your trading account.

Can You Put Your Emotions Aside?

Loss is a part of trading, and the fear of loss can cause an existential crisis. It's primal. For that matter, greed is also a form of fear: the fear of missing out on something.

Here's a trick for overcoming the fear of trading: trade smaller. Small wins compound, and small losses keep your powder dry for the next trade. If you're afraid of the trade, then you have not adequately accomplished your preproduction work, and you are probably trading too large. Your emotions are your most important indicators, and you can use them to improve—if you listen to what they're telling you.

Ideally, you want to not have any emotional attachment to the outcome of any trade. That is a skill that most people have to work very hard at acquiring. If you feel uncomfortable with a trade, that typically means you are overtrading your capacity. You're assuming too much risk. Listen to yourself. When you are ready to trade for real and are risking the right amount, you should not feel uncomfortable with a trade, win or lose.

The big banks and hedge funds have invested heavily in computer algorithms to do their trading, because the machines take all the emotion out of it. Nothing will undo a trader faster than emotions, namely the Big Three illustrated in figure 13.

fig. 13

DOUBT   **FEAR**   **GREED**

Trading is war. For every trade you place, someone is taking the other side. There is an opposing argument for every trade you make. The key to succeeding in the battlefield is to make sure that every trade is part of a larger, proven tradeplan. Any given trade is just one battle in the war. You are going to lose some, but what's important is that you win more than you lose. That's how you win the war. That's how trading helps you achieve your financial goals.

Figuring Out the Style that Works Best for You

Trading comes in many different flavors. Most traders settle on one or two that fit their personality and their circumstances. They look at charts that cover the times of day and lengths of time that they are interested in trading. Check out this menu featuring some of the predominant trading styles:

In the Short Term...

Scalping takes advantage of small price moves. It involves fast, repeated buying and selling of currency pairs throughout the day. Scalpers are looking to pick up small profits rather than play overall trends, but the profits have to be large enough to overcome the spread costs. One loss can wipe out a lot of small gains. It is sometimes defined as "trying to pick up nickels in front of a steamroller." Most of the big traders have algorithms that do nothing but scan the market for scalping opportunities. Small traders will have a hard time finding scalping opportunities. This style is best suited for experienced traders and requires a specially designed trading platform.

Day trading involves placing short-term trades, always looking at the market in real time. Day traders close out all their trades by the end of their trading day, which reduces their risk of being affected by an adverse event outside of trading hours.

... And a Little Longer

Swing trading calls for holding positions longer than in day trading or scalping. Most swing traders look for positions that play out over days or even weeks. I have had some trades last for a few months. They just keep going and going and going.

Long-term trading, or long-term position trading, is where traders make decisions based on long-term trends. They rely on both fundamental analysis and finding trends that play out over their target time horizon.

This begins to cross over into investing, which is the practice of buying a financial asset to hold for the very long term and relies almost entirely on fundamental analysis.

Figuring Out What Makes Sense

As you consider the different ways to trade, think about what makes sense for you given your circumstances and your interests.

This is just like opening a business. Don't let it become personal. Create a plan, develop it further, and follow procedures.

In trading, our edge is our ability to put the odds in our favor each time we place a trade. The preproduction planning work creates the edge. To maintain that edge, traders must remain disciplined and emotionally detached. Good traders know how to deal with their emotions and run their trading like a business.

Practice and Patience Are Necessary

The way to become good at anything is to practice. Repetition is the key. You want to practice your trading maneuvers over and over again until you no longer have to think about it. You just do it, like a reflex. This will take time. I recommend that new traders place 25 consecutive perfect trades in a demo account before moving on to trading with cash, and then another 25 consecutive perfect trades with the smallest position size before risking more capital. Make a mistake, and start over. It can take a while to master, but the training will pay off. Be patient. All businesses take time to build, and a trading business is no different.

By "perfect" I don't mean that every trade has to win, I simply mean that each trade has to be executed with precision and accuracy in accordance with the predetermined rules of a proven tradeplan. We'll get into the nuts and bolts of creating tradeplans in part III of this book.

Once you accept the need for practice and patience, the next step is making a long-haul commitment to being successful as a trader.

In It for the Long Haul

Quite simply, if you want to succeed at this, you must be willing to be a good student for as long as it takes. Reading books like this and watching videos by trading gurus are only a piece of the puzzle. What's most important is what you learn and practice on your own, that you complete your "autodidactic education" in trading. Commit to learning things the proper way, the first time, following specific steps that build on one another and that will lead you down the path with the greatest chance for success. For the beginner-level forex trader, reading this book from cover to cover will kick-start you in the right direction.

If you find after reading this book that you gained valuable insight into the world of trading and are interested in a more holistic view of my approach, beyond just forex, be sure to check out *Day Trading QuickStart Guide*, also from ClydeBank Media.

The world of trading is replete with irony. Some traders say the worst thing that can happen to a new trader is making money, because then trading seems easier than it is. You may have heard that it's better to be lucky than good. Not so with trading. You might get lucky and have a good win on a bad trade. You think you did well, but all you've really done is reinforce what could become a bad habit. You won a battle but are on track to lose the war. I've seen overconfidence cause many a casualty on the battlefield of trading.

Setting Up a Demo Account

If you want to learn to trade, start by opening a ***demo account***, also known as a simulated (sim) trading account. Building experience by working with a demo account will help you better understand how trading works. There are three main reasons to use a demo account:

» You will learn how to place trades flawlessly and consistently.
» You can begin developing the habits of running your trading like a business.
» You can start studying and learning a strategy with the demo account's charts.

The downside of using a demo account is that traders sometimes reinforce bad habits that carry over into real trading. Because it is a demo account, they tend to not take it seriously. With this attitude, they are setting the stage for real-life losses. One of my favorite pieces of advice to the beginning trader is "Practice how you intend to play." A music teacher once told me this when I was learning to play drums. "Practice hard, play hard. Practice like a wimp, play like a wimp." Heed this advice with your trading. Treat your sim account as if it were real.

When you are comfortable entering error-free trades and have been able to achieve 25 consecutive mistake-free trades, with a tradeplan that you have now proven because it consistently grows the balance in your demo account, it's time to graduate to trading with real funds.

If you cannot make money in your demo account, *do not* move on to trading with real money. Trading with real money adds a layer of mental pressure. If you're not generating a profit when nothing is at stake, you will not be profitable in the real arena.

Diving In

Ultimately, the best way to learn about forex is to do it. When you are actually trading, the ideas in this book will become much clearer to you.

Later in this book, we'll talk a lot about tradeplans. Your tradeplan is your road map, which tells you what to trade, how and when to trade it, and what limits you will set. It's the master SOP (standard operating procedure) guidance brief that tells you how to run your trading business. It is your key to successful trading. If you were opening a business, you would write a business plan. If you are going to trade, you need a tradeplan.

The following are some of the more macro-level questions that need to be answered and incorporated into your tradeplan:

- » What strategy or trading methodology will I use?
- » Which currency pairs shall I trade? Am I going to trade only forex, or will I be trading in other markets?
- » Am I adequately funded? (In general, you want to risk no more than 2% of your capital on a single trade. Do you have enough to do this and still meet your other financial obligations?)
- » What time of day will I begin trading?
- » Am I available to run my tradeplan each day, as if it were a business? Or will I need to begin on a less frequent schedule?

Though some of this information will depend on your personal situation, the next part of this book should prepare you to answer those questions.

Chapter Recap

» Forex trading offers freedom that traditional employment does not. It can be a productive and profitable business.

» Before trading, assess both your practical situation (funds, time you can commit) and your emotional situation. Trading is as much about psychology as it is about money.

» There are many ways to trade forex based on your personal preferences.

» Be patient. Start carefully. Allow time for practice. Expect some losses. As with anything else, you will get better over time.

PART II

TOOLS OF THE TRADE

| 6 |

Choosing a Broker and a Platform

Chapter Overview

» Your choice of broker is critical to your success

» Trades are analyzed and placed through a platform offered by a broker

» The case for using more than one broker and more than one platform

Once you decide to trade, your next step is to make another critical decision: which broker and trading platform you will use.

Not all brokerage firms work with forex. Those that do offer a range of services. Some do a better job with smaller traders. Others are really designed for traders with significant capital and experience. Some have better execution on major pairs; others have a niche in exotics. And some are complete and total scams.

The broker maintains custody of funds, handles trade execution, and provides the documentation needed at income tax time. Traders work with different software platforms to analyze the market and place trades. Some platforms are specific to a broker, while others work with several different firms. The choice of platform goes hand in hand with the choice of broker and is just as crucial to trading success.

Because different traders have different needs, I cannot recommend any one broker or platform. Furthermore, the financial services industry changes a lot. Firms merge. Storied firms fold. New startups enter that do things better than the competition. Therefore, I will give you an idea of what to look for and what questions to ask so you can make the best decision for yourself. There are names, yes, but keep in mind that the firms mentioned may be operating under new names, have different philosophies, or be completely gone by the time you do your research.

Selecting a Broker

Some brokers specialize in forex. Others handle trades in stocks, bonds, and mutual funds as well as forex, futures, and options.

NOTE

All brokers are in the business of making money, but some make money by working with their customers and others make money by taking advantage of their customers.

Different brokers work differently, have different fee structures, and offer different services. In forex, firms can be subject to various types of regulation depending on where they're headquartered. And, let's face it, some have much better customer service than others.

The rules governing forex brokers are different than the rules governing other types of brokers, in large part because there are no organized forex exchanges. Different brokers have different clientele, too. Some specialize in work for companies that are conducting business overseas. Those firms may not be set up as well to meet the needs of traders. Other forex brokers are downright unethical. That alone makes the process of looking for a forex broker a little different than looking for a broker for a retirement account or a college fund.

CAUTION

Romance scams, in which someone online finds a mark, pretends to be in love, asks for money, and then disappears, have been around for a while. A new twist that I've heard about involves introducing the mark to forex trading through the hottie's "broker," who takes the money.

Types of Forex Brokers

Forex has no central exchanges. Instead, networks of banks and brokers execute trades for their customers and for their own accounts. Forex brokers fall into two main categories, *dealing desk brokers* and *no dealing desk brokers*. The differences between them are significant.

» **Dealing desk brokers**, also known as market makers or *A-Book brokers*, are intermediaries between customers and the interbank market. They make fast, efficient trades by taking the other side of a customer's transaction. However, this gives them a direct conflict of interest. In fact, some firms do this under the assumption that their customers are bad traders, so they can make a profit by doing the opposite of what their customers do. They market heavily to beginning forex traders.

» **No dealing desk brokers**, sometimes called *B-book brokers*, work with several interbank traders to collect the best prices on the market, giving traders the best rates on the market. They place trades through electronic communication networks (ECNs) to get trades executed quickly; this is sometimes known as ***straight-through processing***. Customers receive the exact spread available to retail customers on the interbank market, which is often lower than that charged by a dealing desk broker. Because of this, no dealing desk brokers often charge exchange fees or commissions. I find that the cost is well worth it, as the bid-ask spread and execution advantages more than offset the commission costs.

Due to the conflict of interest held by dealing desk brokers, I prefer NDD brokers. I want brokers to make money working with me, not against me. However, dealing desk brokers tend to have low initial balance requirements and thus may be more accessible for beginning traders. If you go this route, be aware of the conflict and consider switching to a no dealing desk broker when your account size allows. Remember, commission expense is only one aspect of trading and is usually much less costly than higher spreads.

Understanding Account Offerings

A trader's money is held in a brokerage account, and different brokers and different account types have different features. Whether considering minimum account size, withdrawal policies, or other factors, some brokers are better for a given trader than others.

» **What is the initial account size?** Some brokers allow customers to get started with small initial deposits. Others require large deposits, because the firms are not set up to handle beginners.

» **How are deposits made?** Brokers have different ways of accepting money into accounts. Most use ACH payments, which are made directly to and from commercial banks. ACH (automated clearing house) is a type of money transfer between the banks, brokers, etc.—it's not unlike direct deposit for individual payments. ACH is a simple, secure process. Some brokers will accept funds through a check mailed to them or dropped off at one of their offices, although this is decidedly old-fashioned. And a few brokers will accept funds by PayPal, wire transfer, or even credit card.

Credit cards are a convenient way to send money, but they are a rotten way to fund your trading account. If you don't pay off the balance in full and on time, you will get slammed with high interest rates. And if the only way you can fund your trading is with your credit card, then you don't have the resources to trade. Do not do this. Beware of any broker or service provider who encourages you to borrow to fund your account.

» **How are withdrawals made?** Inevitably, you will want to take money out of your trading account. Whether it's time to fund that backpacking trip or to switch funds to a different broker, you need access to your money. Ask how it happens, how often withdrawals are allowed, and if there are fees for them. Most brokers allow you to make ACH transfers to your commercial bank account. Some will write you a check and stick it in the mail, even in this day and age.

» **How much leverage is allowed? What are the margin requirements?** *Leverage* is the use of borrowed money to place trades. It's common, and it increases potential return—and also potential risk. *Margin* is the minimum amount of money that must be in the trader's account when using leverage. It is determined as a percentage of the trade. The minimum percentage is often set by regulators, but brokers are free to set a higher margin requirement. Using leverage is often referred to as ***trading on margin***.

Forex traders often use leverage, so you should know what your broker's policies are. Be wary of a broker that encourages you to take high levels of risk early in your trading career. Over the years, US brokerage firms have reduced the amount of leverage that they allow, and I think that's a good thing. Keep in mind that brokers profit from margin trades by charging you interest.

» **What currency pairs are offered?** Right now, most forex firms offer trading in all pairs, major and minor, and many offer crosses with gold, cryptocurrency, or other assets. In general, the larger firms have the broadest pair offerings and the tightest available spreads. If a firm does not offer access to all forex pairs, then it's probably not a true forex broker and should be avoided. For example, a reputable financial firm may be well equipped to handle your 401(k) rollover, but that does not necessarily make it the best firm for forex trading—even if it offers some forex pairs.

» **What about options and futures?** Some forex traders also work with options and futures. This book is designed for traders who are just starting out, so it does not cover strategies using these derivatives. Traders who choose to include derivatives will need a broker that can support them.

Commissions, Spreads, and Fees

Brokerage firms have lots of ways to make money. Many beginning traders go for the firm that seems the cheapest, only to find out the hard way that it would have been better to pay a little more for services. On the other hand, some of the more expensive brokers provide services that small forex traders don't need.

There is absolutely nothing wrong with the broker making a profit. However, they should make their profit while helping their customers succeed. Both parties should benefit from the relationship.

A *commission* is a fee that a broker charges for each trade. It is intended to cover the costs of executing the trade (while generating some money for the broker).

The *spread* is the difference between the bid and ask prices of a currency pair. Some brokers set this as a predetermined number of pips, especially for the major pairs, while others use a variable spread based on market volatility. When variable spreads are in play, some brokers do a better job at execution and can keep spreads low. This is especially true in trades of exotic pairs.

The *bid* is the price that the broker pays to buy an asset, and the *ask* is the price at which the broker sells the asset to customers. The difference is the broker's profit. The wider the spread, the more money the broker makes, and the more the trader pays on a trade. What's more, the moment a trader places a trade, they will need the price to move favorably in their direction for the amount of the spread just to be in a break-even position. In other words, when the trade is initiated, the trader is immediately in a losing position due to the spread, whether it be one tenth of a pip, 35 pips, or anything in between.

The trader is at the mercy of the broker. Brokers can manipulate the spread at any time. And trust me, they will manipulate it in their favor, not yours. I have been bumped out of trades when the broker widened the spread so wide that it caught my stop loss, which took me out of the trade, and then the price moved on to what would have been my profit target. Worse, it didn't even show up on the chart. You wouldn't have known it happened if you didn't experience it. The good news is that there are things we can do to protect ourselves from this danger, so keep reading, as this information is covered in part III.

In addition to commissions and spreads, many brokers charge fees for various services. These may include fees for using margin, carrying an account balance below a certain amount, making withdrawals, requesting paper statements, or using enhancements to the trading platform.

When comparing brokers, traders should consider the costs in total based on their own trading needs. The zero-commission broker is rarely the cheapest. I personally look for the largest, most reputable brokers with the most competitive rates. I prefer to pay a small commission for the lowest spread available.

Trading Tools

Most brokers offer tools to help you trade better, including simulation trading, backtesting, trade recording, charting, and technical indicators. Some have full-fledged platforms integrated into their order-entry system, others work with third-party trading platforms, and some provide both. MetaTrader 4 (MT4) is one of the most widely used charting platforms that nearly every forex broker offers to their customers in addition to their own charting and trading platform. The MT4 platform plugs directly into your trading account. Many brokers also offer the more modern MT5 platform, which is even more capable than MT4.

Make Sure the Broker Is Regulated

Here's a reality: forex trading is not well regulated. People need to trade money all the time in the course of travel or business, but there are no central exchanges. Legally, there is no difference between exchanging some cash at the hotel's front desk while on vacation and trading four-hour charts of the NZD/CAD pair. In practical terms, a regulated broker is a huge protection against hassles and scams.

In the United States, forex brokers are regulated through the ***National Futures Association*** (NFA), a self-regulatory organization for derivatives exchanges. The NFA is authorized by the federal government through the **Commodity Futures Trading Commission** (CFTC), which oversees trading in agricultural and financial contracts.

Although the NFA's primary concerns are the options and futures exchanges, it includes **Retail Foreign Exchange Dealers**, which are firms that handle currency trading outside of business contracts, as well as options and futures on currencies.

Offshore brokers, based outside of the United States and often in different tax haven nations such as St. Vincent and the Grenadines, the Cayman Islands, Seychelles, or Vanuatu, sometimes promote membership in trade associations as a replacement for regulation. These groups have no teeth. The brokers allow very high levels of leverage and very small account sizes, a recipe for high fees and massive losses. Traders who run into problems have no avenue for complaint or remediation.

One forex trading scam involves taking customers' funds as soon as they open accounts, under the assumption that most new forex traders will wash out. They encourage risky trades with high leverage. Sure, they let their "customers" enter "trades," but the trades are not actually executed. Scams of this nature are usually discovered in the very rare instances when a trader makes a profit and wants to withdraw money, or when enough people complain and begin to push back. Spend some time on a message board like Reddit and you'll see plenty of sad stories.

Although brokerages regulated by the NFA and the CFTC can only take accounts from US citizens or permanent residents, traders outside of the US are not stuck with the shady offshore firms. Many nations have strong forex regulations. For example, forex firms in the European Union are regulated by the Markets in Financial Instruments Directive (MiFID). In Japan, the Financial Services Agency provides oversight of forex brokers. These organizations help ensure that brokers are willing and able to meet their obligations to customers, and customers can get redress if any problems develop.

Traders in the US should look for brokerage firms regulated by the NFA and the CFTC, and traders in other countries should look for brokers that are regulated in their place of residence. There may be extra paperwork involved in opening an account with a regulated broker, but the protection offered by regulation is worth the hassle.

Check Out the Customer Service

Once you have narrowed down your broker choices, read some online reviews, too, for more information about the quality of service. Then call each one to get an idea of wait times and customer service practices. This is a quick way to find out whether it's easy, or even possible, to speak with a person rather than be funneled to an auto-attendant. If you reach a live representative, ask some questions to see if they can talk to you about execution, leverage, and trading costs.

Because forex is a 24-hour venture, customers should be able to talk to someone at any hour. This is especially important for traders who will be working outside of normal business hours.

fig.14

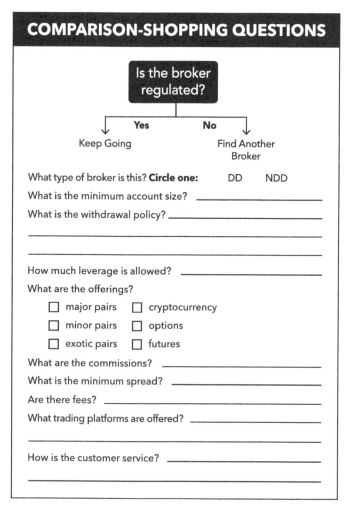

COMPARISON-SHOPPING QUESTIONS

Is the broker regulated?

Yes → Keep Going

No → Find Another Broker

What type of broker is this? **Circle one:**   DD   NDD

What is the minimum account size? _____

What is the withdrawal policy? _____

_____

_____

How much leverage is allowed? _____

What are the offerings?

☐ major pairs   ☐ cryptocurrency

☐ minor pairs   ☐ options

☐ exotic pairs   ☐ futures

What are the commissions? _____

What is the minimum spread? _____

Are there fees? _____

What trading platforms are offered? _____

_____

How is the customer service? _____

_____

Broker evaluation checklist

A printable version of the Broker Evaluation Checklist (figure 14) is available with your Digital Assets. Visit go.quickstartguides.com/forex for access.

Selecting a Trading Platform

The broker's role is to place the trade, clear the funds, and maintain the paperwork. In the context of the entire financial system, these are vital functions. However, any regulated broker should be able to do this for you. Forex traders need more.

That "more" comes in the form of a ***trading platform***, which is a software application that allows traders to analyze the market. Some brokers offer a proprietary platform, and others work with various independent platforms. They have different characteristics and capabilities, and the choice often comes down to personal preference. MetaTrader 4, also called MT4, is one that is commonly used by forex traders, but there are others.

Exactly What Is a Trading Platform?

A trading platform is software used specifically for trading. It connects to the brokerage firm and allows users to open, close, and manage market positions. It also allows traders to analyze price patterns and thus develop new trading strategies. Most platforms are free, but some cost money up front or have charges for additional capabilities. Because the trading platform is a trader's direct connection to the market, the choice is important.

Platforms vary in scope and complexity. Some are really simple to use: open up the app and get going, with no fuss. Others have detailed analytics and can support traders who are designing their own algorithms.

Choice of platform is closely linked to choice of broker, as the broker will offer a particular platform and may or may not support others. Some brokers use their own proprietary software, and others use an industry-wide platform such as MetaTrader 4 (MT4) or the newer MT5. Sometimes a first-rate broker cannot support a trader's platform of choice. In that case, a work-around such as an application programming interface (API) can be created to enable the trader to pair their preferred broker with their preferred platform. Also, many third-party apps can be plugged into charting platforms, which can greatly enhance capabilities and overall user experience.

Features to Consider When Choosing a Platform

When comparing platforms, look at the following:

» **Ability to execute trades quickly**. This is a function of the ease of order entry and of the connection speed. Traders need to be able to react quickly to any market condition.

» **Reliability**. Some platforms are desktop applications, others are web-based, and a few are available in both formats. Many are adapting to a more mobile world and can be used on one's smartphone or tablet as well. The choice will depend on hardware and software characteristics. Some platforms can be glitchy, prone to freezing and crashing. One way to research this is to ask around on message boards like Reddit.

» **Quality and usability of the analysis tools**. Ease of use is in the eye of the beholder, and most platform operators will allow traders to play around with a demo account to see how they like it. In addition, a good platform will allow for *backtesting*, which is a way of testing a strategy by looking at how it would have done using past market prices. Finally, a platform should allow a trader to analyze past trades in order to see how they performed, a critical step for developing the all-important tradeplan, which we'll get to later.

» **Automatic trading**. Over the last decade, trading has become highly automated. Hedge funds and banks use algorithms for almost all their proprietary trades. Some platforms offer similar capabilities to traders, with algorithms that offer suggested trades, as well as programming capabilities that allow traders to enter their own algorithms. This way, they can automatically place orders if certain preloaded conditions are met. Of course, if any of the platform's algorithms were sure things, the company would not be giving them away. Whether using the platform's algorithms or your own, run some backtests and forward tests to see how they work in different market conditions. Don't ever run automation (aka robots) unattended unless you are an advanced trader. I have seen many instances in which the robot thought a trade was executed at a certain price but in reality it wasn't executed at all, or vice versa. Robots can't think for themselves, and things will always go wrong. I have found that automation adds complexity and is often more difficult, not easier.

Some Forex Brokers and Platforms

This list includes some of the largest forex brokers and trading platforms as of the time of publication. There are many others. And keep in mind that the landscape is always changing, thanks to mergers and startups. This list is not an endorsement, just a starting point for further research.

In general, I think traders should choose large, well-known, reputable, competitively priced brokers, preferably those that do not take the other side of customers' trades. Some of these firms run into trouble, to be sure, but they are not scams operating under the guise of being a forex broker. The list is alphabetical.

ATC Brokers

ATC Brokers is a straight-through processor that specializes in forex and works with both retail and institutional clients. It offers a proprietary platform that is based on MetaTrader 4. In addition to forex (including micro lots), it handles trades in silver and gold.

Interactive Brokers

This brokerage offers a special kind of account that allows you to trade every type of instrument, all from a single account: futures, forex, equities, options, bonds, mutual funds, etc. This makes it a great choice for someone who is active in multiple markets. Although Interactive Brokers has its own platform, accounts can also be connected to NinjaTrader charting and a third-party data feed. IB is a huge, international, reputable broker.

Forex.com

Forex.com is a retail forex brokerage operated by GAIN Capital, a major institutional forex broker. Its standard retail product offers dealing desk broker execution and a proprietary platform. The firm also supports MetaTrader4.

MetaTrader 4 and MetaTrader 5

MetaTrader 4, or MT4, is the most widely used forex platform. It's not a broker, but it is the charting and trading platform that works with most forex brokerage firms. Brokers will provide their own version of MT4, usually as a download from their website.

Among its features are trade execution, charting, and indicators. It supports custom trading programs and includes basic algorithms in the package. It has some limitations, such as its inability to easily scale out of positions, but many of those problems can be solved with third-party plug-ins. One in particular that I personally recommend is FX Synergy, a trade manager interface for MT4, by Pecunia Systems. It vastly improves the experience of trading with MT4, and I use it with my own forex trading. You can find a link with your Digital Assets that will give you a 20% discount. Go to go.quickstartguides.com/forex.

MetaTrader 5 is the next generation of MetaTrader. I've been hearing for years that everyone is moving to MT5, yet MT4 remains the "go-to" platform.

Despite my stubborn reliance on MT4, I will concede that MT5 is definitely a significant upgrade. For one thing, it is a 64-bit platform, whereas MT4 is 32-bit.

NinjaTrader

NinjaTrader is both a brokerage and a trading platform. As a brokerage, its expertise is in futures and options, not forex. Its basic trading platform is available for free to use with other brokers. However, traders need to upgrade, for a fee, in order to use such necessary features as advanced order types, automated trading, and backtesting.

Plenty of active traders find NinjaTrader to be worth the money, because of its robust technical analysis tools and excellent charting, real-time analysis, customizable technical indicators, and Chart Trader. Additional apps and add-ons are available from third-party developers. One excellent benefit is that it can be used as an interface with Interactive Brokers. Also, some of my own forex trading strategies, such as Counter Punch Trader and Counter Punch Xpress, are programmed and available for NinjaTrader users.

In addition to the cost of its license fee, the NinjaTrader platform requires the use of a supporting broker to trade forex, which incurs another cost. Also, there is no mobile app as of this writing, unless you trade through NinjaTrader.

Oanda

A large and reputable broker with its own forex trading platform, Oanda is especially known for offering 70 currency pairs. It also supports trading in commodities and index instruments. It is well known for its pricing transparency, platform technology, regulatory oversight, and comprehensive product offering. Accounts can be opened with very little money. The firm is regulated in several jurisdictions, including the United States, the European Union, and Japan. It also offers MT4 as an alternative trading platform.

Thinkorswim

Thinkorswim is TD Ameritrade's proprietary trading platform. It's especially good for derivatives, and I use it for trading equities, options, and occasionally futures. TD Ameritrade's forex offerings are more limited and are available only from 6:00 a.m. to 5:00 p.m. daily, but this is worth considering for those trading the New York session.

TradeStation

TradeStation has a robust platform. I use this brokerage for all my charting, backtesting, strategy, and tradeplan development. I also trade futures through TradeStation. The firm has one major problem for forex traders: it does not offer forex trading. But you may want to use the platform to make trade decisions and then execute them with another broker.

The Case for Having More Than One Account

There are situations in which traders have accounts with more than one broker. Most traders will be perfectly happy with just one, especially when starting out, but there are reasons to consider having a relationship with a second firm. Here are a few of the more common ones.

For Different Styles of Trading

If you want to day trade and swing trade the same currency pair (or if you want to day trade the same pair with multiple methods or tradeplans) then you will need multiple accounts to do so. Attempting to use the same account can lead to roadblocks and frustrations, such as those created by the FIFO (first in, first out) rule followed by US brokers, which requires that traders must close their earliest trades first in situations where there are several open trades involving the same currency pairs and position size. Another snag with US firms is that they will generally not allow you to make simultaneous trades in the same pair but in opposite directions. For beginners, such flexibility may not be needed, but as your approach to trading becomes more sophisticated, you will likely find a lot of benefit in maintaining multiple trading accounts for your various methods and trading plans.

In the Event of a Problem

The world is very strange, and random events can shut down even the biggest brand-name companies. Having a second broker is a nice backup plan in the event that something goes wrong with your primary broker.

Having Access to Different Tools

You may find that one broker has outstanding execution in the pairs you like to trade, but another broker has the charting tools you want on its proprietary platform. Having two brokers gives you access to the best of both. For me, however, the number one reason for having multiple brokers is flexibility. I will often day trade a pair, like GBP/AUD, but I also want to place longer-term swing trades with the same pair. Or I may want to take a longer-term position in a tax-deferred, self-directed retirement account.

Chapter Recap

» Your primary trading relationship is with the broker, which is the company that holds your money, executes your trades, and offers you services that may help you trade better. Do careful research, and look for the most reputable brokers that offer the most competitive rates.

» The trading platform is the software that you use to analyze the market and place your trades. Some brokers have proprietary platforms, and others work with a handful of independent platforms. The choice of platform depends very much on your personal style and the capabilities you require.

» Start your research by looking at some of the bigger names in currency trading. I have listed a few brokers and platforms in this chapter as a starting point, but the list is hardly definitive.

» Some traders find that it makes sense to work with more than one broker or platform.

| 7 |

Using Technical Analysis
When Buying and Selling Pairs

Chapter Overview
» The difference between technical analysis and fundamental analysis
» The important role of price charts in technical analysis
» Using support and resistance in technical analysis

Now that you've chosen a broker and a trading platform, it's time to kick off what will surely be a long and (hopefully) happy relationship with the many charts that your platform will create for you.

Successful traders have a reason for each trade they enter. They can articulate that reason for every one of their trades. They do this with *technical analysis*, a system of research based on price activity. The data is summarized in price charts that traders can use to measure the direction and sentiment of the market. Many trading platforms offer technical analysis tools and signals that will notify traders when certain conditions occur.

In *fundamental analysis*, on the other hand, one considers all the factors that influence the value of a currency. This involves looking at economics, geopolitics, international trade, and investment flows. This work ends up influencing the trades placed by governments, corporations, and major investors like hedge funds. Their trades affect prices, and that, along with a million other unknown variables, works its way into the price itself. It is the study of price action itself, separate from the many known (and many unknown) underlying factors, that forms the basis for *technical* analysis.

The last chapter covered choosing brokers and platforms, which provide the charts and indicators that forex traders use. Here and in the following chapters, we will get into what you will do with those platforms. Let's begin with an introduction to the research systems that guide forex trading.

Technical Analysis vs. Fundamental Analysis
Neither technical analysis nor fundamental analysis is "better." They are

both tools with very different uses. Technical analysis is far more useful for traders, especially those who have a short time horizon. Some people have strong feelings toward one or the other, but what matters most is having the right tool for the job.

Fundamental Analysis

Fundamental analysis starts from the premise that the market is not fully efficient, so work done to uncover global or industry trends can help identify mispriced assets and profitable investments. The goal of fundamental analysis is to come up with a fair value of an asset by evaluating all aspects of the business, along with the industry, the market as a whole, and the domestic and global environment.

Because fundamental analysis is a time-consuming process of trying to identify long-term investment possibilities, it will not help most traders find good opportunities. It is used in the forex market, but for reasons that would not be of interest to traders. George Soros used fundamental analysis to identify his legendary short against the British pound, and his market activity created price changes that showed up in technical analysis. I used technical analysis to trade against the pound at the same time, as you may recall from this book's introduction. I knew nothing of the fundamentals going on, only that the charts showed a great opportunity.

Technical Analysis

Technical analysis is based on three concepts. First, the market is efficient, meaning that everything that is known about a currency pair is reflected in the price at any given moment. (Some traders will say that the market discounts everything, which means the same thing.)

Second, the price is always trying to find its accurate value. The price is either in balance or out of balance. When it's in balance, the price will be consolidating, exhibiting low volatility and tight price ranges. It is very hard to make money as a trader in such conditions. In fact, this is when many traders tend to take losses. When price is out of balance, then either the buyers or the sellers have taken over, and that's what moves prices and creates the best trading opportunities.

Third, history tends to repeat itself, and certain price patterns show up over and over again. We can use these patterns to identify "probable next outcomes." This leads us to an important concept that helps us stack the odds in our favor when trading: Since certain patterns help us predict the next probable outcome, we can say that the immediate past can predict the immediate future with a high degree of accuracy, and when these patterns are identified properly with technical analysis, they can give us great trading opportunities. As traders, all we can hope for is to stack the odds on our side with every trade. Nothing is a one-hundred-percent sure thing when trading, but if the odds are always on our side, it becomes a numbers game. This is how good traders make money.

My approach to creating trade strategies begins with the idea that the immediate past predicts the immediate future. I look for a pattern that commonly appears, one that predicts what will most likely happen next with a high degree of accuracy. This creates a tradeable event. As traders, all we can hope for is to put the odds on our side and then properly manage our risk. This way, we win more than we lose and can increase the value of our trading accounts over time.

Price charts are graphs that show both the changes in the price and the changes in supply and demand that created the price changes. You can find the charts on your trading platform. They do not show why the prices are changing, only that they are. Technical analysts look at charts to see patterns, momentum, and trends, among other things. They use that information to place trades in the hope of making a profit.

With the information in price charts, traders have a sense of overall market sentiment. Is something big happening, or are the charts showing buy and sell activity that is not creating price changes?

Let's face it, there are many reasons to buy and to sell. Some traders are hedging, some are speculating. Some are buying or selling currency to support a company's international expansion, and some are selling currency to help manage a nation's exchange rate. Others, like me, are merely placing trades for no other reason than to turn a profit, looking to take advantage of a pattern where the likely outcome is predictable with a sufficient degree of accuracy. All these activities come together and are reflected in price charts.

Price Charts: An Important Technical Analysis Tool

A price chart shows the activity in a currency pair over a given time period. It can be as short as a few minutes or as long as several decades. It is the very heart and soul of technical analysis.

There are many different types of price charts, but all show how the price has changed over time. The charts place price on the vertical y axis and time on the horizontal x axis. The oldest data is to the left and the most recent is to the right.

Traders sometimes talk about the future as being on the far right side of the chart. In other words, it is the next few price changes that will show up soon but are not currently visible because they haven't happened yet. Although we can't know the future with certainty, the data on the left side of the chart gives a good idea of what has a decent probability of happening next. "The immediate past can predict the immediate future."

Types of Price Charts

Figure 15 is an example of the most basic price chart, a line chart. It's a five-minute chart; this means that each price that is plotted takes place five minutes after the last plot, and that it updates every five minutes.

fig. 15

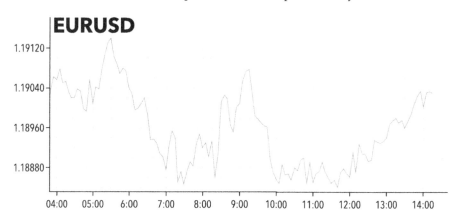

Even the simplest chart carries a lot of information. Figure 15 shows a line chart for the EUR/USD pair. Over a three-hour period, from 11:00 until 14:00, the overall trend was upward. The chart also shows a strong move down earlier in the session and then several attempts to get below a certain price level, with the inability to do so prior to the price heading higher. This is all valuable information for traders. With the right technical analysis techniques, trading opportunities could have been carried out based on this chart.

Looking at a Bar Chart

Figure 16 offers a close-up view of bars from a bar chart. Each bar shows the open, high, low, and close (OHLC) price for the time period being evaluated. The four points are as follows:

» The *open* is the first price in the time period; it is a small horizontal line on the left side of the bar.
» The *high* is the highest price for the time period, found at the top of the bar.
» The *low* is the lowest price of the period, found at the bottom of the bar.
» The *close* is the price at the end of the time period, shown as a small horizontal line to the right of the bar.

Did you notice that the bar on the left is different from the bar on the right? The bar on the left, the up bar, closes at a price higher than the open price; the bar on the right, the down bar, closes at a lower price. On a screen, the down bar is usually red and the up bar is green. Because we are printing in black and white, the figure shows the down bar as being filled in and the up bar unfilled.

GRAPHIC

fig. 16

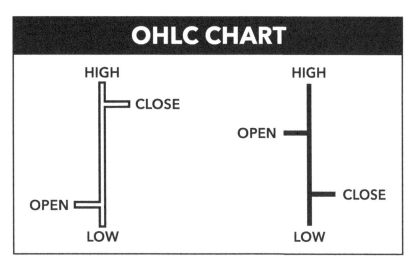

Because each bar includes both the high and the low for the given time period, its length shows the range of price movement. The longer the bar, the greater the trading range.

A bar chart consists of a series of bars. Figure 17 shows the same total length of time as the line chart in figure 15 for the EUR/USD pair. Each bar represents five minutes of trading.

fig. 17

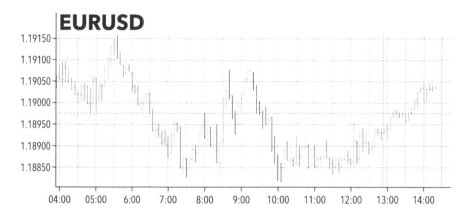

Bar charts can be created for almost any time period. With standard charting platforms like MT4, traders can look at 5-minute, 15-minute, 60-minute, 240-minute charts; and daily, weekly, and monthly charts. More capable charting platforms let you look at more dynamic types of charts that are independent of time, like tick charts or range bar charts.

Looking at a Candlestick Chart

Candlestick charts provide the same information as bar charts, but in a different graphic format. I prefer them because they're much easier to read. It's also easier to see specific price patterns that can be highly predictive and that would be nearly impossible to see or interpret with the simple price bars shown in figure 17. Look at figure 18, for example.

fig. 18

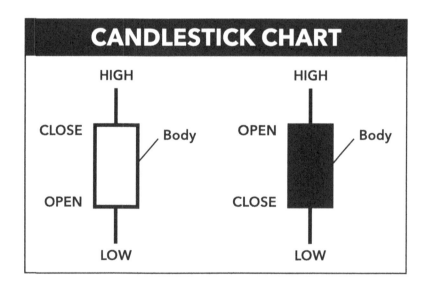

Notice how they look like candles that can be burned at both ends?

The length of the candlestick (including the "wicks") specifies the high and the low, as with a bar chart. The difference is that a rectangle, also called a body or a candle, is drawn to show the open and the close of the pair for the time period. Traditionally, if the asset price closed lower than when it opened (a down bar), then the chart block is filled in, as with the bar on the right. If the pair closed higher (an up bar), then the block is left unfilled. A recent refinement that makes candlestick charts much easier to read is filling in a candle with red if the currency pair closed lower and green if it closed higher.

Figure 19 shows the EUR/USD pair a few minutes after figures 15 and 17 were drawn. You'll notice that the right edge of the chart shows a new bar. You can also see how the candlesticks bring different information to the fore.

fig. 19

Because traders can make money whether a pair is up or down, green does not mean good and red does not mean bad. They are just colors. I prefer candlestick charts because they contain a lot of useful information in an easy-to-read format. I switch to OHLC bars when I'm looking for a longer-term perspective because they are more compact, so more bars will fit on a screen.

Reading a Price Chart

OHLC and candlestick bars carry a lot of information. A string of bars carries even more. By breaking bars down into discrete time periods and identifying the key price levels that mark "support" (an apparent lower limit on the price) and "resistance" (an apparent upper limit on the price), traders gain an understanding of market dynamics and insight that may help forecast a pair's next move. The trader can analyze different scenarios based on what the price has a good chance of doing next. (Technical analysts—or the typical home trader like me—add more indicators and lines to help them interpret what the price action is saying. Keep reading to learn all about it.)

Trading Time Periods

Every trading platform's charting tool set allows users to specify the time periods used to determine a bar's open and close. Different trading styles call for looking at different time periods. Sometimes weekly bars make sense; other times 15 minutes is an appropriate period. MT4, one of the most popular platforms for forex, uses a wide range of time-based charts, with increments of as little as one minute or as much as 240 minutes—or beyond, to daily, weekly, or monthly charts (where one bar represents a day, week, or month, respectively).

I use platforms that offer other types of charts, like tick charts and range bars, which gives me a unique edge and a different point of view from which to make trade decisions. These types of charts are based on the dynamics of price action rather than time. Let's face it: in five minutes, a lot of price movement can happen . . . or very little. A time-based bar doesn't care about the price action. It closes at the end of five minutes, no matter what. I like a chart that doesn't care about time. It cares about whether the price has moved beyond a certain range, like 20 pips for instance, or whatever the range of the bar is set to.

Figure 20 shows the USD/JPY pair on a monthly basis. Each candlestick represents a month of data.

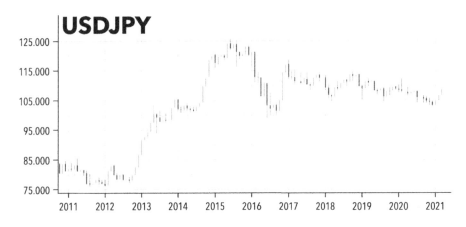

fig. 20

Figure 21 displays the USD/JPY on a daily basis.

fig. 21

Figure 22 shows the USD/JPY on an hourly basis.

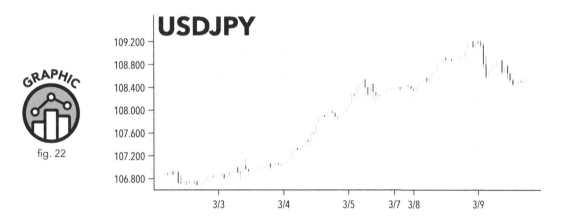

fig. 22

And figure 23 presents the USD/JPY with a five-minute time frame.

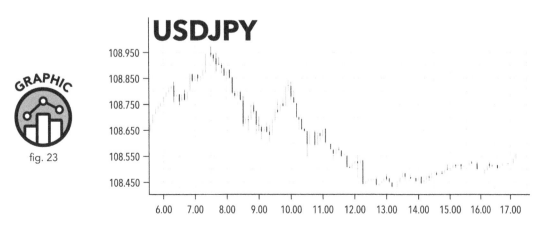

fig. 23

No time frame is "right." Each is suited for a different purpose. Day traders will look at five-minute charts; some will even use charts as fast as one minute. Swing traders and position traders will pay more attention to hourly or daily charts. The various charting tools make it easy to change the time periods, which can help generate trade ideas.

One reason for changing the time periods on a chart is that markets may show one type of trend over one time period and another over a different period. You might see what appears to be a sideways pattern on a five-minute chart that turns out to be nothing more than a blip in a downtrend on an hourly chart. Likewise, a currency pair may be sidewise for months, but when viewed on a faster (lower time frame) chart it can be seen to have days of uptrends followed by days of downtrends during those months.

The Trend Is Your Friend

Markets often trade in trends, which represent some of the most profitable trading opportunities. You can easily spot them after the fact by drawing lines on the price chart that show how they have moved more or less in a single direction for a period of time. Trends are not sure things, however. You may see an uptrend and place a trade in its prevailing direction just as the market decides to reverse direction. While the trend is your friend, we all know that some friends are more loyal than others. If a market is trending higher, that is bullish and indicates a good time to look for an appropriate long position. If a market is trending lower, then it is bearish, and opportunities to go short should be considered. Eventually, the trend either ends or pauses, at which point further analysis is required. One of the most profitable trades, but also one of the most difficult to identify, is trading the reversing direction of a trend that has reached its end. Many traders incorrectly identify a trend as failing when it is merely catching its breath before resuming again. Or they are correct in their assumption that the trend is ending and a reversal is imminent, but their timing is wrong; hence the term "trying to catch a falling knife." They end up being right but still lose money. As soon as they are out of the market with their losses, the market starts moving in the opposite direction, as they had predicted. This is quite common, and the battlefield of trading is littered with the corpses of bad trades with the right idea. Timing is everything, and yet it is the most elusive aspect of good trading. By the way, I prefer to let the knife hit the floor and then start looking for my reversal opportunity. I like my fingers, and my trading account!

Of course, it's easy to see what has already happened. Many novice traders have a wonderful time imagining the untold riches they could have or would have made. With real trades, an entirely different and often cruel scenario unfolds that flies counter to such fantasies. That's why I want you to prepare carefully before starting to trade.

Trends fall into two main categories, *uptrends* and *downtrends*. Uptrends are characterized by both higher highs and higher lows, while downtrends are markets with lower highs and lower lows. Trends are caused by a market that is out of balance. Markets with no clear uptrend or downtrend are said to be *sidewise*, or *range-bound*, and represent a balanced market. Trends work over the long term, medium term, and short term and in all time frames. A short-term trend on a 60-minute chart will look like a long-term trend on a five-minute chart. Understanding how trends work helps you find good trading opportunities with good odds of success.

What appears to be a sidewise pattern on a five-minute chart may be nothing more than a blip on the radar in a larger, hourly chart downtrend. A simple strategy is to identify the "fast" trend on a slower chart (long term), and then trade in that same direction on a faster, short-term chart. Many successful strategies use some element of this concept.

How to Draw Trend Lines

Trend lines are simple additions to a price chart that help make the direction of the market clearer to you. They also mark distinct support and resistance levels, helping you identify possible entry and exit points. Learning to identify those points is a first step in learning chart analysis.

Using Trend Lines

Trend lines help show the magnitude of an uptrend or downtrend. They are nothing more than lines that accentuate the trend, and with most charting packages you can drop them on a price chart with a few clicks of the mouse.

For an uptrend, the trend line is drawn across the series of higher lows; for a downtrend, it is drawn across the lower highs.

Figure 24 shows two trend lines. One is a downward trend, which is followed by an upward trend.

fig. 24

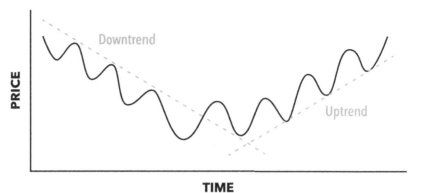

Trend lines can be drawn along opens and closes, too. I often like to draw them in candlestick charts using the opens and closes in the candles, with the wicks showing attempts to break through the trend. These represent those traders who have attempted and failed to catch that falling knife. One of the most profitable uses of trend lines is identifying support and resistance levels—pull-back zones where new positions can be entered into. Another use is identifying potential breaks in the trend that offer warning signs that the trend could be ending. As long as the trend line holds when the price comes back to it, the odds are better that the trend will continue. Contrarily, if the price breaks the trend line on a closing basis, the caution flags should be waving, as the trend could be coming to an end (but not necessarily).

The trend lines themselves mark the support and resistance levels created by the trend. In a long trend, when the price comes down to its ascending trend line (support), long positions can be taken and profits made as the price turns up to make new highs. In a downtrend, we can wait for the price to come up to its descending trend line (resistance) and enter short positions. When a market is in a trend, the odds are that the trend will continue. Of course, you have to be careful because trends *will* come to an end; so we turn to additional technical analysis methods to help us.

Start with Higher Time Frames

Regardless of your trading time frame, start trend line analysis with higher (longer) time frames. These will produce the more reliable trend lines. After all, shorter time periods are merely subsets of longer ones. Looking at the long-term trend can show you the limits of the short-term trends within it. When the trend is down on a five-minute chart as well as a slower chart, shorting the market when the price hits the descending trend line on the five-minute chart is one way that traders time their entries to get short with the more powerful higher time frame. This allows them to capture profitable moves. Naturally, the opposite opportunities exist with long trades.

Use Swings as Anchors

Chart patterns are specific shapes and series of candlesticks that can indicate trends, good trading opportunities, and even times when it's best to remain on the sidelines. Two specific patterns are helpful for drawing trend lines: the *swing high* and the *swing low*. The swing high is a bar that has a high higher than the bar to its left and to its right. The swing low is a bar with a lower low than the bar to its left and the bar to its right. Some traders actually insist on the swing high being a bar that is higher than the next *two* bars on its right and the two bars to its left, and swing lows being lower than the two bars on either side, because they mark more dependable swing levels. Swing levels show us important support and resistance levels on the chart, and the more significant levels seem to affect price action over and over again, because other traders can see these same levels.

You can see an example in figure 25.

fig. 25

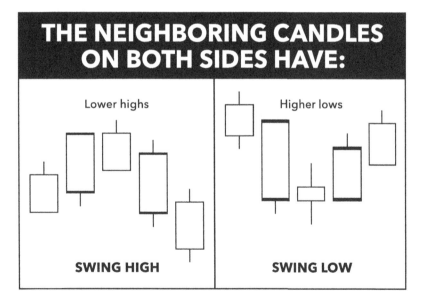

The swings help indicate the start and end of trends, so they are perfect anchor points for trend lines. Look for a swing pattern, then follow it back to an earlier swing pattern to see what the trend has been.

Don't Worry about a Little Bit of Overlap

When a trader draws a trend line, it will generally touch several candles without breaking through them; however, this is not absolute. You may discover a wayward candle or two breaking through your otherwise valid, usable trend line, especially in a longer-term trend.

Furthermore, short-term trends sometimes deviate from long-term trends.

Interpreting price charts and drawing trend lines can be subjective. It should not be forced. If the trend is not there, it's not there, and drawing a line that *almost* shows a trend will not make a trend magically appear.

fig. 26

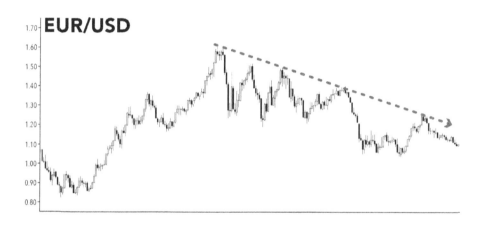

Support and Resistance

Support is the price level where buyers recognize that a pair is a good value, so they step into the market and begin buying. It shows where there is a concentration of demand or buying interest. The support level is sometimes called the demand line, because that's the price, when reached, that will cause traders to demand more of the pair. *Resistance* is the opposite of support. It is a price where an asset looks a little expensive and there is a concentration of supply and selling interest. Traders are willing to get out while the price is high. It is sometimes called the supply line, because that is the price, when reached, that will cause traders to sell (supply) more of the currency.

Support and resistance (or SR) can be easily identified with trend lines and/or horizontal lines at key price levels that are easy to see on the chart. SR levels will often show up on a chart based on past SR levels and can be used to predict where SR levels will be going. Many trading strategies use tactics based on SR levels, including most of my strategies.

Support and resistance levels will often form a range in which buyers and sellers trade back and forth. They test these support and resistance levels until something happens to cause the price to break out of this range. We'll get into more specifics when I show you some actual trade examples in later chapters.

The concept of support and resistance is a key element in technical analysis. Figure 27 shows a ten-minute chart for the GBP/CAD pair. The horizontal lines represent support and resistance levels.

fig. 27

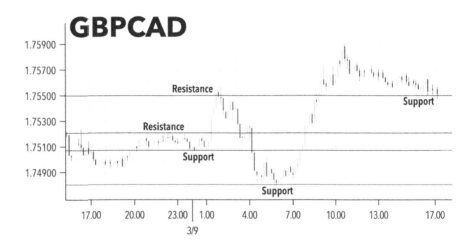

Support and resistance lines should be drawn at price levels that have been hit on several occasions. They are levels that have been tested, not one-off occurrences. The more often a price has served as a support or resistance level, the more significant it is when the level is broken.

Support

The support lines show price levels where buying interest overwhelms selling interest. Buyers see a good price and place their orders. Those with short positions need to buy to close their trades; this is known as going flat. Their increased demand relative to the supply in the market causes the price decline to stop, bottom out, or pause. A support line looks a lot like a floor, while the opposite is true for resistance levels. Over time, support becomes resistance and vice versa.

Support levels come with risk. The more a support line is tested (the price lowering and bumping into the support line), the more likely it is to break, and when that occurs, sellers will overwhelm the buyers, who will find themselves trapped as support gives way. Buyers will then capitulate and begin selling their losing positions, adding fuel to the fire.

Think of a support level as a sale price at the grocery store. If sweet potatoes are on special this week, then stock up and cook them for dinner every night next week. The price will go up again and then come back down later. Grocery stores cycle through their sales on staples, and savvy shoppers pay attention. But the regular promotional cycle is different from an end-of-season clearance. By December, everyone has moved on from pumpkin spice, so fall-themed products are marked down again and again until they're gone. It is a breakout from the regular cycle. The price on a clearance item is no longer supported, and it will decline until next September when everyone's thoughts return to pumpkin spice. The best time to buy the pumpkin spice is when no one wants it anymore. That's when the price for that item will be at its lowest and the strongest price support will be found, as suppliers sell out of their last bit of inventory.

Resistance

Resistance is the opposite of support. Resistance occurs when selling interest materializes and slows or overpowers buying interest, stopping rising prices in their tracks, causing the price to stall or reverse direction. Think of resistance as the ceiling in a price advance. When the resistance price is hit, traders who hold the asset believe they have received a fair value, so they take their profits. Interested sellers also see these same levels and will want to initiate new short positions. As their supply hits the market, prices fall.

Do Not Overcomplicate Your Chart

Technical analysis may include the recognition of many different price patterns and the use of many different indicators. Some are easier to use than others, and some are more useful in certain situations. Beginning traders have a tendency to try out every tool in a charting platform in an attempt to confirm their trading ideas. In no time, there are so many lines and dots on the screen that it becomes almost impossible to make a decision—especially a good decision. "Analysis paralysis" is too often the outcome.

Chapter Recap

»   Technical analysis looks at changes in prices and the strength of the
    force causing the change. Fundamental analysis looks at economic
    and political conditions that affect currency prices. Many traders,
    including myself, rely on technical analysis, which incorporates the
    information and the sentiment in the market at a point in time.

»   Price charts show how supply and demand create price changes.
    Certain patterns are associated with market behavior that plays out
    in more or less predictable ways.

»   Support and resistance lines show the market's gauge of valuation,
    and so, by indicating possible entry and exit points, they help
    traders make trading decisions.

»   Drawing trend lines is a good first step in technical analysis. They
    connect points on the price chart to clarify the direction of trends.
    This information can help predict future price moves or show areas
    where more analysis is needed.

| 8 |
Understanding Chart Patterns

Chapter Overview
» Trends either continue or reverse
» Price action forms patterns
» Chart patterns help you recognize trade opportunities

Price charts and the study of price action power the majority of trading strategies. They carry so much information! They also form the patterns that we can study to determine high-percentage probable outcomes that we can use to place trades with the odds of winning on our side.

There are many chart patterns. Some occur often and some are rare. These patterns typically appear in all markets and in all chart time frames. Here, we will focus on some patterns that are well-known, predictive, and easy to read. When identified and applied in the context of a proven tradeplan, they put the odds of generating profits in our favor. We will also look at some common reversal and continuation patterns that work on most charts and can be learned to help you complete trades.

Patterns reflect the dynamics of supply and demand as they play out over a market cycle, often indicating people's reaction to news and other factors. We see certain patterns repeat themselves over and over again on just about every price chart and time frame, and many of these patterns resolve in a predictable fashion. The immediate past is a good predictor of the immediate future, so patterns can indicate profitable trade opportunities.

Trending and Consolidating Markets
Markets often follow trends, and there are trends within those trends. No trend lasts forever, though, and identifying when a trend might be waning is a worthy skill for a trader to develop.

Trends occur over the long term, the intermediate term, and the short term. Different trades work for different time frames, of course. I find that starting from a longer time frame and drilling down to more recent time frames gives me great insight into what is going on and helps me find more trades that have a good chance for success.

Understanding Trends and How to Identify Them

When currencies trend, they often reflect macro changes in the world, and therefore they tend to trend for a long time in the same direction. Catching these trends can be very profitable for a trader. How do we identify them, though? The ascending trend line offers clues as to good, low-risk places to take long positions. We can look for the strength in each leg up (known as an "action move"), use certain indicators to help identify where a downward leg might end (known as a "reaction move"), and then try to catch the "subsequent action move," where the dominant trend reasserts itself.

Of course, even the strongest trends don't last forever. As an action move wanes, there is always the possibility that the macrotrend may be losing its steam. We can use certain indicators, which we will get into in the next chapter, that help us determine when a trend might be tiring out.

A seemingly simple yet effective trade idea—if you get it right—is to merely buy when the price pulls down to its trend line and place a stop loss a little bit below that same line (so if the price falls below the line, then you will automatically exit the trade). This tactic offers the prospect of strong rewards, and when it goes wrong, you get "stopped out" with much smaller losses. But certain questions must be answered, such as these: How close does the price need to get to the trend line before entering the trade? How far below it should we place our stop loss? Where should we exit the trade? Of course, many other traders see the same trend line and might be attempting the same maneuver. The brokers see it too, and nothing is as easy as it seems. This is when we begin to realize the importance of tradeplans. In chapter 9, I'll show you a different type of approach that answers these questions, with specific tactics on how to trade this idea with great odds of success.

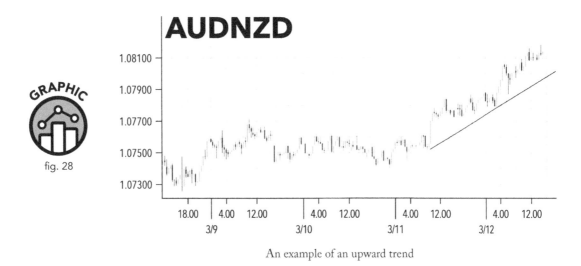

An example of an upward trend

A downtrend is the opposite; the price chart shows a string of lower highs and lower lows. As forex traders, we don't care which way a market trends because we can make money regardless of which direction the prices go. We can look for pullbacks (reactions) and then take advantage of the action to the downside by shorting the market.

Eventually, markets try to find and then establish trading ranges where they can operate for various lengths of time, moving up and down inside of that range. As I noted, when prices are trending, it usually reflects a macro event in the world, which causes a rebalancing of the value between currencies. One currency weakens while another strengthens. The pair will ultimately find a balance (of sorts) that establishes the new trading range. When the price moves to within 10% to 15% of either side of the range, you can begin to look for reversal trades, but this requires a specific tactic and can lead to danger when breakouts occur. When the price moves to the upper side of its range, for example, you might establish a short position, placing a stop loss just outside of the range. If it breaks out to the upside, you will find yourself on the wrong side of the move and will get stopped out with a loss. You will also get stopped out on "fake" breakouts, which happen all too frequently. That's when the price seems to be breaking out, hits your stop loss, and then moves back down into its trading range, perhaps heading lower, to where your target would have been. Your idea was right, but you're still stopped out with a loss! I believe that trading within 10% to 15% of either side of the range is where the least profitable trading occurs. In fact, the strongest trending moves and the best trading scenarios happen inside the 70% in the middle.

Breakouts beyond the trading range do occur, though, and this too offers tremendous trading opportunities. At some point, the macro news in the world changes; the price breaks out of its range and moves to find a new trading range. Learning how to identify this dynamic will vastly improve a forex trader's profitability and overall results.

Consolidation

Markets trend and markets consolidate. Much of the time, a price will be in a *consolidation* phase. This means that the price will move sideways on the chart, not really following the trend but not breaking out of it either. This is a period when the market action is evenly split between buyers and sellers. The market is balanced, and this is when traders lose money and learn the true meaning of frustration. Experienced traders know that breakout moves are on the way and that the possibility of an extended move, a new trend, or a continuation of a trend that has paused is becoming more and more likely. When a market is trending, it is out of balance, as one side exhibits all the power; bulls push the market higher and higher while bears push it lower and lower. This is where the best trading profits are made.

Consolidation is a pause in the trend. After the consolidation, the price can resume in the direction of the trend, or it can change direction. Consolidations happen in any time frame and show a market that is in balance. There are few opportunities for traders to find profits inside the consolidation. The profitable opportunity occurs when the price finally breaks out. Many profitable trade strategies take advantage of this repetitive scenario. The market continually shows action, reaction, and then subsequent action, and consolidation is typically the reaction part of this pattern.

Reversal

A reversal is when the direction of a price trend changes, from going down to going up or vice versa. Whereas a pullback or "reaction" within a trend is a short-lived change before the trend continues in the same direction, a reversal establishes a new trend in the *opposite* direction. Sticking to my "action, reaction, subsequent action" theme, I like to refer to it as a new action in the opposite direction. Reversals happen in all time frames. A reversal of trend in a five-minute chart could be nothing more than a pullback or consolidation to a larger uptrend in an hourly chart, for example. Or it could be part of a stronger action move on the slower chart, and these present very profitable trade opportunities. A reversal can be long and drawn-out following a consolidation, which winds up becoming a "topping" or "bottoming" pattern, or it can happen faster and more abruptly, the most extreme of which will turn on a dime, creating what we call a "V-shaped reversal."

Chart patterns and chart analysis are fundamental elements of technical analysis. They can help you identify likely scenarios and determine whether a trend is continuing, consolidating, or reversing. Chart patterns are predictive and can help you determine when price breakouts and reversals might occur. They provide information about good trade entries, stops losses, and profit targets.

Common Reversal Patterns

Markets reverse when things change. The reasons vary: political change, war, natural disaster, you name it. Sometimes it's more technical: a price hits an established support or resistance area, stalls out, and heads the other way. Nothing stays the same forever. For traders, the reasons for a change are less important than the fact that the change is taking place—and that we can spot it.

Regardless of the reason, changes occur in supply and demand. This leads to reversals. As market participants test the amount of existing support or resistance, certain patterns form. These reflect market action and market psychology. Understanding what these patterns indicate can really ramp up your trading game.

Head and Shoulders and Inverted Head and Shoulders

The head and shoulders formation is one of the most reliable reversal patterns. It works like this: First the price is rising (or falling, in a downtrend). It pulls back lower, forming the left shoulder. Next it rises again, this time to a new high, forming the head. Then it falls again, then rises, but to a peak not quite as high as the head, forming the right shoulder (see figure 29).

The indication in figure 29 is that a reversal, a new trend in the opposite direction (downward), may be underway, but nothing is ever guaranteed with trading. The market is still in charge, and what appears to be a head and shoulders reversal pattern will at times fool you and end up being an extended consolidation that can still end up resuming in the direction of the prior trend. When identified correctly, though, the head and shoulders pattern is one of the most dependable reversal patterns.

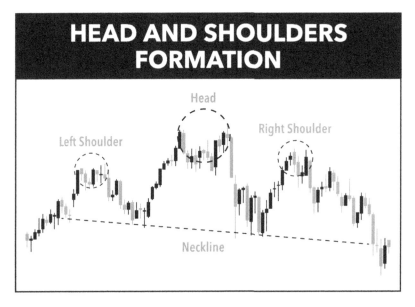

A stylized example of a head and shoulders formation

The pattern does not emerge out of nowhere. Patterns reflect market psychology and form in all markets and time frames. The head has the appearance of the resumption of the trend up. Greed or fear of missing out on the next move motivates buyers to enter the market.

The right shoulder is the first indication of trouble in paradise for the buyers, and they begin to exit their position. Sellers have taken over and those caught on the wrong side of the trade begin to panic, adding more fuel to the downside and causing the price to break through the floor—break its neckline lower. Greed and fear drive the markets. Once that neckline is broken, the head and shoulders pattern will be confirmed and traders will look to initiate new positions. Support becomes resistance, and traders know this. Some of the best trades can be taken when the price breaks below the neckline and then pulls back to it. New shorts can be initiated at the pullback to the neckline with stop losses placed just above it, for a low-risk trade with potentially large rewards. Measuring the distance from the top of the head to the neckline and then projecting that distance down from where a short trade was entered offers a very good target.

A reverse head and shoulders, also known as an inverse head and shoulders, plays out in the opposite end of a cycle following a downtrend and culminates in a new trend to the upside. A market in a down cycle surges to new lows, forms the left shoulder, and then rallies. The rally turns lower again, breaking out to new lows, forming what will become the inverse head as the market then turns and rallies again. To complete the pattern, the market moves lower a third time, testing the recently established lows without dipping below them. It rallies up again, forming the right shoulder. Just like the head and shoulders ending a long rally, a neckline can be drawn in the same way with the inverse head and shoulders. If the price breaks above the neckline, continuing the upward trend established by the right shoulder, the head and shoulders pattern has been confirmed and a new trend to the upside has been established. Many traders form long positions upon the initial breaking of the neckline, but a more reliable, less risky trade can be placed when the resistance becomes the support and the price pulls back down to test the neckline from above. Traders go long, placing stop losses a short distance below the neckline for a low-risk, high-reward trade. The distance between the head and the neckline offers a good measurement for a reliable trading target.

fig. 30

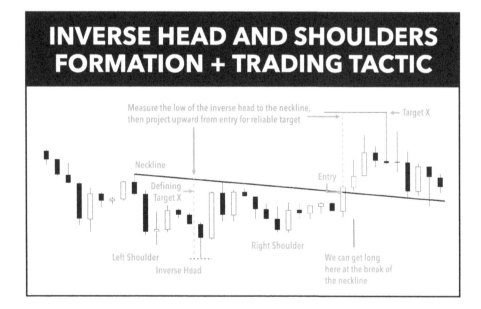

It can take some time and study to be able to recognize head and shoulders formations in different pairs and time frames, but the work will pay off.

1-2-3 Top and Bottom Reversal Patterns

Another common pair of reversal patterns are the 1-2-3 and the inverted 1-2-3.

A standard 1-2-3 reversal may begin at the end of a downtrend (see point 1 in figure 31). The price rebounds upward until it hits resistance (point 2), then moves down again, attempting to break through the initial swing low level. But it fails to make a new low and, in fact, makes an equal or higher low (point 3).

A horizontal line could be drawn across the end of the reaction (point 2). If the price moves up again and breaks that horizontal line, then there's a good chance that a trend in the opposite direction is underway.

fig. 31

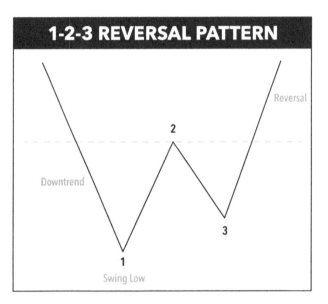

These formations can help us to identify the tops and bottoms of price action. For a 1-2-3 bottom formation (figure 32), after attempting to move higher, then moving back down to test the lows again, traders in real time should be looking to see if the prior low (point 1) has been broken. In other words, they're asking whether the price can break to new lows or not. We call this "testing the lows." If the price does break to new lows, then the bottom has not yet formed. When working in real time, we can start by labeling a low as "point 1" after it occurs. Then we wait. If a pullback occurs, we can add the number 2 to the point that forms just before the price heads lower again to test the newly formed low at point

1. Then, if the price fails to make a new low and begins to rally off of it, the lowest point of that failed attempt will be our point 3.

fig. 32

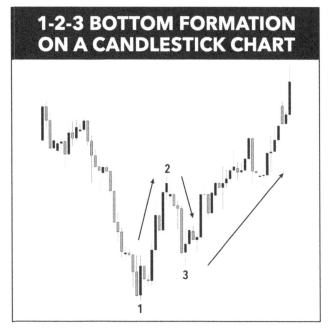

In this chart the 1-2-3 pattern helps us identify the bottom of the price action after the movement from point 2 to point 3 fails to establish a lower low and then proceeds to move up past point 2 and higher, defeating any would-be resistance at that level.

fig. 33

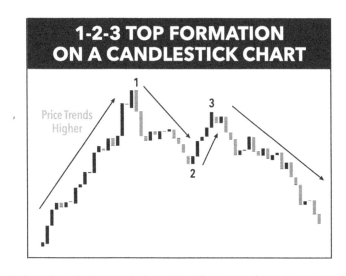

In this chart the 1-2-3 pattern helps us identify the top of the price action after the movement from point 2 to point 3 fails to establish a higher high.

The 1-2-3 top formation reversal pattern (depicted in figure 33) shows how an uptrend reverses into a downtrend following the expression of the pattern.

Point 1 is the low (or the high in a 1-2-3 top formation) that will initiate the pattern (potentially). But if the next low is lower (or high is higher) than point 1, then the 1-2-3 pattern did not form. If the low is higher (or the high is lower), then we have a point 3 that can be used as the entry point for a long (or short) trade.

Engulfing Candlesticks

"Engulfing candlesticks" show sudden reversals in a trend. These occur when one candle is significantly larger than, and positioned in the opposite direction from, the previous candle (see figure 34). In a reversal of a downtrend, the entire body needs to be larger than the prior candle's body, with a higher close than the prior bar's open, and a lower open than the prior bar's close. In other words, a bar closes down, then the next bar opens below that close and then pushes higher, closing above where the prior bar opened, completely overlapping, or "engulfing," the prior down bar. In a reversal of an uptrend, the opposite is true (see figure 35). The body of the engulfing candle needs to be larger than that of the previous candle, with a lower close than the prior bar's open, and a higher open than the prior bar's close.

fig. 34

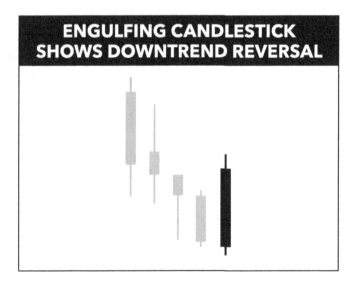

ENGULFING CANDLESTICK SHOWS DOWNTREND REVERSAL

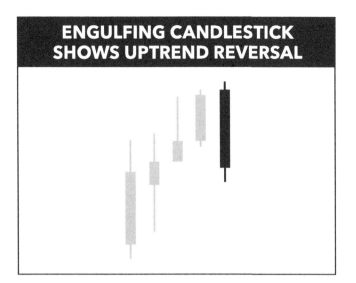

ENGULFING CANDLESTICK SHOWS UPTREND REVERSAL

NOTE

When the engulfing candlestick is preceded by four or more candlesticks of the opposite color (as is depicted in both figures 34 and 35), then an especially strong reversal may be underway.

Common Continuation Patterns

Continuation patterns show momentary pauses in uptrends or downtrends. They are sidewise patterns that form as the market consolidates recent gains or losses. The market takes a pause as a reaction to the preceding price action, what I often refer to as an "action move." Prices rest for a while and move sidewise before resuming the trend. The most common continuation patterns are triangles and flags.

Triangle Patterns

Triangle patterns, sometimes called pennants, are formed when there is a pause in the trend. They are often followed by a resumption of the trend, but not always.

They come in several forms, as illustrated in figure 36:

» **Ascending triangles** tend to show up as a consolidation in an uptrend; they occur when prices move to a series of higher lows, but with resistance that appears as a horizontal row across the recent highs. Ascending triangles are associated with bullish markets and signal that the trend should be resuming soon. Of course, we need the price to break through resistance and move higher to confirm this as a continuation pattern. Resistance becomes support, and a move back lower to the new support level is often a great place to initiate a new low-risk long position.

» **Descending triangles** are the opposite and tend to show up as a consolidation in a downtrend, finding support along a horizontal line and then attempting to move higher off of that support several times, forming a series of lower highs. We can treat them the same as ascending triangles and look for ways to get short once the price shows us it wants to move lower. Support becomes resistance, and as the price breaks below support, it can come back up to test the new resistance level, which is a great place to initiate a new short position for a low-risk trade to the downside.

» **Symmetrical triangles** occur as a consolidation in a trend, either up or down. We let the price action itself tell us whether it will resolve as a resumption of the trend or a reversing move in the opposite direction. Sometimes it will fake heading one way and then do an about-face and move strongly in the opposite direction.

ASCENDING TRIANGLE   **DESCENDING TRIANGLE**   **SYMMETRICAL TRIANGLE**

fig. 36

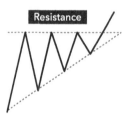

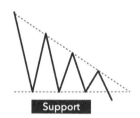

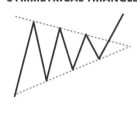

I can't emphasize this enough: *Nothing is certain in trading.* Despite what's depicted in figure 36, ascending triangles and symmetrical triangles may break downward, and descending ones may break upward. The market does what it does without regard for what you're looking for.

Flag Patterns

Flags are consolidations that form a rectangular pattern on a price chart, showing clear levels of support and resistance before eventually breaking out. Flag patterns typically take shape in the middle of a trend where the price becomes confined in a small range between two parallel lines. They usually, but not always, resume in the direction of the trend and make for excellent trading opportunities. Uptrend flags have a high chance of breaking out to the upside, and downtrend flags tend to break out to the downside. These make for trade setups where we can define our risk and target objective and create trades that are completely planned from start to finish with a high degree of winning.

Figure 37 is a rough illustration of bull flags and bear flags.

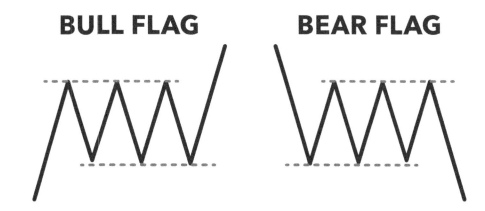

BULL FLAG   BEAR FLAG

fig. 37

The bull flag shows up in a strong uptrend. The flag may slope slightly downward (see figure 38), but its tests of the support and resistance levels show that there is indecision as to whether there is enough strength to continue the uptrend. Eventually, the buyers overwhelm the sellers. The price breaks the resistance level and the bullish trend resumes. In other words, the action forms the flagpole, and the market then consolidates, pausing in reaction to the strong move that just occurred. This pause is what forms the flag. It resolves when the price breaks out to the upside, resuming the trend higher in a subsequent action move. An upward breakout from a bullish flag makes for an excellent trade opportunity and has a strong chance of succeeding.

Of course, flags have flagpoles. The flagpole here is the distance up or down of the prior action move that is then followed by the flag formation. The prior flagpole length becomes the objective for the breakout from the flag. That is another way of saying that it can be used to determine the target price for a trade based on the flag pattern.

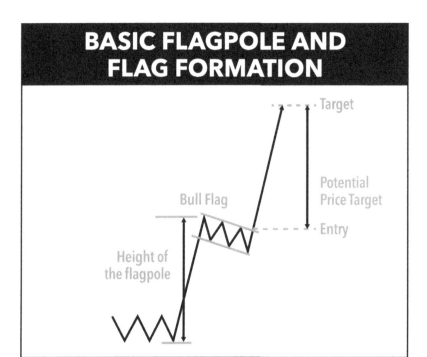

BASIC FLAGPOLE AND FLAG FORMATION

Target

Potential Price Target

Bull Flag

Entry

Height of the flagpole

fig. 38

The height of the flagpole is the amount that the price increased before the flag formed, the "action." The price moves within the support and resistance levels of the flag for a time, which is the "reaction." The "subsequent action" is the price breakout. When the breakout occurs, we may see another flag at the same amount of increase. For example, if the flagpole is 40 pips, then the price target will be 40 pips higher than the point where the breakout higher occurred. Some traders take part of their position off at the midway point, 20 pips higher. Stop losses should be placed slightly below the lowest point of the flag pattern.

Tips for Using Patterns

Patterns can be tricky to identify, especially when you're starting out in trading. Pattern analysis is supplemental to trend line analysis. Identifying the trend is always the first step. Traders study patterns. They look for past reversals and consolidations to see what they looked like, how many bars were involved, and how great the price changes were as the pattern played out.

I have tried to show you a mix of simple schematics and actual price charts. There are many more chart patterns, some more complex than others, and I encourage you to continue studying them. You can learn to specialize in a particular pattern or two and focus on mastering them and trading with them. I know many traders who are skillful with one particular trade setup and style of trading, and that's all they do. Trading doesn't have to be complicated. In fact, the simpler you keep things, the better.

The next step is to open up a charting platform, look for past patterns, and identify trading opportunities.

As you work with price charts, you will be able to see new patterns forming, and you can place trades accordingly. Keep notes on how the trades worked so that you can improve your pattern recognition and your overall trading. A simple log of the trades you make, the reason for making them, and the outcomes can help you improve your trading and develop new tradeplans.

Included with your Digital Assets, you will find free digital resources to help with trading, including the Ultimate Trade Analyzer (UTA) spreadsheet, that will help you plan your trades. Find this and other assets at go.quickstartguides.com/forex.

Chapter Recap

» As a trend plays out, the price will offer clues as to whether the trend is continuing, consolidating, or reversing. These clues are used to find good trade opportunities.

» Charts display patterns. Over the years, traders have identified many standard patterns where the likely next move in price can be predicted, and these present high-probability outcomes. Traders can use these to plan trades. Head and shoulders and 1-2-3 patterns often indicate reversals, while triangles and flags indicate consolidation and likely continuation of the prevailing trend.

» The main chart patterns show how forex pairs are trending, consolidating, and moving. They summarize the activity of all market participants in a way that traders can analyze and work with.

» New traders should practice identifying patterns on past price action to see if they can recognize them and to note what the outcomes were.

| 9 |
Understanding Indicators

Chapter Overview

» What indicators are and what they can do
» How indicators can predict, confirm, and confuse
» Types of indicators

The next step in technical analysis is incorporating *indicators*. These are calculations based on price and volume activity that are used alongside or overlayed on top of price charts. Indicators can give traders powerful signals about when to buy and sell currency pairs. Charting and trading platforms calculate them automatically, adding them to price charts and even sending alerts when they hit predetermined criteria.

This chapter covers the four main categories of indicators: moving averages, oscillators, momentum, and volatility. It looks at how these indicators work with forex and offers some tips on how to use indicators for better trading.

Introducing Indicators

Indicators are technical analysis tools primarily used to forecast price changes on price charts. They are calculations that consider the volume and price, among other things, of a certain financial instrument, helping traders to make decisions about when to enter and exit the market.

Most trading platforms have features that enable indicators to be added right onto the charts or placed in a special window, usually beneath the chart. There are lots of examples in this chapter.

Most traders incorporate one, two, or many indicators into their trading system, based on what works for them and their trading style. Beginning traders are often tempted to look at far too many indicators, and that leads to analysis paralysis. There are just so many out there, some of which may appear to conflict with each other! As you study and practice your trading, take note of the indicators that give you a statistical edge and put the odds in your favor.

Finding a combination that works well for you can help you achieve an edge that will increase your chances of succeeding in the market.

Avoid the Indicator Trap

As powerful as indicators are, they have drawbacks. The main problem is determining which ones to use. There are hundreds of indicators with a seemingly unlimited choice of combinations and settings. Selecting and applying the right indicators can be a daunting task, and new traders often end up trying to use way too many. Trying to keep track of too many indicators at once can be like adding too many ingredients to a recipe that would have tasted great if the cook had only known when to recognize that the dish was finished.

The Limits of Volume

If you look at general trading materials, you will see references to price changes relative to the volume of shares, bonds, or contracts traded. Volume is a key component of many indicators because it reveals the emotion and excitement behind the price changes. Although trading platforms show the volume of activity in different pairs, volume has less value in forex than in other markets. There is no central forex exchange, so no broker or bank sees the full spectrum of activity. Banking activity leads to steady increases in the money supply. In theory, central banks can add currency or take it off the market at any time. Therefore, volume measures have less importance in currency trading than in, say, stock trading. In fact, many charting platforms will show zero volume on forex charts or only show the trading volume from that particular broker, which is not very useful.

Using Moving Averages

The *moving average* (MA) is, hands down, the winner of the indicator popularity contest, and for good reason. It's easy to compute, easy to understand, and very useful. When added to bar charts, it makes spotting trends and potential reversals much easier. It can be calculated for different time periods. It helps identify support and resistance, changes in trend direction, congestion and consolidation, and profitable trade setups. It is the first indicator that most traders learn and, for some traders, the only one they use. Moving averages are not perfect and do have pitfalls, so it's important to understand their strengths and weaknesses.

Most people know enough about basic arithmetic to calculate an average. Add up the value of all the observations and then divide by the number of observations, and there you have the average.

The GBP/USD closed at 1.4201 on Monday, 1.4094 on Tuesday, and 1.3958 on Wednesday. The average of these prices is (1.4201 + 1.4094 + 1.3958)/3 = 1.4084.

The moving average is the average of the prices over a fixed period, such as 5 bars, 10 bars, 20 bars, etc. As time passes, each bar is updated, and the moving average adjusts to include the most recent bar while leaving off the bar furthest back in time.

The GBP/USD closed at 1.4201 on Monday, 1.4094 on Tuesday, and 1.3958 on Wednesday. The average of these prices is (1.4201 + 1.4094 + 1.3958)/3 = 1.4084. On Thursday, the GBP/USD closed at 1.4170. The three-day moving average on Thursday is the average of the prices on Tuesday, Wednesday, and Thursday, or (1.4094 + 1.3958 + 1.4170)/3 = 1.4074.

Simple Moving Average and Exponential Moving Average

A simple moving average (SMA) is a term used to describe a moving average where all values recorded within the specified period are assigned equal weight.

Figure 39 shows the 20-day SMA on the AUD/USD.

fig. 39

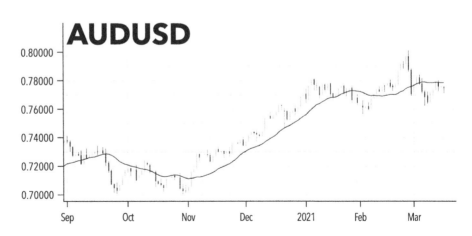

The 20-day SMA added to the AUD/USD daily chart

The exponential moving average (EMA) is a variation of the SMA. The calculation gives greater weight to the most recent data, so the EMA adjusts faster to the latest price action. This matters because the current market's price action is more relevant than what happened further in the past.

Figure 40 shows the AUD/USD over the same time period as in figure 39, but with the 20-day EMA plotted in addition to the 20-day SMA. Notice how the EMA forms a clear and slightly more precise support in the uptrend, particularly in the months of November through February.

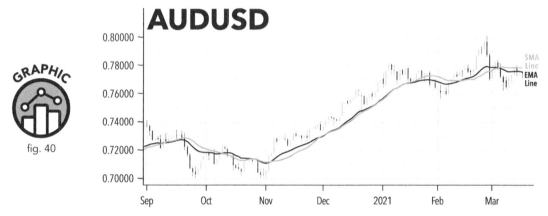

fig. 40

Compared to the SMA, the EMA is more sensitive to recent price bars.

Moving Average Ribbons

A moving average ribbon drops several different EMAs onto a chart for purposes of comparison. Figure 41 shows EMAs ranging from five days to 200 days on the same AUD/USD candlesticks as in figures 39 and 40. The shortest time period featured is known as the base period. Ribbons are easy to create and manage in most trading platforms. If the EMAs are moving in the same direction, then the trend has significant strength. The figure 41 example shows market weakness, as the prices frequently close below the averages and trend lower through September, October, and November, making lower highs and lower lows. You can see the various degrees of lag from one EMA indicator to the next, since they are based on the different "speeds" of each MA. The faster (shorter time period) lines are more heavily influenced by recent data than the others. They always appear to turn in a new direction before the slower lines do, with the faster lines crossing over the slower ones, one by one, as the trend heads in a new direction (lower, as is the case in the latter half of September and then higher in November, as we see in figure 41). Notice the false alarm in October where the fast EMA crossed up and over the slower previous EMAs, only to head lower again.

EMA crossover strategies are valuable at times, but they are prone to give bad signals during periods of low range and consolidation. We can see that is exactly what happened in October, as the price proceeded to trade mostly sideways before breaking out to the upside in early November. However, were we to zero in only on early November, we'd see that the EMA crossover worked very well to signal a highly profitable move up. It is because of this lack of consistency that many traders apply additional indicators to moving average ribbons, either to weed out some of the bad signals or to provide additional confirmation of the good ones (or both).

fig. 41

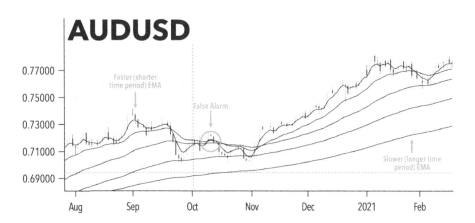

Here are a couple of other basic things to remember when using moving average ribbons:

» When your moving averages fan away from each other, it's a sign of increased trend strength.

» When the price pulls too far away from its MA, there is usually a reversion to the mean underway (a pullback to the MA), which can help you identify good trade setups. Later in this chapter I'm going to show you an in-depth trading technique I use that capitalizes on this tendency.

Volatility Indicators

Volatility indicators show how much the pair moves up and down during a time period. These indicators can help measure the intensity of price movement, offer insights into market activity levels, and show excellent trade setups.

Some financial markets are more volatile than others. As traders, we want volatility, because that means prices are moving. Sometimes, though, there will be violent reactions that we want to avoid. In forex, volatility is most often seen after serious world events or news, when prices reflect knee-jerk reactions, brokers widen their spreads to obscene levels, and many traders are caught on the wrong side of the market. I always recommend that day traders stand down in front of major news events for these reasons. Wait for the price action to normalize. The clue that this has occurred is when broker spreads come back down to earth. From a bigger-picture point of view, pairs with the most average volatility will tend to provide the best trading opportunities.

Buyers and sellers push the price around. Some have information, some are following the price action itself, and others are merely making guesses. As long as they are acting in the market, prices will respond. Sometimes this happens in a big way, as I just described, when pairs show wild swings after a major news event. Sometimes it happens at a lower level, when traders sort out small differences in valuation. Also, it's important to be aware that the same price patterns appear on countless traders' charts, and untold numbers of traders are using the same popular indicators. Although you can find success by following the big players that significantly move the market, it is also advisable to find your own "voice" and establish your own edge in the market with the right mix of indicators. This is typically accomplished by extensively testing with specific techniques discussed in this book.

The two volatility indicators that I like for forex are Bollinger Bands and Keltner Channels.

Bollinger Bands

Bollinger Bands® were developed in the 1980s by a technical analyst named John Bollinger. The indicator can be applied to any time frame and any investment type. This is important, because some indicators are great for the stock market but worthless for forex. Indicators based on volume, for example, have no value in forex trading.

The Bollinger Band starts with an EMA, usually 20 days (bars). One line is drawn above the EMA and another below it, each two standard deviations away from the EMA. Standard deviations are measures of how much any one item in a series is likely to deviate from the mean, so the Bollinger Bands show the likelihood of the price trend moving up or down from the EMA. Bollinger Bands are laid over the price chart (see figure 42).

fig. 42

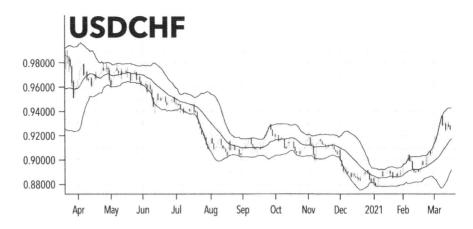

Another way to put it is that Bollinger Bands forecast the potential high and low prices for a pair relative to their moving average. Traders look at the width of the bands. The wider they are, the greater the volatility. If they are normally apart and then squeeze together, that can indicate that an explosive move is imminent as the market works through a period of consolidation.

Bollinger Bands are useful for showing a market that is building up pressure before a breakout. The longer a pair stays in a tightly compressed market, the more likely there will be an explosive breakout. Fake breakouts may also appear that can lead to strong moves in the opposite direction.

Keltner Channels

Keltner Channels, like Bollinger Bands, employ three bands, the middle of which is an exponential moving average. The upper and lower bands show the average true range (ATR), which is how much the highs and lows each day deviated from the previous day's close.

fig. 43

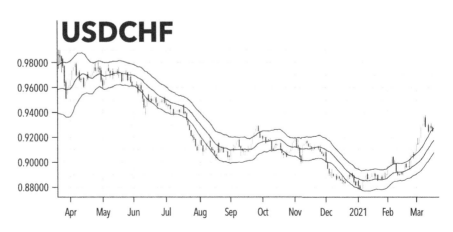

Figure 43 shows how the Keltner Channel tracks the EMA. Some traders who use it buy when the price closes above the upper band and sell when the price closes below it. Others look at trades above and below the middle line. Still others have different ideas.

When working with Bollinger Bands and Keltner Channels, many traders will watch for the "Bollinger Band squeeze," which can be observed when the Bollinger Band is laid on top of the Keltner Channel: the Bollinger Band is compressed (squeezed) inside the Keltner Channel. This shows that pressure is building, and there are good strategies for trading breakouts from this condition.

Oscillators

Oscillators are used in technical analysis to help confirm trends and signal possible reversals. Unlike the moving averages, which are typically plotted directly onto the chart, oscillators are most always plotted at the bottom of the price chart. They move back and forth (oscillating) between a minimum value and a maximum value. Think of them as the market's polygraph test. They show when the market is overbought—meaning prices are too high—or oversold, with prices being too low. These situations can reverse on a dime. The trend simply ends, leaving unaware traders stuck with a losing position.

Most oscillators are best used in conjunction with other indicators. Think of a detective doing an investigation. A polygraph alone is not sufficient evidence for a conviction, but in combination with other clues, it could seal the deal. Price charts should be the first point of reference, with oscillators acting as confirmation rather than as primary signals. Just because a market is overbought, for example, doesn't mean that it won't continue trending up. Strong trends can go on and on despite the market's being overbought or oversold.

Three of the most common oscillators are the relative strength index (RSI), stochastics, and moving average convergence/divergence (MACD). These are used in different ways to help traders manage the risk of their positions and alert them to possible trend reversals. They can also be used as confirming indicators when teamed with other indicators and patterns as part of a specific trade setup or tradeplan.

Relative Strength Index

The relative strength index (RSI) indicator, created by one of the fathers of technical analysis, J. Welles Wilder Jr., can be used to confirm the end of a correction in a trending market. A "correction" refers to the market returning, sometimes hastily, back to a preestablished trend after diverting from it or after leaning too heavily into it. The RSI is available in most charting packages. It tracks closing prices and the total lengths of green and red candles (price bars) over a period of time, normally 14 days, to gauge how strong a trend has been. The result of the calculation is a value between zero and 100. In general, the higher the RSI, the stronger the trend leading up to a given point.

Figure 44 shows the RSI on the AUD/USD, tracked below the price bars.

fig. 44

The RSI is shown below the price bars. Note that the RSI is a moving average and has its own trend lines.

When the RSI goes above 70, the indication is that the market for the pair is overbought. It is reaching the point where long trades become riskier, as the uptrend is showing signs of becoming tired and there may not be enough new buyers to support further increases in the price. When it goes below 30, an oversold market is indicated. Short trades become riskier because most of the downside move has probably already happened. Everyone who wants to sell has already gotten out, creating such low valuations that the pair looks attractive to new buyers. The exception to both these scenarios is when a trend is so strong that it remains in an overbought or oversold position for a long time and continues to trend in its prevailing direction. Despite what the indicators tell us, as traders we have to remember that the market itself is always in charge.

Normally, the RSI should move higher and lower with prices to confirm trends. If the RSI is moving in a different direction than prices, that's a sign that a market reversal is on its way. For example, if the price makes a new trend high while the RSI makes a lower trend high, there is divergence between the two, and that's an early sign that a trend is getting tired. Of course, the opposite is true with a downtrend. The price makes a new low, but the RSI is unable to follow and makes a higher low. You can see both occurring in figure 44. The only problem is that it can take a while for the reversal to happen. In general, traders should track divergences and not jump into a trade as soon as the RSI gives a signal, without sufficient confirming information. Yes, "trends are our friends," but more money has been lost trying to guess when a trend will end than in just about any other scenario. Just because a market becomes overbought or oversold doesn't mean it's going to reverse anytime soon—but it might.

Stochastics

Stochastic means "random." The stochastics indicator looks at the difference between the high and the low price over a given time period compared to what would be expected if the difference was random. Stochastics are plotted on a vertical scale from zero to 100 and are used to validate range boundaries. Some traders use stochastics to trade up and down inside of an established range. Range-bound trading can work well for a while, so long as the price trades inside the boundary. When it approaches the top of the boundary and a fast stochastics indicator is overbought, a trader can take a short position and put their stop loss just on the other side of the resistance level, the outer channel boundary. The opposite can be done on the low end of the range when the stochastics have become oversold. This style works well at times because the risk can be defined in advance and kept low in relation to the potential reward on the trade. You must be on the lookout for breakouts, though, because ultimately, the price is going to break out of the range (see figure 45).

When prices are trending upward, they tend to close near the highest recent price. This causes stochastics to move above the 50 level. When the stochastics hit 80, the pair is generally considered to be overbought and possibly due for a reversal. In a downtrend, the candles tend to close near the lowest closing price, giving a reading below 50. When it hits 20, the pair is oversold and possibly due for a bounce.

fig. 45

Moving Average Convergence and Divergence

The moving average convergence/divergence indicator (known as MACD, which is pronounced "Mack D") is something of an anomaly insofar as it is both a trend-following indicator and a momentum indicator. It can be used as an oscillator as well. The MACD is made up of three exponential moving averages and is displayed in three parts:

» A signal line (gray line in figure 46), which is the 9-day EMA

» A MACD line (black line in figure 46), which is the difference between the 12-day and the 26-day EMAs

» A histogram—a series of small vertical bars at the bottom of the chart representing the difference between the signal line and the MACD line. If the two lines are equal, the histogram will be zero. If the signal line moves above the MACD line, the histogram is positive, and if the signal line is below the MACD line, the histogram is negative. The wider the difference between the two lines, the longer the histogram bar.

Figure 46 shows the MACD for the USD/CHF pair.

The MACD is a trend-following momentum indicator that can show when a sustained trend may be coming to an end. The inverse head and shoulders pattern (from mid-December to mid-January) signals a possible trend reversal, and the MACD (by diverging from the price action) offers more evidence that the downward trend may be ending. "Divergence" in this scenario refers to the fact that the price action is making a new low (the head of the inverse head and shoulders pattern) while the MACD line makes higher lows within the same window of time.

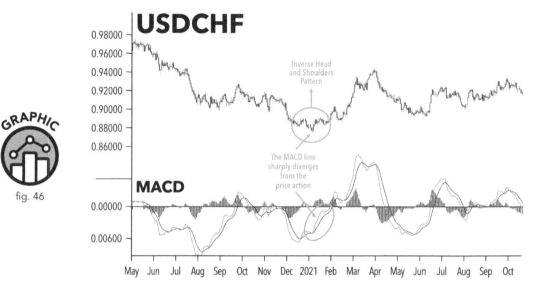

fig. 46

If the MACD moves above the signal line, the market for a currency pair may be breaking out on the upside. Likewise, if the MACD moves below the signal, then a downtrend may be underway. Be careful to check the price chart, as the MACD can be a lagging indicator, meaning that it will often give a signal after the action has already occurred. It may be too late for a trading opportunity by itself, but the MACD can still offer corroborating information as additional confirmation.

Like all indicators, the MACD is just a piece of the puzzle. Look at figure 46 and notice how the price made a new low at the start of 2021 but the MACD made a higher low. See how the price turned and reversed higher with a strong move? We can also see, in mid-December, that the signal line had moved up and over the MACD line before the trend reversal occurred. While the MACD is usually a lagging indicator, sometimes it can give a heads-up prior to the price action, as it did in this example. In fact, if you look closely, you can see that the exact point of this reversal was the head, in an inverse head and shoulders reversal pattern. The MACD divergence and the crossing over of the two lines contributed to identifying this pattern while it was forming. Pretty darn cool, huh?

Momentum Indicators

In forex trading, ***momentum*** refers to the speed at which prices change, both up and down. There are many different *momentum indicators*, one of which is actually named momentum indicator. These are oscillators that can help you get on the right side of the direction of the trade. They can also help identify reversals or other turning points in trends.

Momentum in the market is about the strength of recent price trends. When traders play momentum, they are betting that an asset price is moving (or will move) strongly in a given direction. Furthermore, they are betting that the asset price will continue moving in that direction until the trend loses strength.

I'm going to cover a few momentum indicators here that I think work especially well in forex.

Average Directional Index (ADX)

The average directional index (ADX) is one way to gauge the strength of a trend. It is often used with two accompanying indicators, the negative directional indicator (-DI) and the positive directional indicator (+DI). Together, these three indicators are known as the directional movement index (DMI), developed by J. Welles Wilder Jr. Figure 47 shows the USD/CHF pair with the ADX data shown in the middle pane, directly below the chart, and the DMI data shown below that, in the lower pane. The lines can look quite busy when plotted all on the same pane, so I plotted the actual ADX above the DMI. Although the ADX was developed for use with daily charts, it also works well with other time frames.

When the price of a pair is increasing, +DI is higher than -DI. If +DI is lower than -DI, then the price of the pair is declining. If the +DI and -DI lines cross, then the upper line signals where the trend is going. This unique indicator set can aid in showing us when a market has become overbought or oversold. Notice in figure 47 how the DMI+ (or "DM+" or "+DM") spikes up to the 40 level, right about the same time the ADX does the same. It was reflecting the strong move up in the price action. I have found that when either one of the DM lines and/or the ADX rises to around the 35 or 40 level, the market is either overbought or oversold. In this case, since the line that rose to that level was the DM+, and the market rallied up (the rising ADX reflecting the trend strength in that move), we can easily see it had become overbought.

Notice what happened next. In April, the price broke out to a new swing high, but both the ADX and the DM+ made markedly lower highs.

Immediately following, the market sold off. Though these indicators, like so many others, are lagging in how they reflect what's happening with price action, there are ways to use them as "leading" indicators as well. In this case, the indicator was able to alert observant traders that long trades had become more risky, first by rising above 40 and then by diverging from the new high prices that were being made, by posting lower highs themselves. These "leading" signals reflected increasing odds that trading the downside could (and did) offer greater opportunity.

GRAPHIC

fig. 47

Notice also that in January (off the chart), prior to the strong move up, the DM+ was above the DM- and the ADX line was rising from a low level. That information might have presented an opportunity to take advantage of that move up.

If the ADX line is above 25 and rising, then the trend is considered to be especially strong. If it is below 20, then the trend is weak. You can see a horizontal line at 20, to clearly mark this level. Typically, the ADX will fall below 20 when the price is moving sideways, when the trend has reversed, or when prices are so volatile that it's difficult to identify a trend. I have used the ADX as the basis for some custom indicators because of its ability to show trend strength. The ADX will slope higher during a strong trend, whether that trend be up or down. A rising ADX line reflects the strength of the trend.

I sometimes draw another horizontal line at 10.00 or 11.00 to show me when the market has become so "sleepy" that it may be poised for a breakout. If I can get a position placed in front of a breakout from sleepy price action, it can lead to a very happy result. Of course, I would use one of my complete strategies to do such a thing, not just an indicator like the ADX by itself—though the ADX can indeed be a valuable piece of the puzzle. Combining this idea with my exhaustion concept described in chapter 14 can offer some very interesting opportunities.

Average True Range

Average true range, or ATR, also developed by J. Welles Wilder Jr., is a measure of volatility often used by forex traders. It's a moving average showing how much the pair moved between its high and low, on average, over a period of time. In other words, it shows the pair's average trading range over the period it's applied to, usually 14 bars.

fig. 48

Like all these indicators, it too is a lagging indicator, but it has some uses. I typically combine it with a multiplier that helps me create dynamic entries, stops, and targets that adjust themselves to current market conditions. If the ATR is rather large, I use it with the multiplier to push the entries, stops, and/or targets a little further away—the idea being that if the market is trading with greater range, additional price action confirmation can increase the odds of the trade working out. If the ATR contracts, it means trading ranges have recently lessened, so using it in this way would pull the entries, stops, and targets closer to the trade entry point. This is a somewhat advanced concept and beyond the scope of this beginner's guide, but I wanted to mention it to show how the creative use of standard indicators can give a trader a real edge in the market. Figure 48 shows the ATR on the USD/CHF daily chart.

Price Rate of Change

The price rate of change indicator measures the percentage of change in price between the current price and the price however many periods ago that the trader specifies, such as 5 days or 14 days. The number is positive if the price has increased and negative if the price has decreased. The closer the indicator is to zero, the less clear the trend.

fig. 49

Figure 49 shows the price rate of change indicator for the USD/CHF, calculated using a 14-day time period. It appears below the price. Do not confuse price rate of change with volume rate of change. Volume is meaningless in forex.

Finding Indicators that Give You the Greatest Edge

Indicators can be used to manage the subjective elements of price charts and patterns by helping to interpret the action and reaction so that you can anticipate the subsequent action. They can also confuse a forex trader who keeps adding items to a chart or messing around with indicators to "curve-fit" them to past data. Traders will tinker with the inputs and adjust the indicators so that they perfectly match and signal past price changes, expecting these perfect configurations to continue to work going forward. They won't! You cannot curve-fit indicators to past data and expect it to be effective in the future. Think of it like trying to fit a shoe to a foot that is always changing in size, constantly growing, shrinking, changing its various dimensions at every moment. The markets are ever-changing, and I can't tell you how many traders have crashed and burned attempting to curve-fit their indicators.

Traders should use indicators, but they should use them carefully. After developing some experience working with price charts, add one or two indicators to see if they improve your ability to recognize tradeable patterns that you can prove will give you an advantage, an edge. Also consider making some trade decisions based on charts while also noting what a few indicators are showing. Then go back and evaluate whether there were any clear patterns in the trade results based on what the indicators showed. Personally, I focus on the price action and use indicators to help corroborate my ideas. The example I mentioned previously—where the MACD helped corroborate the formation of the head and shoulders pattern on the USD/CHF, signaling the reversal in trend—is a good example of what I mean. The MACD by itself was probably not enough to rely on, but if we were trying to decide whether to place a long trade coming out of the right shoulder, we could look to what the MACD showed us as confirming information to help support that trade idea.

Evaluating trades by looking at what different indicators have shown is a form of **backtesting**. This is the process of seeing how trade ideas would have done in the past, using actual market conditions. Rather than making changes to your tradeplan based on new-to-you indicators, see how these indicators would have worked in the past. See if they would have helped to confirm or disconfirm your trade ideas. By backtesting enough of a sample set with a specific trading approach, you will get an excellent idea of whether or not an indicator will help you.

Your goal is to figure out a set of mechanical rules that can be proven. You may notice, for example, that when the price does X and the MACD does Y and your momentum indicator confirms Z, then you have a setup that you can test. In your tests, you want to see if that particular scenario wins more often than it loses over a lot of trials. With all the extensive testing I have done over the years, I've found that after a sample set of 75 to 125 examples at a minimum, I see the statistics (results) begin to stabilize. Of course, we want to continue testing going forward (**forward testing**) with each new session to be sure our results continue to hold up. By doing this, with proper use of the right mix of indicators, we can establish effective trading tactics that will give us a real edge in the market.

More information on backtesting and mechanical rules can be found in chapters 14, 15, and the conclusion of this book. You will also find detailed info on both of these topics in my *Day Trading QuickStart Guide* title, also available from ClydeBank Media.

No indicator can guarantee successful trading. There is no machine that makes money all the time—or if there is, no one is sharing the details. Traders are working with different pairs, in different market sessions, with different commission structures. However, there are ways to prove that certain patterns lead to profitable trading decisions the majority of the time. The immediate past predicts the immediate future. Indicators are tools that can be used to guide and improve your trading. Like all tools, they are most powerful in the hands of those with knowledge and experience, and they can be injurious when used incorrectly.

Chapter Recap

» Indicators are calculations based on price charts. They give traders more information about the magnitude of price trends and the likelihood of upcoming changes.

» There are four main types of indicators: moving indicators, oscillators, momentum indicators, and volatility indicators. These can be found in most major charting packages, along with a seemingly endless array of other indicators.

» Many traders find that the number of indicators available overwhelms their ability to use them well.

| 10 |
Applying the SMA Indicators
In the Trading Room

Chapter Overview
- » The SMA in action
- » Identifying setup bars
- » Setting entries, stops, and targets
- » Applying the bid-ask spread

When learning to trade, it's helpful to see actual examples of trades. In this section, I will walk you through a few trades that paid off for me. The logic behind them will help you see how indicators are used in practice.

Using the 20 SMA on a Five-Minute Chart

I am a fan of the 20-day simple moving average, also known as the 20 SMA. It shows me reliable pullback zones. This indicator is a great way to see the Action → Reaction → Subsequent Action concept play out.

I wait for an action move to occur, then I use the 20 SMA to mark the possible end of the reaction move that follows. Markets trend and markets consolidate. An action move could be the beginning of a new trend direction or the middle of an established trend. The move that typically follows a strong move (action move) is known as a pullback or consolidation (a reaction). In a trend, a new action move has a good chance of occurring after this reaction, and, in fact, the subsequent action move that follows often mirrors the prior action move (see point 3 to point 4 in figure 50). Because the immediate past often predicts the immediate future, this is predictable and tradeable, offering good probability. I am now looking for the likely subsequent action move. Figuring out where the reaction will end is the critical judgment call. This will determine if and where I place my trade. It is critical that I get it right, and the tool I use is the 20 SMA. It does a pretty decent job of indicating where the end of the reaction might occur, while also marking the beginning of the new action move.

Figure 50 is the five-minute chart for the GBP/AUD on 11/6/20 from 19:10 p.m. through the early morning of 11/7/20. Just before 20:15 p.m., the price crosses up and over the 20 SMA (point 1 to point 2) and then pulls back (point 2 to point 3). This is the first action move and the first reaction move. When the price pulls back to the 20 SMA, I will look to enter my trade based on a trading tactic that uses this pattern to anticipate the subsequent action move (point 3 to point 4). The number labels on the figure identify the important points of the price action:

fig. 50

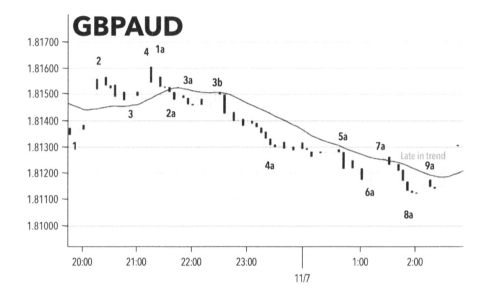

As we begin our exploration of actual trading scenarios, it will be helpful to visualize them as they would happen in real time. For this reason, we've created a Forex Investing QuickStart Guide Trade Chart Visualization webpage where you can visualize the charts, such as the one featured in figure 50, as they would develop in real time without seeing the entire progression of the price action all at once. Visit go.quickstartguides.com/forex for access.

» **Point 1a to Point 2a** shows the first action move in the opposite direction. At first, we need to be alert to the fact that it could be another reaction to the action move that just happened (from 3 to 4). As it pushes beyond the 20 SMA, though, ultimately closing below it, we learn that this is not a reaction, but a new action move in the opposite direction. When we see this new action move to the downside, we can begin to look for a new reaction that will follow and use our 20 SMA to indicate where that reaction might end (support becomes resistance), and the subsequent tradeable action move will begin.

» **Point 2a to Points 3a and 3b** shows the pullbacks to the 20 SMA, setting up two great trade opportunities down to point 4a. Often, but not always, there is more than one trade opportunity. This example gave us two chances to enter a low-risk trade to take advantage of the likely subsequent action move down, and, as you can see by what followed, it was well worth it.

» **Point 4a to Point 5a** shows the price stalling a bit around the 1.81300 price point until the 20 SMA catches up with it, which sets up a pullback trade short to point 6a. This is common. *Consolidation patterns often turn out to be the reaction.* Thus, the 20 SMA, on this chart, proves quite versatile and effective at marking the potential end of the reaction. It helps us establish the setup to our subsequent action, point 6a in this case.

» **Point 6a to Point 7a** The four successive up bars may indicate that the trend is beginning to tire out, but it's got one last gasp to spend. The pullback to point 7a and the 20 SMA sets up a final trade down to point 8a. Of course, this is easier to see in hindsight than it is when you're watching and waiting at the right edge of the chart. However, if you study and test the action, reaction, subsequent action dynamic that occurs on all charts and time frames, then you can count on the 20 SMA to provide you with a huge clue as to where the reaction moves might be ending. You may then trade accordingly within the purview of your tradeplan (see chapter 15).

» **Point 8a to Point 9a** shows the pullback trade failing as the market is ready to head higher now. The process may begin again to the upside. It appears that the 20 SMA (at point 9a) marks the beginning of a new action move lower, but instead the price quickly pivots and turns higher, with multiple bars closing up and above the SMA, for what could be a new action move in the opposite direction—up. We must now be on the lookout for the next reaction and tradeable subsequent action to the upside.

The modest 20 SMA does a great job of marking the likely end of a reaction move. It is not perfect, so we will protect ourselves with well-placed "stops," or stop losses. These are orders to the broker to close the position when a predetermined price is hit, and their use is discussed in greater detail in chapter 13.

Ongoing consistent success at trading requires having enough humility to be able to admit when our trade isn't going to work. We don't have to be right all the time, and in fact we won't be. No one can achieve that. We just have to be right *most* of the time. Traders who think they are smarter than the market, like Harvey the Engineer, have a hard time understanding this. Do you want to be right, or do you want to be profitable? It's best to answer that question right away and establish your true reason for trading from the start. This will help you remain focused on what truly matters when risking your hard-earned cash trading the markets.

Using the 20 SMA on a 15-Minute Chart

The 20 SMA is a great way to look for Action → Reaction → Subsequent Action dynamics on longer charts, too. A 15-minute chart may show one or two excellent setups in a session. I particularly like watching the 15-minute chart during the London or New York morning trading sessions.

Forex market hours and trading sessions are discussed in chapter 3.

As we saw in our previous example, the 20 SMA has an uncanny way of showing us where reactions may end. In general, I like to see a pullback of one third to two thirds from the prior action move. For me that's the sweet spot for setting up a trade with a suitable risk-to-reward ratio. For example, if the action move was 21 pips, the reaction should be from 7 to 14 pips. I can use the 20 SMA to see where the reaction might end, and then it gives me a trade setup with very good odds of succeeding, by trading the subsequent action move. Furthermore, using the 20 SMA helps me to stay flat (not initiate a position) at the sight of price action that may look like a reaction move but is in fact a new move in the opposite direction. When the anticipated reaction moves past the 20 SMA, I become suspicious and consider the possibility of a new action move in the opposite direction. We saw this occur a couple of times in the previous examples, and we'll see it happen later in this section as I walk you through a series of trades.

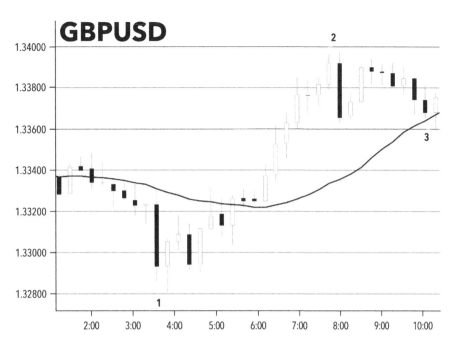

GBPUSD

This particular sequence begins late during the European session, around 4:00 a.m. in New York (eastern time), and extends into the US morning session.

To keep things simple, I split forex hours into three tradeable sessions. What I call the Asian session begins at 6:00 p.m. eastern time. This is the longest session and can stretch to 11:00 p.m. or midnight, depending on the tradeplan. The European session runs from 2:00 a.m. to 5:00 a.m. eastern time, and the US session runs from 8:30 to about noon. These are not official sessions, but they are how I like to divide up the trading day when creating tradeplans. Some traders also like what I call the "bridge session," between 5:00 a.m. and 8:30 a.m. eastern. This may be very good for certain pairs, but I'm always sleeping at that time, so I don't pay it much attention. I am also asleep for the European session, unless I'm in Europe, but I realize many traders are wide awake and on that side of the world. The European session is a very active one for forex traders.

At point 2 in figure 51, 16 bars and 4 hours later from where we started at 4:00 a.m., the upward run in the price runs out of gas and reverses down. The US morning session is underway. Remember, each bar on this chart represents 15 minutes of time. We've been waiting quite a while for this setup to take shape, but now we can see that a new action move was established back at point 1. Is the big down bar at point 2 the beginning of a reaction move? The price did move higher again, testing the swing high that was just established, but it failed to make a new high and instead turned down, making a lower swing high as seen in the diagram in the bars following point 2. From there, the price declined before finding support at the 20 SMA, at point 3.

Q: What's the meaning of the term "swing" or a "swing level" in trading?

A swing high occurs when a price bar marks a higher high than the two bars to its left and the two bars to its right. Similarly, a swing low occurs when a price bar marks a lower low than the lows of the two bars to its left and to its right. Swings show us near-term support and resistance levels on the chart. If the price attempts to move higher to make a new swing high but fails to do so and instead makes a lower high, we say that it failed to make a "new high," or a "new swing high." Now we have to see if the price will head lower, and if so, will it be merely a pause in the uptrend (a reaction move), or is it going to be a new action move in the opposite direction? Determining this is paramount to the success of these SMA-guided trade ideas that I'll be reviewing with you in this section. As I explained earlier, we will use the 20 SMA to help us mark the likely location of the end of a reaction move and the beginning of a new action move continuing the trend.

At point 3, notice that the up bar has a wick that stabs down below the 20 SMA before closing higher. This is bullish, and so I added the two arrows to the chart to indicate my intent to trade long here. This is the "setup bar," the bar that presents information we need to enter a trade using a ***bracket order***, a special kind of order that places our entry between our stop loss and a series of targets. We'll return to the setup bar throughout this walk-through as we make key decisions about our trade. One thing we notice right away is that, in this case, the price action in the setup bar indicates that the reaction move has probably ended. It meets our criteria, in that it stopped at the 20 SMA and closed higher with a very bullish bar, and the move down to the SMA is approximately one third to two thirds the length of the prior action move. Moreover, whenever you see a bar like this, where the price action attempted to move below the SMA (as indicated by the tail that stabbed down below it) but then fails to continue lower and winds up closing on or above the SMA, that usually is a strong indication that this could be a very good setup bar. It's a bullish sign. That's what we're looking for with this setup.

As a reaction move ends, a subsequent action move back up, in the direction of the prevailing trend, is possibly beginning. Now comes the hard part. The chart is hindsight. It shows what *has* happened. Now we have to imagine what could happen next. Trading happens at the right edge of the chart where we can't see what will happen next. We can see the action move that just occurred and the reaction move that has met our criteria so far. To the right, though, where all trading takes place, we see only blackness. But we have the information we need now to envision a trade opportunity. After all, my trading philosophy leans on the idea that the immediate past—the action and reaction moves in price that just happened—predicts the immediate future, the likely new action move that often resembles the prior action move. That is our trade opportunity. As traders, we have to realize that this trade opportunity could win or lose. We are not trying to be right. We are taking advantage of the odds that this trade setup has a good chance of winning, and we are protecting ourselves within the rules of our plan in case the trade doesn't work out. Trading is a numbers game and as long as we are winning more than we lose, and more often, this trade setup will make us money over time, accomplishing our reason for trading, which we established from the start.

We place an order to go long a couple of pips above the high of the setup bar. As noted, we will rely on our setup bar as we determine the parameters of our trade in accordance with the rules we have established for this trade setup. The key to this trade succeeding is our being able to correctly identify the end of the reaction move, and for that we are relying on the 20 SMA and the fact that the setup bar closed above or on it, as well as the ensuing price action itself. Some setup bars will cancel if, for example, the price can't move the extra 2 pips to hit our entry and instead moves lower again.

Start by measuring the length of the setup bar (18.3 pips) and adding it to the high of that same bar, to project our targets. On the right side of figure 52, you can see that I projected five targets above the high of my setup bar, at 1x, 1.5x, 2x, 2.5x, and 3x, where x is the 18.3-pip length of the setup bar itself. Note that the high of the setup bar is at 1.33776.

Each of these target values would be an excellent place to take profits. The larger targets would obviously be the most profitable, but only if the market could trade that high. Knowing what we know from what just occurred, the prior action move offers us the chance for a large subsequent action move, so our higher targets are worth shooting for. But the smaller targets have a higher chance of succeeding, and they are profitable. Because forex is flexible with position sizing, we can scale out a percentage of our position (take some profits) after hitting each successive target level. By scaling out of our trade like this, we can profit from the easier-to-hit targets while also giving ourselves a chance to hit the more ambitious targets.

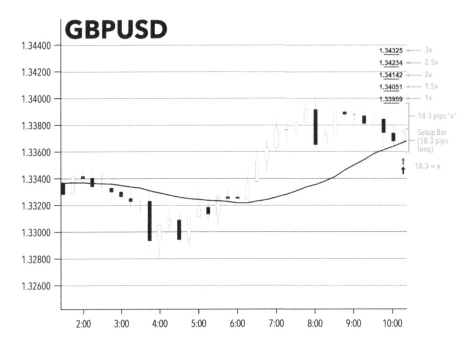

fig. 52

Now that you understand how I create targets for a trade, I'm going to walk you through how I decide where to enter a trade, or, in trader-speak, how I "place my trade."

The high of the setup bar is 1.33776, which we'll round up to 1.3378. When day trading forex, I'm generally looking to place my entry about 2 pips beyond the setup bar in the direction of my trade. If we add 2 pips to 1.3378, we end up with 1.3380, but I don't like to place trades at price points that land on multiples of 10. Such "key levels," as I refer to them, often create psychological support/resistance levels that the price struggles to get through. I want to see the price push through the key level of 1.3380 before I get into the trade. So, I'll move the entry up 1 pip to 81, and I will therefore place my buy order / entry order for this long trade at 83 to account for 2 pips of spread. (I will explain shortly why I always account for spread (see chapter 3) on the buy side of my orders. Spreads can cover more or less than 2 pips, so it's important to see how your broker is pricing the pair at the time of entry. It's never perfect, because they are always changing the spread, but if you can get set prices with your broker, you should opt for that because it makes figuring out your setups much easier.) The higher entry point means that the price action has to confirm the upward trend, just a little bit, at least enough to not only push past our setup bar but also to push through the key level price point of 80. This small "key-level adjustment" might not seem like much, but it will sometimes save losing trades. Our trade won't enter until the bid price pushes 3 pips above the high of the setup bar. If the price fails to push through these 3 pips or heads lower, then we have avoided a likely losing trade.

Notice that with this technique we are allowing room for the price action to guide the trade, not the other way around. We want to let the market lead the way. This helps us see how the market is moving before we commit our funds.

At this point in our trade setup analysis, it's important that we recall our discussion in chapter 3 about the bid-ask spread. In fact, if you're not clear on that concept, now would be a good time to stop and reread that section from chapter 3. The charts we use when setting up a trade, including those featured thus far in this chapter (figures 50 to 52), display only the bid price for the currency pair. We can still use these charts to execute great trade setups, but we must account for that fact. To understand the logic here, consider the simple 3-pip bid-ask spread in figure 53.

GBPUSD	
0.9995 bid price	**0.9998** ask price

fig. 53

If I want to go long on a hypothetical trade on the forex pair ABC/XYZ, I might decide that I want my entry to be, let's say, 1.0001. The bid-ask spread is currently 0.9995/0.9998, 3 pips, but I believe the price is headed up. I don't want the order to be filled any lower than 1.0001, because I want the upward price action to be confirmed beyond the round-number "key level" point of 1.0000. Therefore, since I see that there is a 3-pip spread on this pair, I'm going to place my actual buy order at 1.0004 with the intent to get long if and when the bid hits 1.0001. How does this make sense? Well, I know that the broker will not fill my buy order (1.0004) until the ask price climbs up to 1.0004—at which point we will have a bid-ask spread of 1.0001/1.0004; in other words, the price as it is reflected on the chart (the bid price) is now where I wanted it to be for my desired entry (1.0001) even though my order will actually be filled at 1.0004, the ask.

We always have to "pay the spread" on the buy side of every trade. The buy side is the entry for longs and the exit for shorts.

In our current trading example with the GBP/USD pair (figure 52), we were trying to get long at 1.3381. But we'd determined that we were *not* going to place our buy order at this price, because the broker will fill us on the ask and the bid will have only gotten to 1.3379. We needed to first look at the spread for the pair (which should be viewable on your charting platform; simply locate the current bid and ask prices for the pair). We ascertain a spread of roughly 2 pips, and we therefore decide to place our entry order at 1.3383. This way, the bid will have hit 1.3381 and the broker will fill us at the ask, 1.3383.

NOTE

Depending on your broker, the spread can be even less than 1 pip for the GBP/USD pair, because it's commonly traded.

To recap, our 1.3383 buy order price is derived from identifying our setup bar, moving 2 pips up from the high of the setup bar (from 1.3378 to 1.3380), moving up one more pip to get past the key level (to 1.3381), and finally moving the price up another 2 pips to account for the spread (to 1.3383).

DETOUR

When going short on a trade, you are buying when you exit the trade (you sell to enter). Therefore, you only need to account for the spread on your exit (aka your target and your stop). When the bid hits your exit, you get filled at the ask, paying the spread as you exit the trade.

When you *enter* a short trade, you are filled at the bid price and, since the charts are drawn using bid prices, you can place your short trade entry order right at the bid, as displayed by your chart. It's the same with exiting a long trade. You will exit at the bid. You only need to account for the spread when you are entering your long trades or exiting your shorts.

MY TAKE

Practice makes perfect. There's no way to develop a firm command of trading mechanics without persistent study and repetition. You'll get the hang of it if you don't give up. Correctly executing trades should be practiced in a sim account until you can do it perfectly each time.

Let's see how the trade played out (figure 54).

Figure 54 shows that the price action did push higher, triggering us into the trade on the very next bar (remember, when the chart shows us breaking past our entry of 1.3381, it means that the bid price hit 1.3381; therefore, the ask price hit 1.3383 and our order got filled at the ask).

fig. 54

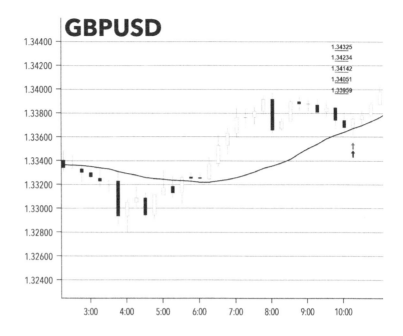

Also, keep in mind that each bar in this chart represents 15 minutes of trading. As you peruse the book you can see it all happen in an instant, but it can be difficult to imagine what it feels like waiting for a full 15 minutes to see if your entry price was hit. Often a setup bar will require numerous bars to form after it before the price action moves up and through your entry. Real trading includes the passing of time, which always proves to be a great unforeseen challenge to most inexperienced traders.

fig. 55

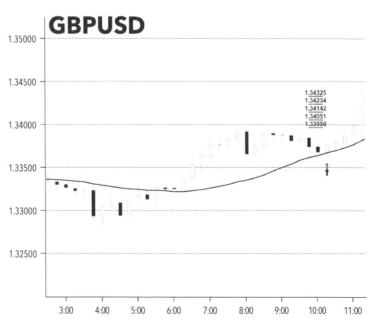

Three bars and 45 minutes later, the price exploded and smashed through the remainder of our targets, as you can see in figure 55. This trade took seconds to identify and set up, but in reality, an entire hour passed before the targets were hit, which is relatively quick for a 15-minute bar chart. Many trades take a lot longer.

Knowing where to find and how to use the best available trade tools is crucial. Trade tools allow us to set up the entire trade instantly. Rather than succumb to the tedious and time-intensive task of monitoring the trade in real time, you can set everything up in a few clicks. Furthermore, you can request that audible alerts be sent to your mobile phone to notify you when targets are hit or when you stop out. These trade tools also allow you to automatically scale out of your position and lock in your profits after hitting various targets. The Digital Assets at go.quickstartguides.com/forex provide a great entry point for discovering and exploring the tools I use in my own trading.

It's interesting to see what happened after this trade. Figure 56 shows how the price started to drift sideways as our subsequent action move came to an end. According to our Action → Reaction → Subsequent Action formula, the point where we closed our trade was the end of our subsequent action (points 3 to 4), and the sideways drift (price consolidation) became the new reaction move, as we later learned (see the next example in figures 56 through 60).

fig. 56

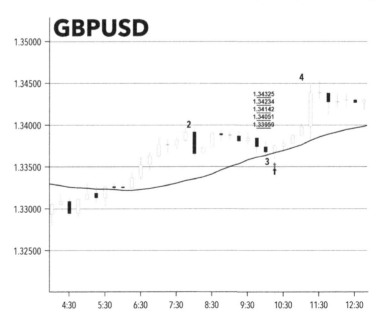

The next few bars, shown in figure 57, help set up our next trade. At point 5, the price comes down to hit the 20 SMA bar even as the 20 SMA trends up. We can see that this sharp stab lower suffices to constitute another possible reaction move (points 4 to 5), meeting our criteria of being approximately one third to two thirds the length to the prior action move (points 3 to 4). Now we can try to take advantage of this new trade setup that has just formed.

fig. 57

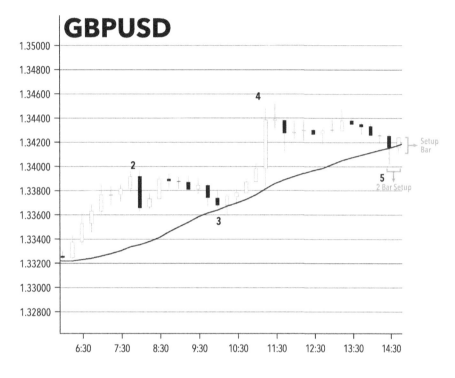

There are two big concerns. First, it's getting late in the day. The New York session will be closing soon, and that increases the risk of trades placed at this time. I've noticed it's a time when many pairs just don't trade well, unless there is some headline news to generate activity. The price action tends to be much less reliable for certain pairs and charts in the afternoon. Second, spreads become abnormally large between the close of the New York session and the open of the new day's trading, which happens in Australia. We can get bumped in or out of trades due to spreads becoming too large.

Still, for the purposes of this walk-through, to learn how a sequence of trades can and will unfold at the right edge of the chart, let's go through the exercise of placing the next trade. In this case, we will use the low of the down bar's wick and measure to the high of our setup bar, which is the next one to the right. While the setup on the first trade was a single bar, this trade uses a two-bar setup (see figure 57). We'll measure from the lowest point of those two bars to the high of our setup bar. Remember, for long trades the setup bar must close up and above the 20 SMA. For shorts, it must close down and below the 20 SMA.

The high of the setup bar is 1.34248, which we will round up to 1.3425. Then we will place our entry 2 pips above the high of our setup bar and add 2 more pips to account for the spread. If the price pushes high enough so that the ask hits our entry order, it will pull the bid price up as well so that it will land on our target entry of 2 pips above our setup bar. We will get filled on the ask at 1.3429, but for the purpose of our chart (which is comprised totally of bid prices) we are entering at the bid, 1.3427.

The thing to remember is that when we buy, the broker is going to fill us at the ask price, which is above the bid. We need our bid price to hit our entry point at 2 pips above our setup bar. If the bid can't get to our entry point, we don't want the order to fill because it means that the price action doesn't have enough energy to confirm the possible beginning of the next action move. This is a very important concept that I often refer to as "price action confirmation." The market is in charge and we are letting it lead the dance. Also, to reemphasize: because the charts that we use to create and test these trade setups are based on bid prices, all our trade decisions need to be based on the bid as well. We need the bid to hit our entry, and then we will get filled on the ask and pay the spread. If the bid can't hit our entry, we will remain flat. Some traders try to cheat a little and get in at a lower price. They prefer not to pay the spread and will try to get in 2 pips earlier. That is a flawed way of thinking, though, because it defeats the whole purpose of price action confirmation. What if the price can't break out to our calculated entry point? Then the trader gets filled on a trade that doesn't meet the requirements of the trade strategy and ends up holding a losing position. Don't be penny-wise and pound-foolish. The spread cost is a necessary trade expense and is not worth saving if it means giving up our price action confirmation as a result.

We'll place the entry buy order at 1.3429. The low of the down bar that precedes the setup bar is 1.3402, so we will place our stop at 1.3399. This is 2 pips below the lowest point of this two-bar setup plus an additional 1 pip off the key level of 1.3400. Remember, since our stop, if it's hit, sells us out of the position via a sell order, we need not worry about the spread.

fig. 58

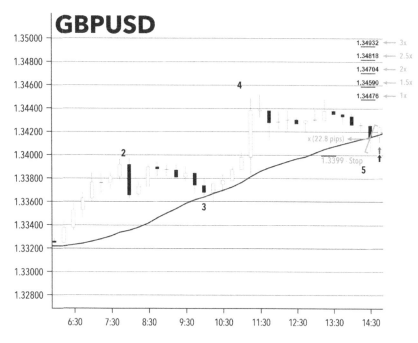

The new target prices are on the right of figure 58. As with the earlier trade, these are set at 1x, 1.5x, 2x, 2.5x, and 3x the length of our two-bar setup (22.8 pips), added to the setup bar's high of 1.34248.

In figure 59, we can see how the trade played out.

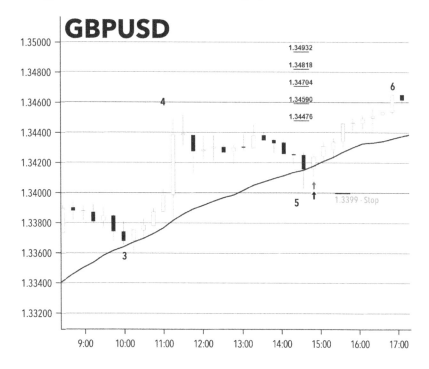

fig. 59

This would have been a good trade. It hit the first two targets. Now we're coming to the end of the New York session, which calls for a decision: close out the position or hold it into the opening of the Sydney session. Holding on could be risky, since spreads tend to be large as a new session opens. A larger spread could push down the bid price and make it easier for us to stop out if the trade breaks against us.

At a minimum, we may wish to scale out of our position somewhat and lock in some profits before pursuing those higher targets. But let's continue to follow the price action. Markets don't stop. They continue in a sequence, one bar after another, and we as traders must be able to spot the best trading situations in order to achieve consistent success. In figure 60, we see that the price has again started down, coming back to the 20 SMA and then going below it.

fig. 60

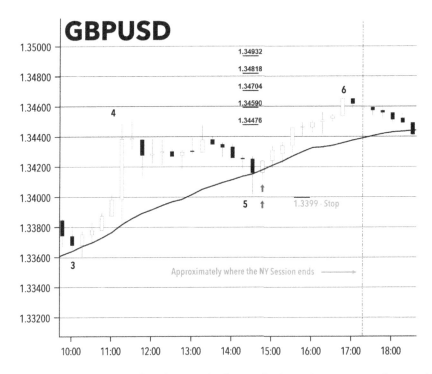

This drop below the SMA is not bad in and of itself; a strong up bar could still give us a setup. In our prior examples, the setups had bars with long tails piercing down, but they still ended closing up, above the 20 SMA. That kind of setup bar is excellent and often leads to winning "subsequent action move" trades. It's quite possible that that will happen again. In this case, though, we should also note that the 20 SMA itself is beginning to lose a little momentum. It's flattening some as its upward slope begins to diminish.

We have had a few good action moves up already, and we are not in our prime trading time. Trends do come to an end, so we want to stay vigilant for clues that could alert us as to when this may be occurring. We have to consider that maybe this move lower is not a reaction at all, but an action move in the opposite direction. We will let the price action tell us.

fig. 61

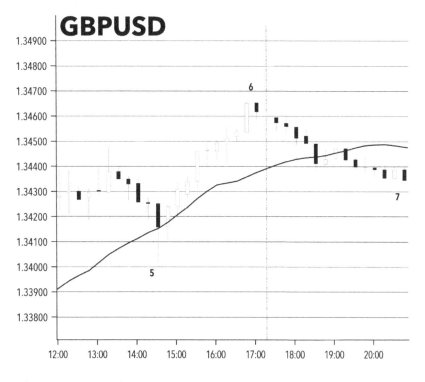

As we can see in figure 61, it appears a new action move down has begun. The price tried to hold up at the 20 SMA, but with multiple bars closing below it, the support we'd be looking to identify in a new long setup was not there. Note that the second bar to close below the SMA, an up bar, stabbed back up through the 20 SMA from below but then closed below it again—support became resistance! We have to pay attention to this. Then, as the price continued to tell its story, it pulled back to the 20 SMA again, closing above it. This could be perceived as another setup bar to go long, and we might have placed a trade, although, if we did so properly, that trade would never have been filled. The fact that bars were closing below the 20 SMA makes this setup less reliable, but regardless, an entry 2 pips above this prospective setup bar would never have been hit, *which highlights the important role that price action confirmation plays on the success of this setup.* The next bar closes below the 20 SMA, which would cancel the long setup.

We now need to seriously consider that the move from point 6 down through the 20 SMA might be a new action move down. In fact, from this shifted perspective, we must now consider the reaction, the pullback back up to the 20 SMA, and then the first down bar (occurring around 19:15) as a new short setup. Do you see the possible setup bar? It's the second black bar that closes below the 20 SMA. Is that a valid short setup bar marking the all-important end of the reaction move, or is the initial action move lower still forming? Figure 62 reveals that the latter interpretation is the accurate one.

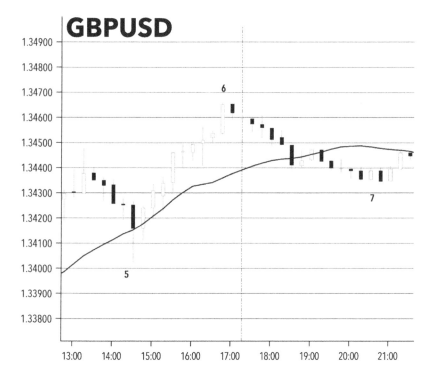

fig. 62

How could we have made the right decision here (regarding the prospective setup bar near 19:45)? Let's think through our rules. We have our pullback and then our first down bar, but it doesn't quite meet all of our criteria for identifying the end of a reaction move—namely, this prospective reaction doesn't extend one third to two thirds the length of the prior action move.

The price did indeed continue lower, ending at point 7, terminating what appears to be a new action move to the short side. We then get another pullback to the 20 SMA and our first down bar. Can this be used as a new short setup bar? Let's think it through.

Does it meet our one third to two thirds pullback rule? Maybe. It appears closer to meeting that standard than our previous setup bar prospect did.

Rather than split hairs here, I'm going to go ahead and place my entry on the short and let the price action take charge and show me the way. If I'm off base, the price action will not allow me to enter the trade.

The low of the new setup bar, even though it is small, is 1.34434. To place a trade, we would start by rounding down to 1.3443. An entry 2 pips below that would be at 1.3441, which is 1 pip in front of the key level of 40. We will adjust the entry below the key level by 1 pip to 1.3439.

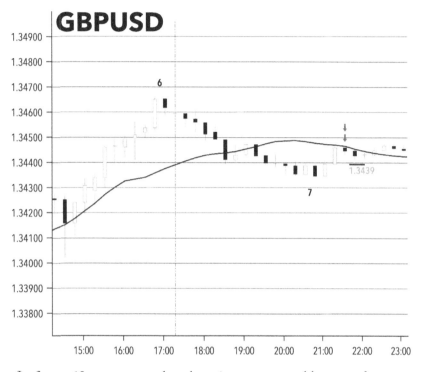

fig. 63

In figure 63, we can see that the price was never able to get down to our 1.3439 entry, so the order would not be executed—another example of how we let the market lead the dance and the importance of our entry rules that always ask for additional price action confirmation. Also notice that we are late in the Sydney session, and, as stated previously, it's not the best time to be trading this pair.

Price action confirmation is essential to keeping the odds firmly on our side. We avoided a losing trade by maintaining the discipline inherent in our tradeplan rules.

At this point, do we know what the price is doing? What is it saying to us? Take a moment and write down what you think might happen next.

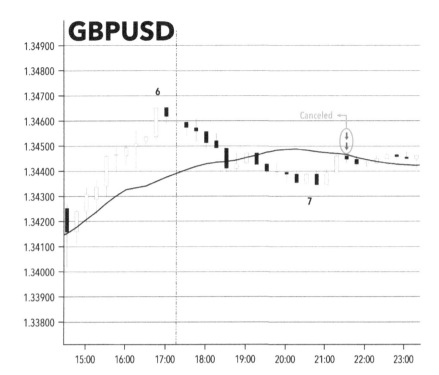

fig. 64

Since the short trade did not fill, it is possible that we are not in a reaction move at all, but a new action move up again. Action moves are not always followed by reaction moves. "Higher time frame influences" could be at play. In other words, if we widen out the lens of the price action, what seems like a reaction move on our faster charts may be a quite obvious and insignificant section of a slower action move that can be visualized easily on a chart with a higher time frame. Our trade setup rules help us mitigate the ever-perplexing and unpredictable nature of price action. We just saw this with our short setup that never triggered in. I try not to overthink things. It's easy to become confused. The rules of this trade setup tend to do the hard thinking for you, keeping the odds firmly planted on your side. Trades that don't trigger in and need to be canceled are a part of the process and should be integrated into your tradeplans. Moreover, action moves followed by new action moves in the opposite direction are going to happen. That's why it is so important to qualify our identification of where reactions should end. We use our 20 SMA, our one third to two thirds requirement, our time-of-day considerations, and our price action confirmation technique to help us get into the right trades the majority of the time.

If you keep winning more than you lose, then you win!

Chapter Recap

» The moving averages are powerful and easy to use, making them a good first step for a trader who wants to work with indicators. Study and backtest moving averages and any indicator in your existing trading strategy before using them in actual trades.

» Less is usually more. We saw that just by using one indicator, a simple moving average (SMA), in addition to a specific price pattern and well-thought-out trading rules, we could identify reliable trade setups.

| 11 |
Using Trading Systems

Chapter Overview
» Incorporating patterns, indicators, and stops
» Proprietary and custom trading systems
» Training and support for new traders

Trading is a little bit like cooking. Take a few ingredients, use them in the right proportions, subject them to heat, and the result can be amazing. Or it can be deadly. Take one simple ingredient, salt. In large amounts, it can be lethal. In small amounts, it makes everything from carne asada to crème caramel delicious. And without it, we would die.

In forex trading, traders bring together different currency pairs, trading sessions, and time frames. They combine charts, patterns, indicators, and leverage and expose them to the heat of the market. The results can be huge profits or crushing losses.

This chapter covers the ways that people develop trading systems and includes some of the factors to consider when evaluating your own system or one developed by someone else.

Defining a Trading System
Traders approach trading systems in different ways. They can develop and execute their systems manually, program their own strategies and indicators, or subscribe to a proprietary methodology. Some traders do all three.

Developing a Manual System
A manual system is one in which traders place their own orders rather than automating their trading. This is how most traders start. It involves developing an approach to the market, such as looking for momentum or playing off of volatility, and then identifying how much risk to take. It is refined by identifying which price patterns to use to enter and close trades and adding any indicators that will support the trading decisions.

This involves a lot of work, but the advantage is that doing the work creates a strong platform for future success.

Custom Programming

Most brokers and trading platforms allow customers to create their own trading algorithms or bots. These allow for automated trading whenever certain parameters are met in the market. They can simplify trading, but they require the up-front work of creating and testing the algorithm, as well as ongoing work to maintain and refine it. Many things can and will go wrong. If you are going to run an automated trading system, you have to pay attention and be prepared to take over control when things do go wrong. Automated trading adds complexity and often makes trading more difficult, which is counterintuitive to what one would think.

Automated trading has one enormous advantage. It can reduce the emotions involved with trading: doubt, fear, and greed.

For forex traders who have logical minds and experience with programming, this can be a winning approach. It is not for everyone.

Systems often need to be refined, because markets change. Also, as commonly traded systems become more widespread, they work less often, because too many traders are chasing the same signals. The best trading strategies have the ability to self-adjust, to actually tune themselves in real time to market conditions. These are the trading systems I always recommend. They have the best chance of remaining evergreen and working regardless of how markets change.

Using a Proprietary System

Many trading firms have developed their own trading systems that they make available to customers. They are often based on software platforms that connect to direct-access brokers. They vary in the amount of commitment required of the trader, from using preprogrammed trading bots included with some platforms to becoming an employee at a proprietary trading firm.

Most of these systems are available as subscription or membership services. They offer a combination of proprietary indicators, tested strategies, training, and support.

Good proprietary systems have the following characteristics:

» Ability to trade multiple markets and time frames
» Ability to tune themselves in real time so that the precalculated trade setups are based on market conditions at that moment
» Ability to scale and trail, meaning that they can help with taking out profits and adjusting stop losses as the markets play out
» Offer precise and concise tradeplans
» Offer full-immersion training
» Emphasize capital preservation
» Stack the odds on the side of the trader

The downside? Many do not perform well, and others are scams. Do the research on proprietary systems just as you would any trading system. If you do decide to go this route, you'll have to work hard to learn the strategy so you fully understand it. Even an exceptional strategy is dangerous in the hands of an ill-prepared trader.

Using Custom Trade Methodology

Many indicators are named for the people who developed them. Trading platforms list ridiculous numbers of indicators, but there are others in use that are not widely known. Many traders develop their own. Proprietary trading firms have in-house technical analysts who do nothing but develop and test indicators.

Some of these indicators are combinations or refinements of existing ones, and others are based on new theories of technical analysis. Many are offered to traders through subscription services or as software purchases. For example, many are available as add-ons to MT4 or NinjaTrader.

Advantages of Using Custom Indicators

Good custom indicators contain easy-to-follow trade signals and setup steps. They help manage entry points, stops, and position sizing. Most firms that offer custom indicators also offer training and support in how to use them, but these vary in quality and effectiveness, like anything else. The best ones come with rules on how to use them and can be profitable when used as intended—but plenty of others don't help much at all. Custom indicators should be contributing some kind of information that increases the odds of your trade setups having a positive outcome. If they do, that's a real edge.

Custom indicators can help reduce analysis paralysis by paring down a trading system to a handful of well-thought-out indicators that work together. Also, having a limited set can help speed decision-making, enable faster trade recognition, and make it easier to backtest. Potentially, they can make it easier to learn to trade, too, because they can offer structure that you would not otherwise have.

Finding a Dynamic System for Trading

Whether using your own system or evaluating proprietary systems, I recommend that you look for one that is dynamic. This means that it changes with market conditions. As the volatility of the market changes, the trade setups self-adjust to reflect the market's current condition. Some trade setups will be larger, some smaller, depending on the market itself. I feel that the best trading systems are based on price action itself and don't rely too heavily on the common lagging indicators that most traders are using. Price action is what's happening *now*, when the trade decision needs to be made.

Dynamic trading represents a mindset that acknowledges that yes, everything changes, but the market is always in charge. It allows you to take what the market wants to give you instead of what you want from the market. The market doesn't care what you want.

Indicators that show whether the market is oversold (OS) or overbought (OB) are useful in dynamic trading, because they can be on the lookout for a tiring trend and can be the precursor for effective reversal setups. On the other hand, just because a market is overbought or oversold doesn't mean the trend will tire. Often a trend will go on and on, remaining OB or OS for a long time. This leads to the point that an indicator by itself can help or hurt, and how it's combined with overall trade system rules is far more important. For example, if a market is rallying up and our indicator shows the market is OB, we can start looking for short setups "only IF" something else occurs, as defined by the trade system rules.

A dynamic trading system can adjust its entries, stops, and targets to reflect volatility, which helps you create trade setups that have a greater chance of succeeding at that exact moment in time.

Chapter Recap

» A trading system is a philosophy that represents how trading styles, market indicators, risk management, and position sizing come together.

» Many traders develop their own trading styles. Some work manually, and others develop their own algorithms to automate trading. Still others subscribe to services that offer custom indicators and trading systems.

» A robust trading system is dynamic. It adjusts to changing market conditions. The best ones are based on pure price action and let the market itself dictate what to do, allowing the trader to take what the market wants to give while mitigating risk with smart money management tradeplan rules.

| 12 |

Using Dynamic Systems
In the Trading Room

Chapter Overview

» The snapshot trading technique
» The 1-2-3 setup
» Momentum bars in action
» Tools of the trade

In our last "In the Trading Room" chapter (chapter 10), I covered how we can use information from the immediate past to predict the immediate future, following the Action → Reaction → Subsequent Action framework. An action move and a reaction move that just occurred are now the immediate past, and the subsequent action, which often tends to mirror the prior action, is the immediate future. It hasn't happened yet, but it provides us with a good trade opportunity if we have a system that we can prove will give us superior odds. The 20 simple moving average often marks the end of the reaction and offers a great clue that the subsequent action is about to begin. Using the first bar that closes in the direction of our trade in combination with the lowest point that gets close to, touches, or even stabs through the 20 SMA line helps us measure accurate targets. If we place our entry and stop just outside the range of those two places, we can calculate trade setups with a strong chance of winning.

I have just described an effective, dynamic trading system. It has all the components and qualifications we have been discussing thus far: It uses price action itself. It uses chart patterns that often repeat in all markets and time frames. It uses a simple indicator that by definition is a lagging indicator but is not being used in a lagging manner, but rather to show support and resistance and to mark when a reaction might end. Finally, it uses a trade setup and targeting method that is dynamic to the immediate price action, always adjusting to the current condition of the market. It dances with the market, allowing the market to lead.

Can another indicator be added to improve it? Possibly. The risk, of course, is that you can end up breaking something that didn't need to be fixed and making what was a perfectly effective strategy into something muddled and ineffective. Be slow to make any changes to an already effective trading approach. Test it through and through to prove it has indeed been enhanced. And be sure you can go back to its original form if things don't work out.

Whatever trading system you use, you'll be well served to make sure it incorporates the aforementioned components and qualities.

The Snapshot Trading Technique

While the trade method we just discussed will work on most time frames, we have mostly talked about day trading techniques so far. Now I'd like to introduce swing trading, which involves taking a position that will be in place for a few days, or even longer. For many people, this is a good way to get started. After all, many beginner-level traders have day jobs, and it's fair to say that the average boss is not a fan of employees trading forex while on the clock. Or perhaps you don't have a boss. Maybe you're at home taking care of small children. You'd like to learn how to make money by trading, but you only have so many undistracted hours available in a day.

Snapshot trading is a technique that I learned from Mark Soberman, a trader whom I greatly respect. This technique allows you to integrate strategic trading into your schedule. It's an example of a dynamic technique that allows traders to be flexible. The idea is that you set aside a specific window of time each day to check your charts to see if there are any trade setups you can take advantage of. The technique is best suited for trade charts with 15-minute or slower (longer) time frames. Hourly, four-hour, or daily charts that are too slow for day traders often work well in this situation.

Figure 65 is a snapshot trading example with some trade setups using an hourly EUR/USD chart and the 20 SMA pullback.

Let's say we establish a "snapshot trading window" between 6:00 and 8:00 p.m. (18:00–20:00), which gives us time to get home from work and have some dinner before getting into our charts. Studying the recent activity on our chart, we notice that a setup occurred at the end of the US session at around 16:00 eastern time. Prior to that time, there was a clear action move and a reaction that meets our one third to two thirds pullback criteria, straight to the 20 SMA (see the double arrows in figure 65). That same bar, as it dips low (before going higher) marking the end of the reaction, is also the setup bar. Since it is a single bar setup, we measure the distance of that bar to determine our "x" factor and then project our targets upward.

fig. 65

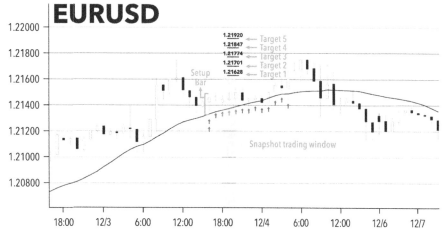

Note how, relative to our previous scenarios, we're using a much slower "higher time frame" chart for the snapshot trading technique.

REMEMBER

The "x" factor is a multiplier representing the distance from the low of the trade setup, in this case a single bar, to the high of the setup bar. We will set our targets using multiples of it. We have seen how sometimes there can be more than one bar in a setup as well, a bar closing down into our 20 SMA, and then a long bar closing higher above the SMA—the opposite being true for shorts. A single bar setup such as we see in this example stabs down into our SMA and then closes up. This is quite common.

In figure 65, notice how many one-hour bars passed before the trade took off and began to hit its targets. I put a single arrow under each 60-minute bar where we could have placed this trade. And, as you can see, this row of single bars (12 hours' worth) extends well into and beyond our snapshot trading window. Because you could place this trade at any point along that series of bars, you do not need to watch every bar to catch the setup. You simply come in during your snapshot trading window, identify the trade, and use the setup bar to calculate the entry, targets, and stop.

NOTE

When placing your entry, targets, and stop, I strongly recommend using advanced order types, specifically OSOs and OCOs, which you can research on your own. I do discuss these order types in more detail in my other book, *Day Trading QuickStart Guide*, from ClydeBank Media.

If our snapshot trading window is between 18:00 and 20:00, then our setup bar (which formed at 16:00) will have long been established by the time we identify it and use it to define our trade. That's okay, as we are operating within longer time frames with this approach.

Even if we weren't at our trading desk when the setup bar formed, we can still set up our orders and "get in sync" with the trade, so long as the following conditions remain in place:

» We are able to get in at or near the entry as defined by our setup.
» The trade, as defined by our setup, has not stopped out.
» The trade, as defined by our setup, has not yet hit a target level (like the break-even target) that would have caused us to move our stops.

If we place our trade and then one of those conditions is met prior to our being filled, we will cancel the trade and remain flat. Through the application of these three qualifying factors, we can take advantage of trade setups that occur earlier than when we are at our computers. Snapshot trading allows us to balance our busy lives while still being able to take advantage of great trading opportunities. Missing some trades because they move too quickly is an acceptable trade-off for not feeling like we have to live at our computers. If you've missed a trade, just know that, like a bus, another one is around the corner.

The high of our setup bar is 1.21482, which we will round to 1.2148. Using this setup bar, we can define an entry at 1.2152, which is a 2-pip entry, a 1-pip adjustment off the key level, and a 1-pip spread to make sure that our entry is on the ask (the EUR/USD is widely traded, so it has very low spreads).

The 60-minute chart is slow, relatively speaking, but it's actually fast as a swing trade time frame compared to other popular time frames like a 240-minute or a daily chart. We use snapshot trading as a means of being able to effectively trade these slower-moving charts, and since these are swing trades by definition, we usually hold them for more than a day, so the time of day for the setup is not that important. We anticipate that our trades may require multiple bars that will often stretch into subsequent sessions.

The three major forex trading sessions are discussed in chapter 3.

As an additional tip, I'd recommend setting an alert that tells you when the price is 90% of the way to target 1. When this alert is triggered, a conservative technique is to move your stop up to your entry (to a "break-even" position) and make your trade risk-free.

Take time to explore your trading platform. Most platforms have automation tools to facilitate strategic stop management. You should be able to tell your platform that if the price hits x, then it should move your stop to y. Automate what you can, and then you can sleep at night knowing that crucial elements of your trade will be handled in accordance with your tradeplan. I recommend checking out FX Synergy's trade manager first. Learn more about it at go.quickstartguides.com/forex.

Returning to figure 65, notice that at 6:00 a.m. the next day, the price came up and hit target 3 before turning around and heading south. Assuming we'd used some form of a "trailing stop" technique—which in this case would involve moving the stop upward several times to follow the price action—to dynamically adjust our stops, the remainder of the trade would have automatically closed at a profit—it would only be a matter of how big.

The snapshot technique may feel a little too easy and stress-free. But keep in mind that you must be disciplined. You must know how to say no when you don't have a tradeable scenario at hand. The rules of your tradeplan must be followed, and your setup criteria must be objectively evaluated. For instance, if you sit down at the front end of your snapshot window to evaluate whether or not you have a viable trade, and you find that a great setup has formed but the price action has already gone too far (let's say it's gone far enough to prompt you to move your stop), then forget about the trade (or cancel the setup if you've already placed it). That wasn't your bus; don't try to catch it. Another bus will eventually come along. Similarly, if you sit down to trade, identify a setup from a few hours ago, and see that the price action has already moved beyond the stop as defined by your setup, then that trade is over and you avoided a losing trade. Keep your eyes out for the next, fresh setup, and be patient and consistent. The price action will often present multiple opportunities for entry—no need to have an antsy trigger finger.

A Final Note on the Snapshot Technique

In chapter 7 we mentioned range bar charts, and we will be applying them in extensive detail in our next trading technique, the 1-2-3 Setup. However, before we depart from this section I should note that range bar charts can also be very useful in the snapshot technique. As a refresher, in a range bar chart, bars don't form on the basis of a given interval of time but on a given interval of price action; that is, whenever the price action moves *x* number of pips beyond a given range, a new bar forms.

In fact, if you want to take advantage of longer-term range bar charts (where the range is set to be especially large and thus fewer bars form over time) then the application of the snapshot technique becomes a necessity. And these longer-term range bars are excellent for swing trading! One never knows when a range bar will close and a new one will open. It can happen very quickly or take a long time, depending on the price action itself. Yet they form excellent trade setups when used on slower swing trade time frames. Snapshot trading gives us a way to take advantage of these dynamic charts without needing to glue our eyes to the screen for eons at a time. We merely open our doors for business during our snapshot window and look to get in sync with setups based on our rules described previously. If the trade is there, take it. If not, don't worry. We can trade multiple charts and pairs as well, to increase our trading activity— we can test and establish numerous swing trade plans, adding another advantageous element to our overall trading business. Diversification!

Snapshot trading gives us the opportunity to be as active as we want to be and take advantage of the superior edge that each established tradeplan gives us, while keeping our hours of operation at a very manageable level in relation to our busy lives.

The 1-2-3 Trade Setup

The Action → Reaction → Subsequent Action sequence is a powerful guide for setting up trades. It's a setup that we've depicted very frequently in previous chapters. Many charting platforms have simple trading tools that allow for variations of this setup, making it easy to see and to manage trades.

As we look for trades, we measure the first action move. When the subsequent action move is 25% along, progressing in the direction of the first action move (up for longs, down for shorts), we assume that this 25% move confirms that the subsequent action move is indeed underway. For the purpose of our next real-world trading scenario, let's refer to this 25% move as "critical confirmation."

Just because we believe that we've identified an accurate pullback (as noted by where our price action pulls back into the SMA), we may not have a subsequent action move on our hands. It could be the beginning of a new action move in the opposite direction. And, while not perfect, the 25% move is critical confirmation and does help stack the odds further on our side. See figure 66.

GRAPHIC

fig. 66

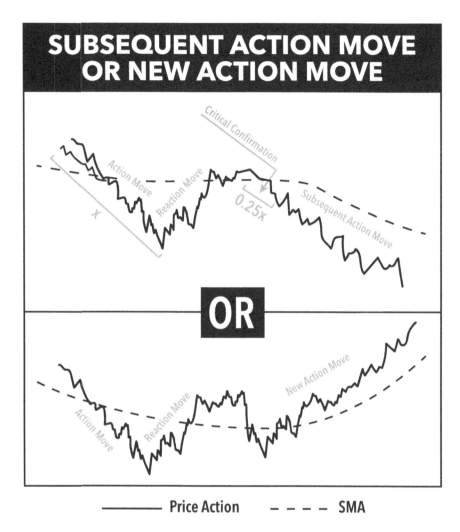

SUBSEQUENT ACTION MOVE OR NEW ACTION MOVE

Price Action — — — SMA

While 25% gives us a nice marker for confirming our subsequent action move, the process of accurately defining the end of our reaction move can be tricky. Just as we did in our previous "In the Trading Room" scenarios, we're going to rely on our SMA (see chapters 9 and 10), which, though not a perfect predictor of the reaction move's end (nothing is perfect in trading), will help us stack serious odds on our side.

Before proceeding any further, let's define and illustrate one other aspect of this setup. Don't worry; it's mind-numbingly simple (see figure 67).

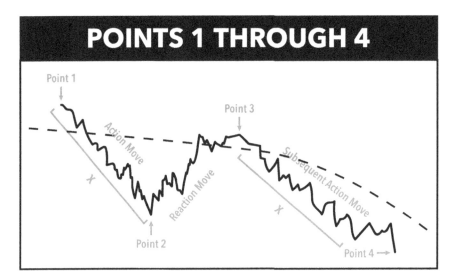

POINTS 1 THROUGH 4

fig. 67

——— Price Action – – – – SMA

Throughout the example that follows, we'll refer to the beginning of the first action move as point 1. The end of the first action move is point 2, which is also the beginning of the reaction move. Point 3 will be the end of the reaction move and the beginning of our subsequent action move. Point 4 is the location of our ultimate profit target.

We will look to trade the move between point 3 and point 4. You'll note that this is very similar to our previous "In the Trading Room" setups, but, as you'll see with the 1-2-3 trade setup, we are going to use trade management rules in a different way.

We will enter into the trade between points 3 and 4, after the price action moves 25% of the way between those two points. Remember, the length of x, as shown in figure 67, is determined by the length of the first action move, as opposed to our setup bar as in the prior setups we discussed. When .25x is reached on our subsequent action move, we enter the trade.

We still have to identify the end of the reaction move, point 3, which should be about one third to two thirds of the action move. Take a look at figure 68 to better understand how this works.

Now that you understand the basic setup for this trade (we enter 25% of the way into the subsequent action move, looking to hit point 4) let's take a step back and talk about the charts we might use in this setup. Deciding which charts to use is critical to our ability to identify tradeable patterns at the right time.

fig. 68

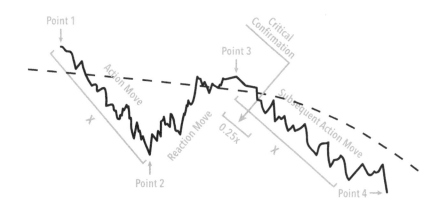

Let's look at a 15-minute chart for the GBP/USD pair during the European session (figure 68). Were we to just use this chart by itself, we wouldn't be able to identify any good trading opportunities. By the time a pullback occurs into our 20 SMA line, the major price action move has already happened. Remember, one of our most challenging objectives here is to identify a suitable point 3. It's the end of the reaction move and what we hope to be the beginning of the subsequent action move. As with our previous trading scenarios, we're looking for the pullback to cover one third to two thirds of the length of our action move.

fig. 69

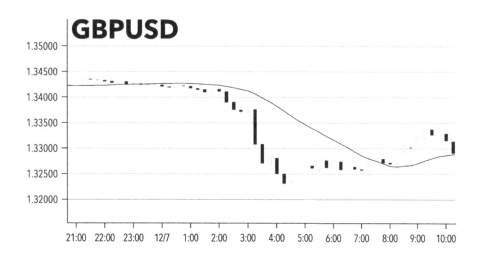

Time-based charts, like the 15-minute chart, provide visibility into price action based solely on the passage of time. If a dramatic pullback occurs smack in the middle of an arbitrary period of time, a trader can be caught flat-footed, unaware that a tradeable action is taking place as he awaits the formation of the next 15-minute or 30-minute bar, or whatever time-based chart he is watching. For this reason, I like to have in my trading repertoire a chart that I know will respond quickly to price action, such as a momentum range bar chart (figure 70).

fig. 70

The parameters of your trade setup can be much more (or less) visible depending on the type of chart you look at.

This is a different type of chart than we have seen before. It is a momentum range bar, in which a new bar is formed every time price action spans 6 pips of movement. Up to this point in our study, we have been using time-based charts. Sometimes time-based charts show great trades. Other times, the bars trend for hours but never give us a place to enter a trade. On our time-based chart in figure 69, a big downtrend took shape, beginning close to 2:00 a.m. and really taking off after 3:00 a.m. Unfortunately, though, as we noted, there was no clear tradeable setup that could be observed using that time-based chart. Now, if we view the 2:00 a.m. price action in our momentum range bar chart (figure 70) we'll get a much more granular look at the price action dynamics that were taking place at that particular time. Let's say that we got to our trading desk shortly after 2:35 a.m. and pulled up this chart. We would be able to identify an action move and the beginnings of a reaction move. An opportunity to go short may be coming.

Range bars don't care about time. The figure 70 chart is set to 6 pips. A new bar prints whenever the pair trades in a price range of 6 pips and then moves 1 tick (one tenth of a pip) beyond the high or low of that 6-pip range. When that happens, one bar will close and a new bar will open. On a range bar chart, a large 15-minute increment will appear as numerous 6-pip bars that occurred inside of that 15-minute bar, allowing us to take advantage of that strong price action. In other words, on the 15-minute chart, we might not have an actionable trade setup, but the momentum range bar chart allows us to "open up" the inside of the 15-minute bar and see the ups and downs of price action, often showing us tradeable action, reaction, subsequent action setups. This is a trick not known to most forex traders, since the typical charting platforms offered by brokers like MT4 offer only time-based charts.

Let's continue to study our 6-pip momentum range bar chart (figure 70). One thing you may have noticed is that the downtrend actually began several hours prior to the action move we've identified. In fact, had we made it to our trading desk a little earlier, we might have taken a short position prior to 2:00 a.m. Note that this earlier downward trend is much more prominent in our momentum range bar chart than it was in our 15-minute chart. For the two hours between midnight and 2:00 a.m., the 15-minute chart looked flattish, but the momentum bar chart revealed a clear and steady downtrend over the same time period. As I've stated, range bars don't care about time. The bars on the chart can form quickly or slowly, depending on what the price action is actually doing.

Returning now to our initial assumption, that we sat down to trade shortly after 2:30 a.m. with our 6-pip momentum range bar chart, let's go ahead and apply the simple trade setup we introduced at the beginning of this section.

Let's label points 1, 2, and 3 on our momentum bar chart.

fig. 71

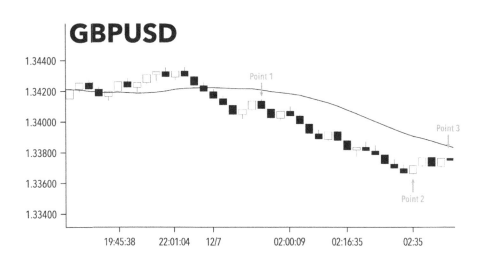

At around 2:45 eastern, we see a clear pullback into our 20 SMA. Now a short trade can be initiated. Point 1 to point 2 is our first action move. Point 2 to point 3 is the reaction that bumps into the 20 SMA.

We can take this trade using a technique I call the 1-2-3 setup. To give credit where credit is due, I will note that I first learned about this style of trading from *Trident: A Trading Strategy* by Charles Lindsay, one of the first trading books I ever read. The 1-2-3 setup idea borrows some of Mr. Lindsay's concepts.

» Step 1 is to measure the vertical distance from point 1 to point 2, our first action move (per figure 71, that distance is roughly 50 pips).

» For step 2, measure the vertical distance from point 2 to point 3. To do this, we have to predict point 3, the point where the reaction should end (that distance is roughly 15 pips). Time to ask yourself, is this my reaction move?

There will be a bit of a gut check at this point, as our prospective reaction move is just under one third the length of the action move (we were looking for 16.6 and we got 15—not off by a huge amount). Also, our upward-stabbing wick doesn't quite reach the SMA (perfection is a rare beast). Some traders would pass on this setup and wait to see if the price action finally did make its way up to the SMA, and if it didn't they would just wait for the next setup, and that's fine.

Once we're ready to define point 3, we can look for the subsequent action move. This is a short setup, so point 4 will be below point 3. Keep in mind, as always, that trading happens on the right edge of the chart. At the time we think we've identified point 3, the subsequent action move has not happened yet. As you may recall from earlier in this section, we must obtain critical confirmation before we enter the trade.

» Step 3 is entering the trade. We can proceed with step 3, placing a trade that will trigger in if and only if the price moves lower from our assumed point 3 by an amount equal to 25% of the distance measured in step 1. That distance is about 12.5 pips, which puts our entry at 1.3370. And after the next two bars form, as shown in figure 72, we can see that the price does move lower, hitting our 25% level and triggering in a short trade at 1.3370.

NOTE

Perhaps we would have made a key-level adjustment to the entry, moving it to 1.3369. In any event, the trade triggered short.

fig. 72

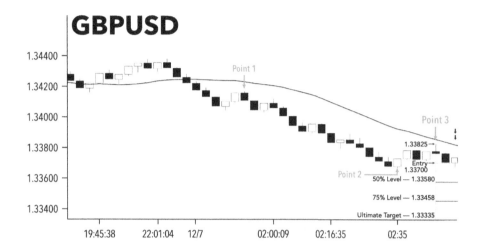

In the figure 72 trade, we will be going short. We'll place our stop 1 pip above point 3, because if the price moves beyond that level, then our anticipated point 3 was not the end of the reaction move. (Remember, this particular point 3 barely missed our one third to two thirds requirement.) If this happens and we stop out of the trade, then we can wait to see if a new point 3 emerges and place the trade again, as a second-chance trade. Predicting the end of the reaction move, a valid point 3, is often elusive and we won't always get it right. Sometimes you need to weigh the risk of predicting a point 3 a little too soon against missing out on the trade altogether. If you always wait to see if a new point 3 occurs that more precisely conforms to the one third to two thirds requirement, you will miss some great trades. Each trader, with time and experience, will need to decide what to do with situations that seem to split hairs, like this one.

Our "ultimate target," which, if hit, will become point 4, is 1.33335 (we'll round it to 1.3334). If we attain critical confirmation and hit our entry (1.3370), then the price has already traveled 25% of the distance of our initial action move (point 1 to point 2, what we measured in step 1). If we hit our ultimate target (1.3334), then the remaining 75% of the prior action move will have been "mirrored," and we will have arrived at point 4. We base this trade on the premise that the subsequent action move often mirrors the prior action move (the immediate past predicts the immediate future), especially when caught early in a trend, as you can see with how this all plays out.

If the trade begins breaking our way—let's say after entry it moves another 25% in the direction of our target (50% of the way total)—then we will move our stop to the break-even point, 1.3370.

A 1-pip key-level adjustment here to our stop from 1.3370 to 1.3371 may be a good idea.

Our stop, if hit, will trigger our exit from the short position and our purchase of the pair. Therefore, let's account for a 2-pip spread, setting our stop loss order at 1.3373. When the bid hits 1.3371, the order will be filled, presumably close to 1.3373. Unfortunately, when trading forex, we must pay the spread on the buy side of our trades–the exit in this case. If we wanted a true break-even position, we would need to place our stop at 1.3368. The risk, of course, is getting stopped out prematurely and then missing the move to point 4, our reason for taking the trade in the first place. Trading is about mitigating risk versus obtaining possible reward. It is often better to make a minor adjustment around a key level, giving the trade a greater chance of succeeding, even if it means maintaining a few pips of risk. Each trader must decide: move their stop to a true break-even, or move their stop enough to reduce a vast majority of the risk so as to give the trade a greater chance of succeeding. Time and experience, which cannot be taught, will better inform you over time as you encounter these types of trader decisions over and over again.

I find that in addition to moving the stop to break-even, it's also a good idea to take some profit, say one third, out of the trade once we are 50% of the way to the target. The 50% level is hit a vast majority of the time and gives you a very high-percentage winning profit level. Take one third of your position off, with the remaining two thirds being either at risk-free or close to it (as you would have moved your stop to ensure that). Risk-free works for me! If the trade keeps running in your direction and goes 75% of the way to the target, then you can take off another third of your position, locking in even more profits. Often, but not always, you will reach the 100% level, a move perfectly mirroring the first action move, at which point you will exit the remainder of your position. It's a great feeling when that happens.

There are different ways to approach taking profits with this trade setup. A trader can hold out for the full target with their entire position, offering a nearly 3 to 1 reward-versus-risk scenario. Be aware that the full target at point 4 might only be reached 15% to 20% of the time, however. On the other hand, the 50% target level will be hit over 80% of the time. That's why I suggested the plan of scaling out one third at the 50% level (while eliminating all or most of the risk), one third at the 75% level, and the final third at the full target. It's a great example of how we use risk as a tool to place and manage excellent, high-probability trades.

There are five possible outcomes with this trade:

» The trade doesn't trigger in, resulting in a risk-free situation. No trade = no risk.
» The trade triggers in and stops out before traveling to the 50% level, resulting in a loss.
» The trade triggers in and hits the 50% level, resulting in a profit while eliminating all or most of the remaining risk.
» The trade triggers in and hits the 75% level, resulting in even greater profit.
» The trade triggers in and hits its full target, resulting in achievement of the full potential of the trade.

As you can see, out of five possible outcomes, only one presents a losing proposition. We also have a break-even scenario and three profitable situations. Three out of five outcomes give us a profit while we also enjoy a risk-free or nearly risk-free position. It's an example of how we use the knowledge that certain patterns continually repeat combined with smart money management. These are the kinds of trades we want to be in.

Reflecting on Risk-to-Reward Ratios

One of the key attributes of winning traders and winning tradeplans is their ability to balance a trade's probability of success against the risk-to-reward ratio. The 1-2-3 setup offers a very convenient, straightforward approach to calculating the latter factor (the risk-to-reward ratio). We just saw how the five possible outcomes stack the odds in our favor. But what about our initial risk, when we first enter the trade?

Let's say you decide to leave your position intact (not take off profits) as you pursue the ultimate target (point 4). In this scenario your risk-to-reward ratio is approximately 1:3. You are only risking 25% (plus 1 pip) for a chance to make 75%. If, on the other hand, you take all your profits and close the trade at the 50% level, then your risk-to-reward ratio would be 1:1, but you're more likely to see your reward materialize (your probability of success is greater). If you decide to take all your profits and close the position at the 75% level, then your initial risk-to-reward will have been 1:2.

Q: What is my risk-to-reward ratio if I follow Troy's preferred approach, scaling out one third of my position at the 50% level and allowing the remainder of my position to pursue the 75% level (or beyond)?

This question is like a moving line in the sand—one that moves in favor of the trader. When the trade is first initiated, the 50% level offers nearly a 1:1 risk-to-reward ratio. It is not a perfect 1:1 because we have to factor in the additional pip we added beyond point 3, where we placed our stop. The 75% level begins as a 1:2 risk-to-reward ratio, which is fantastic. It gets even better, though, because once we hit our 50% level, stops are moved to our entry (or within a few pips of our entry), eliminating or drastically reducing most of the risk. Ultimately, there is actually no risk, because one third of our position would have already closed out with profit and the remaining risk, if any, is house money only. The full target, however, begins with a near-perfect 1:3 risk-to-reward ratio. We are literally risking a pip to make three times our risk! Once our 50% level is achieved and some profit comes off our trade when we move our stop as described, well, that is the closest thing to trader nirvana.

In short, the trade begins with 1:1, 1:2, and 1:3 risk-to-reward ratios on each third of our initial position, respectively. Combine that with our five possible outcomes, of which only one is a losing proposition and three are profitable outcomes, and you can begin to see how all the concepts presented in this book elegantly come together to put you in the most advantageous position you can possibly be in as a trader.

The Trade Continues

As our trade continued to play out (figure 73), you can see that the price pulled back just after 3:00 p.m. to retest the 20 SMA, which at that point had already moved lower. It revealed where the resistance had moved to on this chart (which is why we love this indicator), causing the price to turn lower, passing through the 50% level. Profits can be scaled out, and the stop should be moved to break-even as previously described.

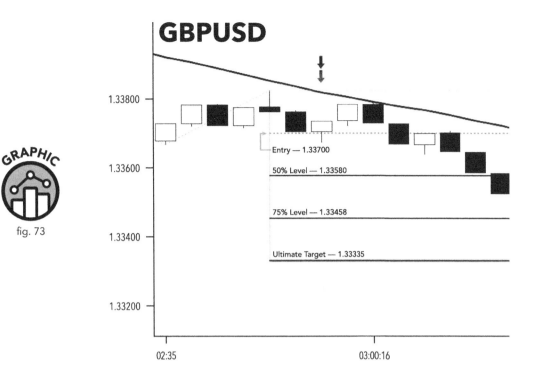

In the next example, figure 74, we can see that after the next two momentum bars formed, the price moved straight down through the 75% level, and any profits taken here (any profits from the initial capital outlay that were not taken off at the 50% level) now represent a 2:1 profit-to-risk ratio from when the trade was first placed. Essentially, for every pip originally risked, 2 pips are made on whatever part of the position comes off at this level. Not bad!

Range bars are deceptive sometimes. Because each bar shows price change rather than time, it's easy to misconstrue how a trade played out in relationship to time. In our current trade, it took 18 minutes for the price to trigger into the trade and move to its 50% level. But the move from the 50% level to the 75% level only took seven seconds! This illustrates the importance of using superior trade management tools so the entire trade can be placed from start to finish with all the steps in place. This way, scaling out at each target level is handled by the actual trade management tool regardless of the element of time. Some tools will literally give you a "cha-ching" sound as you hit each target, which, as I hope you will soon discover, you'll never tire of hearing!

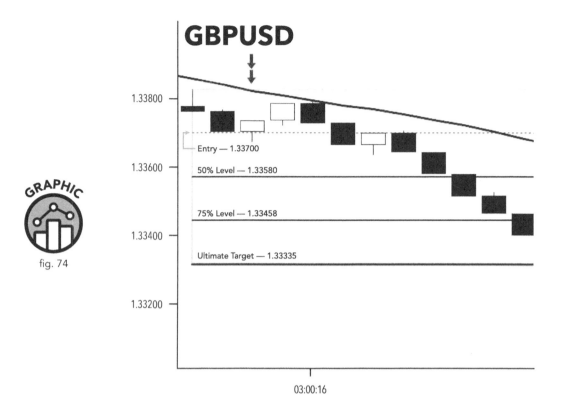

fig. 74

About nine and a half minutes later, the price finally works its way down through our 100% "ultimate" target (see figure 75).

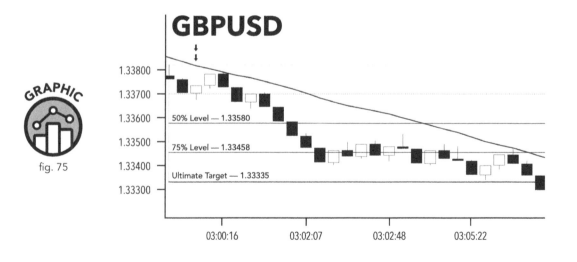

fig. 75

Reflecting on Stops

In the example I've selected, we picked a real winner. Yay for us! But in the real world you'll soon discover that you don't win all the time and that learning how to lose, the right way, is part of being a winning trader. Just as the 1-2-3 setup lends itself to quick, easy, and favorable risk-to-reward calculations, it also allows us to visualize a multitude of trailing stop methods, which you should consider throughout your trade to mitigate your losses and lock in your profits. We've discussed the idea of moving the stop to "break-even" after the 50% level is hit. Well, as you can see from our charts, you can also consider moving your stop to the 50% level after the 75% level is hit. Should you continue to let some of your trade run past the ultimate target (100%), then you can employ the use of a trailing stop and let the market decide when it's time to exit the trade. Once in a while this technique will seriously ring the register as you hit the grand slam trade outta the park!

One of the great things about trading forex is the ability to split your positions and scale out at different places throughout the trade. Thoughtful systematic application of risk management allows you to take advantage of both the small and the large moves. The rules you will use to determine how and when to use trailing stops should be based on a proven tradeplan that you will develop through rigorous preproduction work (see chapters 13-15). Once you put your tradeplan to work, it will take the pressure off of you. You can relax, focus, follow your plan, and allow the market to give you what it wants to give you. We'll be discussing the finer points of risk management within a proven tradeplan in part III of this book.

Reflecting on Tools of the Trade

You may have noticed the nifty lines that are drawn on the bottom of my charts (figures 72–75) to help illuminate my entry and targets. I applied this simple grid using the TradeStation platform, and it's easy to do. It's also ideal for visualizing the parameters of your 1-2-3 trade setup. I use something called the Fibonacci extension tool, which, with just a few clicks, makes the necessary calculation and draws the grid onto your chart.

This tool is designed for use with the Fibonacci trading system, which is not a system I use. Therefore, when I co-opt it for use with the 1-2-3 setup, I immediately turn off the Fibonacci "price extension" lines in the tool's formatting window. Instead, I put in my 25%, 50%, 75%, and 100% projections. With this tool, I can easily measure point 1 to point 2 and then point 2 to point 3 on a momentum range chart—or any other type of chart, for that matter.

TradeStation, while offering excellent forex charts, is not a forex broker. Most of you will be using the charts provided by your actual forex broker and won't have access to the Fibonacci extension tool. If you have trouble locating an appropriate alternative tool, one that's compatible with your forex broker's trading platform, I may be able to curate some options on your behalf. Email me at troy@backpacktrader.com.

Continuing with Our Trade

As you can see in figure 76, that downward movement continued.

fig. 76

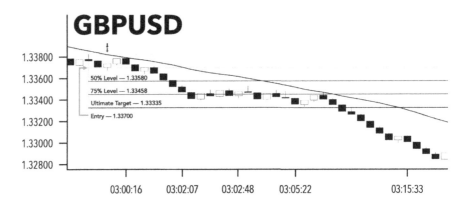

Just because a subsequent action often mirrors the first action move doesn't mean it can't go further.

If using TradeStation, we can use our Fibonacci extension tool to calculate larger targets like 200%, or we can use a variety of trailing stop techniques to take advantage of explosive moves—again, allowing the market to give us what it wants to give us while we manage our risk. I consider the profit I have made on a trade, even if it has not been taken off yet, to be my money now, which I worked hard to earn with the current trade. How much of that to risk for the potential of further gains is a consideration that should be worked out in advance, with proper preproduction, well-tested measurable results, and predetermined tradeplan rules.

The example in figure 76 reinforces just how useful the 20 SMA can be when combined with our Action → Reaction → Subsequent Action dynamic. At the 75% level, we can see that a new point 1 has formed. Point 2 is easy to see because the price reaction move has already begun, working its way back up to the descending 20 SMA at point 3. We are ready to repeat our three-step process: (1) measure the exact distance from point 1 to point 2, (2) measure from point 2 to point 3 and determine whether you have the right length to justify your point 3, thus defining your reaction move, and (3) set up your trade.

As you can see in the bottom right corner of figure 77, I used the Fibonacci Extension Tool to draw the next trade.

fig. 77

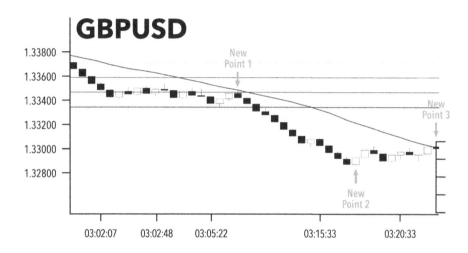

NOTE

Fourteen minutes have passed from the new point 1 to the assumed new point 3. That is less than one 15-minute bar and only three 5-minute bars. These trades would be invisible to us on time-based charts, which, unfortunately, are what most forex broker charting platforms provide. This is why I choose to use the superior charting of a platform like TradeStation, even if it means placing my trades with a different broker.

Figure 78 shows us that less than two minutes later the trade hits our 25% level and triggers in. The price action is dictating everything about this trade. The entry was at 1.3290, rounding the extra digit down. Out of habit, I would place the trade at 1.3289 to avoid the key level of 90. Our stop will be placed at 1.3307 + 2 pips of spread, 1.3309. The entire trade risks 20 pips.

fig. 78

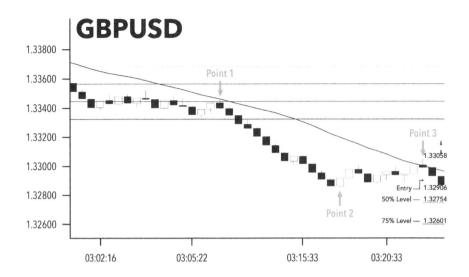

Only 30 seconds later, the price has already moved down to its 50% level, where we can scale one third of our position and move our stop to either break-even or near break-even (after considering our discussion about whether to completely eliminate the risk or keep a little risk to give the trade more room to breathe).

fig. 79

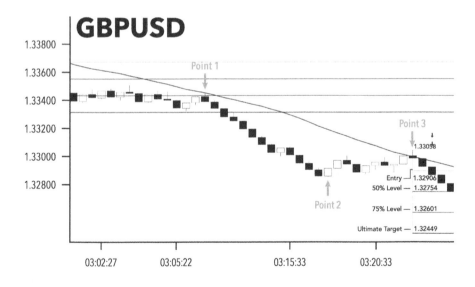

This example, figure 79, reminds us that the price action is in charge. If you snooze, you lose! It is important to have a method by which to properly execute trades with speed, precision, and accuracy. This takes practice with proper tools.

Another thing that I strongly advise: spend money to get the right trading tools. Don't be penny-wise and pound-foolish. Missed trading opportunities are far more costly than the few pennies one spends to upgrade their charting platform.

At the far-right edge of figure 80, we see that the price hit both its 50% and its 75% target levels, providing the superior reward-to-risk virtue that this trade has built into its rule set and demonstrating the anatomy of an excellent trade.

GRAPHIC

fig. 80

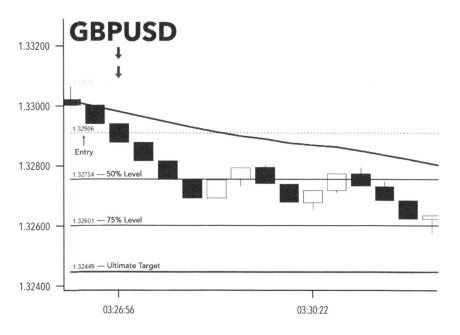

Our 75% target was hit just five minutes after we first hit the 50% level about 10 bars back. On a time-based chart, these 10 bars would have been subsumed in a single five-minute bar. This limited visibility into the price action not only leaves us unable to make key trade management decisions, but trades like this would not even appear in the first place.

At the 75% level, some traders might trail their break-even stop further down (to the 50% level). That's a legitimate approach, though I find that you will do quite well to leave your stop at break-even and hold out for your 100% target. Of course, as always, much depends on your market, the size of your chart, what your preproduction work tells you (chapters 13-15), and your own personal style that will continue to develop with time and experience.

This 1-2-3 trade setup has built into its rule set, from start to finish, the assumption that a subsequent action move will tend to mirror the prior action move, and then proceeds to act accordingly. Moreover, every trade is completely planned from start to finish with all the odds stacked on our side. Check out what happens next (figure 81).

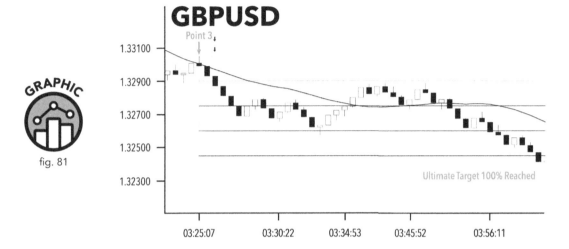

fig. 81

About 28 minutes later, the price had worked its way all the way down to the ultimate target (100%). To reiterate, any profits taken here would have made nearly 3 to 1 in profit relative to money originally put at risk. But remember, these trades don't happen by themselves. A trader must actually place and manage them from start to finish. When it comes to the skill of profitable trading, though, it doesn't get much easier. We get to lean on the old adage, "plan your trade and trade your plan." In other words, we get to lean on our plan from start to finish, and that is as simple as any trading can ever be.

I want to point out a few nuances from the preceding example. We can see that the price came up and actually touched 1.3289 between 3:35 and 3:50 or so. Had we set our stop at the break-even point, at the bid of 1.3287 accounting for spread after hitting the 50% level, we would have been stopped out at break-even before hitting the ultimate target. This illustrates why it often pays more to give the trade the room it needs to breathe with strategic key-level adjustments.

The broker will fill on the ask when we close the short position. When the bid hits 1.3287, assuming a 2-pip spread, we will get filled at the ask, 1.3289, which is our true break-even point.

MY TAKE

As stated, it pays to work around key levels. I prefer to "hide my stop" behind the key level of 90 rather than go for a true break-even stop. At this point I would have already taken one third of my position off anyway, and the trade would end profitably if it stopped out. I'd place my stop at 1.3291 + 2 pips of spread = 1.3293. I'm willing to pay a small "insurance premium" (4 pips total, 1.3289 versus 1.3293), taken off the top of the profits just made from exiting one third at the 50% level, in order to give the remainder of the trade a better chance to hit its larger targets.

If we later stop out at the break-even point after taking our second third off at the 75% level, then we would still have a nice profit on the trade (even after paying the "insurance premium" to hide the stop behind the 90 key level). And what happens if hiding the stop behind the key level works in our favor? We'd then have a chance for the trade to break back down in our favor, possibly hitting the ultimate target (100%). In this scenario we've risked 4 pips of newly made profit for the opportunity to make 50 more pips! That is one heck of a risk-to-return ratio, don't you think? We may not be able to control what the market does, but we can certainly control how we mitigate risk by intelligently managing our trades for maximum benefit. Better yet, all of this is built into this trade setup's rule set and is one hundred percent objective and mechanical. Boom!

One of the things I love about the 1-2-3 trade setup is that there are only five possible outcomes:

1. What we identify as the subsequent action move never exceeds 25% of the action move. We never enter the trade. We remain "flat," as traders say. Outcome: Neutral.

2. The price triggers us into our trade and then turns around and goes in the other direction for a loss. Outcome: Loss.

3. The price triggers in, gets to our 50% level (as we have learned will happen a vast majority of the time), and when it does, we take our profits, then move our stop loss to break-even and let the trade continue to run. The price then turns against us, stopping us out at our break-even point. Outcome: Mildly profitable.

4. Same as scenario 3, except the price proceeds down to our 75% level and another third comes off before turning against us and stopping the rest out at break-even. Outcome: Significantly profitable.

5. The price hits the full 100% target level. Outcome: Immensely profitable.

There's a variation of scenario 5 in which the price continues even further, and we use a trailing stop to lock in even bigger profits.

Returning to our trade: if we continue to follow the price action on this pair using the 6-pip momentum range bar chart, we will find another opportunity waiting for us. Following the successful conclusion of our previous trade, we may have been looking for the larger downtrend to continue. More specifically, we'd look for the reaction move back into our 20 SMA and we'd be ready to go short on the subsequent action move. As I said earlier, this 1-2-3 trade setup tends to work better early in a trend. We've already had two successful trades to the short side; we need to be on the alert that this trend could be losing its energy and tiring out. As you can see in figure 82, instead of a reaction move back up into our 20 SMA, the reversing move (just prior to 4:30) proves instead to be a new action move in the opposite direction, the first clue coming with bars closing above the SMA. A leopard can't change its spots—but price action will often try to pose as a chameleon. Ultimately, though, price action can't hide from itself, which is why the best trading ideas let the price action lead. The new action in the opposite direction pulls back into our handy-dandy 20 SMA, providing what proves to be a new reaction move, setting up a new and profitable trade to the long side. I marked points 1, 2, 3, and 4 (the ultimate target) so you can see how the trade unfolded.

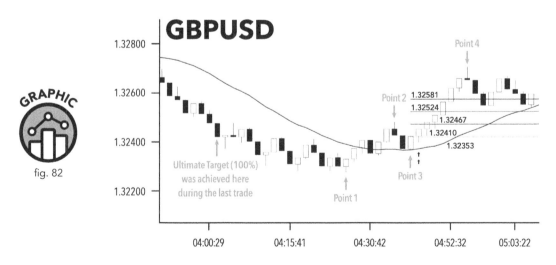

GRAPHIC

fig. 82

The examples I've featured in this review of the 1-2-3 trade setup show how a momentum range bar chart can be useful, even essential, but I want to be careful about the point I'm making. I don't want you to think that time-based charts, such as the 5- or 15-minute bar chart, aren't helpful when trading. The 1-2-3 can and does set up on time-based charts as well.

It's a good idea to have multiple monitors, so you can follow different charts at the same time.

I love the 1-2-3 trade setup. And I recommend it for both beginner and advanced forex traders. It's a good one to learn and to practice. Use a sim account to master this setup. Do not go live with real money until you have proven that you can trade this method with consistent success.

Chapter Recap

> » A trading system is a philosophy that represents how trading styles, market indicators, risk management, and position sizing come together.

> » Many tradeable price action patterns that are undetectable on time-based bar charts will show up on momentum bar charts.

> » Resources such as the Fibonacci price lines extension tool can help traders expediently measure targets and assign appropriate entries and stops.

PART III

INCREASING YOUR CHANCES FOR SUCCESS

| 13 |

Putting Risk Management to Work for You

Chapter Overview
» The necessity of risk management
» Losing streaks are part of trading
» Tools to help manage risk

Risk and reward come in a package. Traders looking for rewards must accept risk. There is no way around that. On the flip side, a trader should not take on risk unless the potential rewards justify it.

Many new traders worry about their strategy. They spend their time trying to figure out what patterns and trading techniques will give them a surefire profit. Surefire profit is the wrong thing to worry about. For one thing, it's not possible. The only sure things are death and taxes. Moreover, the reason to trade is to make money, not to try to achieve something that isn't possible, like surefire profits. When it comes to making money as a trader, the focus should be on *risk management*, not risk avoidance or miracle techniques that never fail. Learning how to anticipate and manage one's risk is paramount to success.

Some of the risk comes from user error, which is why it's so important to study chart patterns and practice entering trades in a demo account. Most risk comes from the market itself, which can gyrate and reverse in unexpected ways. Even the most tenured and successful traders have off days. While risk cannot be eliminated, it can be managed. In fact, risk management is one of the most important keys to successful trading. Risk is a tool to be used and controlled. Without risk, we can't trade for profits. Risk mitigation comes from careful trade planning and trade setup analysis where we choose to take on a certain amount of risk because the odds have been proven to be stacked in our favor by our own preproduction and foundation-building work—and the potential reward justifies the risk.

NOTE

We will get into more detail on the "ditch digging" of trading in chapter 15, but I should note that I write extensively on preproduction, risk management, and foundation building in part IV of the best-selling *Day Trading QuickStart Guide* from ClydeBank Media.

Some people say the worst thing that can happen to new traders is making a lot of money right away, because then they don't learn the important but hard lessons about risk management. Winning with poor trading creates and reinforces bad trading habits that lead to losses later. The best risk management practice is to learn how to trade correctly, for the right reasons, with the proper trading foundation in place.

Volatility Risk

The primary measure of market risk is **volatility**, which is how much the price is likely to move. Of course, volatility is what creates trading opportunities in the first place. Some floating exchange rates are more or less stable, while others move up and down seemingly all the time. The statistical measure of volatility is **standard deviation**. Almost all trading packages include standard deviation with their indicators. The higher the standard deviation, the more volatile the pair—and the more volatile the pair, the better the trading opportunities.

In the forex market, there is an extreme form of volatility risk known as a "gap." A gap occurs when a security's price changes from one level to another without any trading in between. Gaps often occur in response to news or events that occur while markets are closed, so they are less common in the forex market because of its more or less continual weekday operating hours. Still, gaps in the forex markets have been known to occur in response to news events over weekends and holidays. Traders who keep positions open while the market is closed must be especially careful about volatility risk. This risk can be mitigated by using well-placed stops and proper position sizing—but even this can be risky, because large gaps can still pass over stops and cause larger losses (or gains) than were originally planned for when the trade was placed. Spread risk exists in these situations too. Not only are there gaps, but brokers widen their spreads, which can take you out of your trade even with well-placed stops. Worse, it might not even show on the chart that the price hit your stop.

An important proactive step you can and should take to mitigate volatility risk is to choose reputable brokers. There are so many brokers to choose from. Focus on the largest ones with the most competitive rates. Read what other traders say about them. It's best if you select a broker that offers low commissions for smaller spreads. Some brokers offer fixed spreads plus a small commission, and that is often the best choice.

Using Leverage

Leverage, or trading with borrowed money, is central to trading. Forex traders use leverage to build profits and control more currency than they would be able to otherwise. Most price movements in forex are relatively small, especially in the major pairs, so leverage makes larger profits possible. It helps traders get more profit from their winning trades, making trading capital go much further.

There's a catch, though: leverage also magnifies losses; borrowed money must be repaid whether or not the trade plays out.

Figure 83 shows how leverage works. Please note, *what I'm about to show you has nothing to do with how you actually determine your position size* (how much you are going to risk). I just want you to understand how leverage works in relation to lot size (see chapter 3 if you are unfamiliar with forex lot sizes). After I show you how leverage works, I'll make life really simple for you by boiling it all down to what actually matters when making a real trade.

How Leverage Works

Let's assume you're placing a trade with $1,000 of your own capital. With $1,000, you could only control one micro lot, and each pip of movement in your favor would earn only ten cents. On an exceptionally good trade— let's say you get a 50-pip move in your favor—you're still going to earn only $5. Even if it's an amazing trade, with a 500-pip move your way, you earn $50 (see the "No Leverage" column in figure 83).

fig. 83

LEVERAGE RATIO	NO LEVERAGE	5:1	50:1
Initial Trading Capital	$1,000.00	$1,000.00	$1,000.00
Borrowed Capital	-	$4,000.00	$49,000.00
Micro Lots Controlled	1	5	50
Value of a Pip	$0.10	$0.50	$5.00
Value of 5-Pip Move	$0.50	$2.50	$25.00
Value of 50-Pip Move	$5.00	$25.00	$250.00
Value of 500-Pip Move	$50.00	$250.00	$2,500.00

Let's now assume that you determine you want to take on more risk, using the proper position sizing techniques, and give yourself the chance to earn more. That's when leverage may come into play.

Let's say you determine that you want to trade a $5,000 position size, but you don't happen to have that much capital available in whatever account you're using for that particular trade. Your broker will allow you a certain amount of leverage, and leverage allows you to control a larger position size than what you actually have in your trading account. A 5:1 leverage, for example (see the associated column in figure 83), lets you control $5 for every $1 you have. A 50:1 leverage lets you control 50 times what you have.

What Really Matters

Leverage allows traders to control and risk more capital than they have on hand, with the idea of setting themselves up for larger gains. But ultimately, leverage really shouldn't matter when you're considering how large of a position size you should put on a trade.

What does matter, in my view, is how much you're risking on a given trade and whether you're applying sound money management techniques. As you will hear me say time and again, I think 2% is a good target amount to risk—if and only if the trade is part of a proven tradeplan. Let's assume it is; otherwise, I wouldn't take it and neither should you.

As an example, if you have a $50,000 account, then 2% is $1,000. The $1,000 at risk is the value of the pips between the entry and the stop, plus some expenses like spread.

> » If it is a 10-pip trade, meaning that the risk from entry to stop is 10 pips, we can risk 10 full-size lots at $10 per pip. That's $100 total risk per pip x 10 pips of risk = $1,000 of risk, 2% of our total account value.

> » If there was a risk on the trade of 100 pips, then we could risk one full-size lot; 1 x $10 x 100 = $1,000.

Alternatively, if your account value was $5,000, then you'd risk $100 to risk 2%. For a trade with 10 pips of risk, you'd use one full-size lot (10 pips x $10 risk per pip = $100 total risk). For a trade with 100 pips of risk you'd use one mini lot, 100 pips x $1 risk per pip = $100 total risk).

Keep in mind that this example assumes pairs involving the US dollar. Other crosses with other currencies will have different pip values. Fortunately, position-size calculators make it easy. You will also need to refer to your broker platform for a current and accurate value per pip in your currency at the time of placing your trade. For example, at the time of this writing, the GBP/AUD was valued at $7.31 per pip. Ten minutes from now it might be $7.37. Its value will change from moment to moment, because markets are never standing still.

Some brokers allow you to take more risk, because it is more profitable for them. But just because you *could* risk 50:1, for example, doesn't mean you should. In fact, you should not. Stick to your risk profile, whatever it is. I think 2% from entry to stop is a good place to start with a proven tradeplan. As traders like to say, you need to plan your trade and trade your plan.

Another important factor when considering your risk allotment is when trading in correlated pairs. You might think you are only putting 2% risk on your EUR/JPY long trade. Say you also choose to place long trades on the AUD/JPY and the NZD/JPY. Certain pairs are more correlated than others. If the JPY strengthens, it's possible you could lose on all three trades. If you put 2% risk on each, the question must be asked, how much risk was really placed—6%? There are excellent resources for checking one pair's percentage of correlation with others. I recommend doing a Google search for "forex pair correlation."

On the other hand, if you're using a different strategy and have a tradeplan for each of those three JPY pairs, and each one "marches to the beat of its own drummer," or they're different types of charts, then perhaps market correlation is not as much of a concern. I have been in that exact situation, where I had three different JPY trades going at the same time (it may have been GBP or something else, but that doesn't matter), and one lost while the other two won. You may get any mix of results. You may be long on one position and short on the other two, and all three wind up winning. Perhaps one wins in a matter of minutes and another takes several hours and the other takes a few days. They all dance to their own rhythm. The different strategies, charts, tradeplans, or trading tactics may offer enough diversification that the market correlation risk is completely mitigated and doesn't really matter. It is important, though, that you consider market correlation between pairs when making trade decisions in relation to what you are putting at risk in the markets.

Many traders have been wiped out by leveraging too much with overly correlated pairs. This is an important aspect of your overall money and risk management consideration.

Finally, when considering leverage, it's important to take into account the total amount you have at risk across all your open positions. The broker might not let you execute on a trade if you have other open positions and will exceed your account's leverage capacity. You might commit only 2% of your capital on any given trade, but if you have several open trades, at some point you will have committed the maximum amount of leverage afforded by your broker, and you'll need to wait until you have closed positions before you can open new ones.

Make your life and trading even easier. Get my Risk Allocator Workbook by going to go.quickstartguides.com/forex. You can enter your target risk percentage and your trade parameters (entry, stop, target) and the calculator will help you determine your ideal position size.

Using Too Much Leverage

Before we depart from our discussion of leverage, I need to point out a few more things. Going back to the leverage illustration from figure 83 showing how the value of a pip increases with greater amounts of leverage, let me make it explicitly clear: if the pips move against you, then leverage will magnify your losses, just as it magnifies your gain. With one micro lot ($1,000 worth of the base currency) at no leverage, a 50-pip move against you costs $5. You have $995 left of your initial $1,000. If you trade at 5:1 leverage, then the 50-pip adverse move will cost $25, leaving you with $975 of your initial capital. And with a 500-pip adverse move at 50:1 leverage, you not only lose your $1,000, but you now have to pay another $1,500 to the broker to cover your $2,500 loss, assuming the broker hasn't already liquidated your position. That's not so nice.

Right now, US brokers offer a maximum of 50:1 leverage. Most international brokers offer more. But just because you are allowed to borrow that much doesn't mean you should. Concentrate on your tradeplan and your money management rules. Those factors will put you in the best position to succeed.

Not Enough Margin

A trader using lots of leverage could have losses that wipe out the entire account. To protect themselves against losses resulting from traders getting busted by leverage, brokers set margin requirements specifying the minimum amount of cash or tradeable securities that must be in a trader's account. In the United States, margin is set by the Federal Reserve Board to protect the financial system.

If a trader's account value goes below the margin requirement, then the broker will not allow trades to be executed until the trader deposits more cash or securities. This is no different from the bank sending someone to repossess a car if the borrower skips loan payments.

Trading can also be restricted if you have too many trades in place. And if you happen to have too many positions or trades that are open, and some or all of those trades move against you, not only will you be unable to place new trades, but the broker will most likely begin closing some of your open positions. This is why it's wise to maintain a cushion in your account in case trades do move against you. Nothing is worse than having a broker close your trade with a loss before it hits your stop, only to witness it turn back around and run to hit what would have been your profit targets. Your trade decision was masterly and you wound up losing anyway. Yikes! It is the trader's responsibility to know what the margin requirement is and to make sure it's met.

Drawdown and Losing Streaks

A *drawdown* is a loss that occurs whenever your account is below its all-time high-water mark. The only way to stay out of drawdown is to make new equity highs. This might seem obvious, but it is not.

Let's say our stats show that every tenth trade, on average, makes a new equity high. That means that 90% of the time we are in drawdown. Imagine that! This does not mean that we're only winning 10% of our trades. We're probably winning quite a bit more. And even though we're in drawdown 90% of the time, we are making good money trading, because one out of every 10 trades pushes us to all-new equity highs again. With smart risk and money management, we won't go broke in drawdown.

Moreover, everyone who trades will experience a string of losses sooner or later. Understanding them helps to manage the psychological effects—because drawdowns can hurt, psychologically. I'd even go so far as to say that understanding drawdowns is a critical factor in your success as a trader. Many inexperienced traders will quit a winning tradeplan when momentary bumps in the road cause them some pain.

Remember Harvey the engineer and Trish the truck driver? Harvey is sure that he's smart and in control, so his forex losses crush him. Trish knows that they come with the territory. She's not happy about losing money, but she powers through because she knows that things will swing her way if she just leans on her proven system. Consecutive losses happen, but so do consecutive wins. Winning streaks will come back around, and what you will learn with time and experience is that the best trades and the best winning streaks seem to follow the ugliest sessions.

Drawdown Is a Part of Trading

Not every trade is going to be a winner. An awful lot of trades are going to lose. In fact, you can lose 50% of your trades and still come out ahead as long as the value of your losses is smaller than the value of your gains.

Your stop loss orders should be strategically placed to limit the losses you might incur on any given trade, per the rules of your proven tradeplan.

The table in figure 84 shows the likelihood of an extended period of losses. It may be a little challenging to understand right out of the gate, but spend some time studying the chart and thinking about it carefully, because this is an important concept. The first column shows the win percentage of your tradeplan. This is the percentage of trades that, thanks to your preproduction/ditch digging work (chapter 15), you know will win a certain amount of the time. Based on this, the second column shows the number of consecutive losing trades you are sure to experience if you use this tradeplan for an indefinite period of time. The next column shows the average length of a given losing streak with this tradeplan. The next two columns detail what a less likely but possible losing streak might look like. The final column notes the maximum number of consecutive losing trades you should experience when using a plan with a winning percentage defined by the leftmost column.

With this data, we can see that a system that has a 55% probability of generating a winning trade is certain to have streaks of four losing trades in a row and a 1% chance of 10 or 11 losing trades in a row. Even a system with an 80% probability of generating a winning trade is going to have two-trade losing streaks regularly and may have five- or six-trade streaks on occasion. You can go for months with more losing streaks than winning streaks, too.

GRAPHIC

fig. 84

If your trade plan wins X% of the time...	...then there is a 100% probability you will experience losing X trades in a row.	Your losing streaks, *on average*, will last for X trades in a row.	*There is a 10% chance* that your losing streak will last for X trades in a row.	*There is a 1% chance* that your losing streak will last for X trades in a row.	Your max losing streak is...
80%	2	3	4	5 to 6	7
75%	3	3	5	6 to 7	9
70%	3	3	5 to 6	7 to 8	10
65%	3	4	6 to 7	8 to 9	13
60%	4	5	7	9 to 10	14
55%	4	5	8	10 to 11	16
50%	5	6	9	12	19
45%	6	7	10	13 to 14	22
40%	7	8	11 to 12	15 to 16	25
35%	8	9	13 to 14	18 to 19	34
30%	9	11	15 to 16	22	38
25%	10	13	18 to 19	25 to 26	41
20%	12	15	22 to 23	32	51

Source: Van Tharp

A Little Bit of Drawdown Is Manageable

The last column in our figure 84 table shows the maximum number of losing trades that you might experience consecutively for a given tradeplan. This is the worst-case scenario for the length of time that a drawdown can happen, assuming that your win percentage (far left column) is correct (and if you've done your ditch-digging preproduction work and proven your tradeplan, then you shouldn't be making errors when assigning win percentages). It's important to keep in mind that no drawdown lasts forever. The real issue for a trader is not the number of losses but the amount of money that can be lost during this period, and that's why risk management matters.

In my experience, drawdowns of about 20% or so of your trading account are manageable. They are not fun, but they can be overcome when the odds swing back and the winners come pouring in again.

The More You Lose, the More You Need to Gain

A weird thing about the math involved in recovering from a drawdown is that percentage gains needed to make the account whole again are greater than the percentages of the losses incurred during the drawdown period. Let me illustrate: If you had $100 and lost 50% of it, you now have $50. A 50% gain on $50 gets you to $75. In order to recover your 50% loss, you need to have a 100% gain, turning $50 back into $100. The following chart (figure 85) breaks down the math.

RECOVERY AFTER A DRAWDOWN	
DRAWDOWNS	GAIN TO RECOVERY
5%	5.3% Gain
10%	11.1% Gain
15%	17.6% Gain
20%	25% Gain
25%	33% Gain
30%	42% Gain
40%	66.7% Gain
50%	100% Gain
60%	150% Gain
75%	300% Gain
90%	900% Gain

GRAPHIC

fig. 85

Think about it for a minute. A $100 account that experiences a 50% drawdown is then worth $50. That $50 account must now double in order to return to its original $100 value. Money can disappear more quickly in trading than it can be recovered! Therefore, managing your risk and limiting the damage of drawdowns are vital for survival.

Drawdowns are going to happen when you trade. But they are survivable. The key is proving in preproduction that your tradeplan will make money and then managing risk to limit the damage when drawdowns occur, per the rules of your plan. When the drawdowns do occur, and they will, don't feel that you need to make your money back immediately. Trading is a numbers game, and the edge you have in the market works in mysterious ways sometimes. The winners come when they come. Don't try to force it. Your superior odds will swing back around and lift the value of your account to new highs once again—when it decides to do so, not when *you* decide. Revenge trading (trying to make your losses back on the next trade) or anything else that causes you to deviate from your proven tradeplan will only lead to more losses in the end.

A trader who uses careful risk management will cultivate a sense of taking two steps forward for every one step back. With this approach, you let the superior odds that your tradeplan gives you do the heavy lifting while keeping your losses smaller and recoverable. You'll stay in the game, ready to profit when the trades swing back in your favor again.

Using Stop Losses

A *stop*, also called a stop loss, is an order to place a trade that includes instructions to close out the trade if the price hits a predetermined level. If you've followed along with my "In the Trading Room" scenarios, then you are already well acquainted with stops.

The stop will be a lower price for a long position and a higher price for a short one. Stops are critical to successful trading, as they take the emotion out of the decision to limit losses. Traders do not have to admit mistakes or hope that things turn around; the position closes out automatically.

No one likes to get stopped out of a trade. Our predetermined stop losses put into action something I tell my students: "He who learns to walk away lives to trade another day." This means surrendering at the appropriate time, while maintaining the superior edge that our tradeplan has given us, which includes that very same stop loss, without which we would not have a winning tradeplan in the first place! It is a tool to be valued, not feared.

Stops limit losses and protect capital. No trade should be placed without a stop. Ideally, the stop level should be established by the tested rules of a proven tradeplan and attached to the entry order with an OSO (order sends order). Once the entry is filled, the stop as well as the predetermined targets are placed and become live orders, as OCO orders (order cancels order). If the stop is hit, the targets are automatically canceled. If targets are hit, then stops are canceled. These order types are critical and must be learned and practiced until you can execute them perfectly, before placing live-money trades. The good news is that you can use your sim account to get the reps you need to perfect placing trades the correct way, and it costs you nothing but time and effort.

If the trader does not place a stop, the broker will. This is the *margin* stop, the point at which a broker's margin call is triggered. The broker will close positions to save you from yourself (and to save himself too).

Setting Position Size

How much should you trade? There are several approaches to money management for traders—and two very bad practices.

The first of these widespread bad practices is determining how much to trade based on how good you *feel* about the trade. This approach puts your emotions in control and will lead to unwise decisions. Doubt, fear, and greed have never helped anyone be a better trader.

The second bad practice is swinging for the fence or, worse, placing all your capital on a single trade. This falls into the category of gambling, not trading.

Risking relatively small amounts as a ratio of your available trading capital allows the odds to work to your benefit. It ensures that you're able to place another trade after you experience a loss.

Even though your position size is small in relation to your capital, it will accrue over time. This is because of the power of compounding, one of the key powers of successful trading. If you want to learn more about my "12 Powers," I review them all in the conclusion of this book and I cover them in great detail in *Day Trading QuickStart Guide* from ClydeBank Media.

The 2 Percent Rule

You many have noticed that I use 2% as the basic risk guideline. In general, traders should risk no more than 2% of their total trading capital on a single trade. A loss with 2% at risk will leave 98% of capital intact and ready for more trading, should a full loss occur from a given trade.

There are other position-sizing metrics out there. I find that the 2 percent rule creates enough room for trades that work out to contribute to account growth while protecting my account from drawdown. Remember, though: market correlation should also be considered. If you have concurrent trades that you have deemed to be closely correlated, you should tamp down your risk on each of those trades.

While I'm a serious proponent of the 2 percent rule as a starting guideline for most traders, 1% may be more appropriate for some newcomers, especially while they're still learning. On the other hand, after you gain some experience in the arena, more aggressive approaches such as 3% to 5% may be viable if the tradeplan wins at an extraordinary rate and you can afford to kiss your money goodbye without any dire consequences. I'm not saying that will happen—only that you should be prepared for it and be able to handle it. Risking 3% rather than 2% would have a dramatic impact in a very good way, when considering the power of compounding, but you would see your account value evaporate much more quickly should you encounter a losing streak. It's a double-edged sword.

Traders should always consult with their brokers to discuss worst-case scenarios. For instance, if a forex pair gaps big (jumps drastically in price) through a stop (like what happened a few years ago with the CHF Swiss franc) then it's possible that trades could lose a lot more than 2% even when the trader has attempted to configure their position to risk no more than 2%. This problem can be greatly compounded, as I'm sure you can imagine, with multiple open positions, should something like this occur. Worst-case scenarios do happen!

Determining Position Size

Tools like FX Synergy help you calculate the size of your trade. All you have to do is enter your risk parameter as a preset (like 2%), the entry, and the stop. It will then place the trade for you with the proper position size based on your preset parameters. Since it's connected directly to your account via your trading platform, it already knows your account value. These tools simplify the work and eliminate the potential for math errors. In a moment I'm going to walk you through the formula so you understand how it works, but when you're actually trading you will want to use the best tools.

I encourage you to download your copy of FX Synergy at go.quickstartguides.com/forex.

NOTE

In a currency pair, the first currency mentioned is the base currency and the second is the counter (or quote) currency. The price of the pair is the value of one unit of base currency in terms of the counter currency. For example, if the price of GBP/USD is 1.38166, then the GBP is the base currency and the USD is the counter currency. It costs $1.38166 to buy £1.

The position-sizing formula in terms of the counter currency is as follows:

GRAPHIC

fig. 86

$$\text{Amount Traded} = \frac{\text{Account Value x Risk Percentage}}{\text{Value per Pip}} \times \frac{\text{Units in a lot where pip value is one unit of counter currency}}{}$$

Remember, the amount you risk is the number of pips from the entry to the stop times the size of your position times the amount per pip plus spread, *slippage* (when a trader receives a lower trade execution price than intended), and commission. If your counter currency is not the same as your account value, then you have to convert the value of the amount risked into that currency. It seems complicated. But in truth, I never think about this when I'm trading. I just let my tools do it for me.

Here's the process:

» Begin with your starting account value.

» Figure out the pips at risk from your trade's entry to the stop. This might be, for example, as big as 200 pips for a swing trade or as little as 17 pips for a day trade.

» Apply your risk level to those parameters based on the value per pip.

The charting platform will tell you the pip value in the currency of your trading account. For example, I traded the GBP/AUD this morning. My platform shows me that the pip value is $7.78. That's for a full-size lot, 1.0. So a mini lot would be .1, .778 (77.8 cents) per pip, and a micro lot would be .01, .0778 (7.78 cents) per pip.

Chapter Recap

» Risk is part of trading, so learn to manage it from the start. Risk comes from the market and from the use of leverage—both of which are also sources of return.

» Traders will lose trades. Sometimes those losses will stretch for extended periods. Strong discipline will get you through the inevitable drawdowns. Maintain proper position sizes and stops.

» Every trade needs a stop, which is a limit on how much it can lose before it's closed out automatically.

» A 2% risk level is recommended for good money management. It is simple and will help keep your powder dry for trading over the long term.

| 14 |

Managing Trades

In the Trading Room

Chapter Overview

» Identifying and applying exhaustion signals
» The stop and reverse
» Swing trading forex

When I was kid, I watched a lot of westerns. Tonto, one of the main characters in the *Lone Ranger* movies, would put his ear to the ground to listen for what might be coming their way. It could be a stampede of buffalo, a band of outlaws, or a stagecoach. By putting an ear to the ground, he was taking in the action.

If we want to find out what the price action is trying to say, we have to learn how to put our ears to the ground and listen. The indicators you use are less important than knowing how to use them. After many years of time and experience in the markets, I have concluded that the best way to hear what the price action is saying is to listen to the price action itself. The indicators I use assist me with that, in real time at the right edge of the chart. Think of indicators as the stethoscope that helps you hear what's happening in the greatest of detail.

Exhaustion Trades

Markets are noisy. You have to learn to tune out that noise so you can hear the message in the price action more clearly. I like to begin listening by deciding what it is that I am trying to hear. What am I listening for? We know that the immediate past predicts the immediate future. What does that tell me? Where is the market in the Action → Reaction → Subsequent Action sequence?

The market consists of two forces at any given moment: buyers and sellers. When the buyers have the strength, markets go up. When the sellers have the strength, markets go down. So what if we had a way of knowing when the side that has driven the price action has used up all its strength to the point of exhaustion? Is that something that could help us? Yes! With this knowledge we can make an effort to stay away from the tired side of the trade and look for positions on the side that is about to show energy. The price action itself will give us the clues we need.

Early in my trading career, I learned how to confirm that the force that pushes prices up or down has become exhausted. This simple concept works with just about all charts and time frames.

Let's consider it from the buyer's side first. Imagine a currency pair ascending in value. The buyers are many and motivated. However, common sense tells us that this can't last forever. Eventually the buyers will tire out. And it's my contention that just prior to buyer exhaustion, there will be a sign.

The signal is simple: Three bars with lower closes. If we see three consecutive bars with lower closes than the bar prior to those three, we have our first significant clue. We'll call the bar prior to those three the "0" bar, and the three bars that close to the right of the 0 bar are bars 1, 2, and 3 (see figure 87).

These closes don't have to be lower in succession relative to one another—only relative to the 0 bar.

Once we identify our three bars with lower closes, we'll look for the next clue: a display of buyers exerting significant energy *before* the 0 bar. I have found that three or more bars (not necessarily in succession) closing higher and higher (not always immediately) before the 0 bar is sufficient to confirm the exhaustion signal and prompt consideration of a trade setup to go short. In figure 87, this criterion is met quite plainly; there are actually four bars (we include the 0 bar) attaining higher highs, all in succession in this case (though they don't need to be). Remember, what you are ultimately looking for is evidence of overexertion on the buyer side. Later in this section we'll see examples of this signal that aren't quite as tidy and clean-cut but will nonetheless meet the criterion.

If we're viewing things from the perspective of seller exhaustion, we'll simply swap our highs for our lows and vice versa: we'll look for three consecutive bars (bars 1 through 3) to the right of the 0 bar, each closing higher than the close of the 0 bar. And somewhere to the left of the 0 bar we will want to note at least three bars with lower and lower closes that lead down to our 0 bar (which may be considered one of the three) and which itself will close at a new swing low.

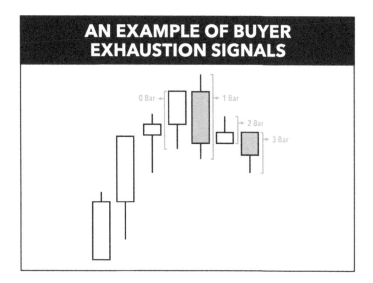

Note that bar 2 is an up bar, but it still closes lower than the close of bar 0.

Let's take a look at an emerging, potentially tradeable scenario where we'd seek to identify seller exhaustion:

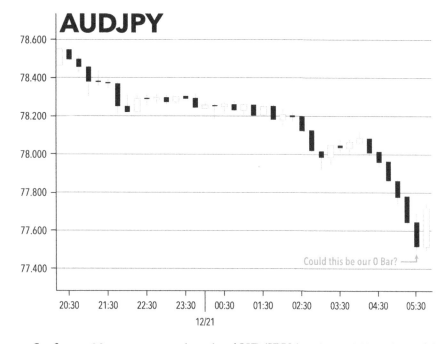

In figure 88, we can see that the AUD/JPY has been falling hard. The sellers are in charge. At the right edge of the chart, we get a bar that closes higher than the bar on its immediate left. Is the bar on the left the 0 bar? We need two more bars to close higher than the close of our prospective 0 bar.

Two bars later, as shown in figure 89, we can see that a total of three bars closed higher to the immediate right of the 0 bar. Note as well that our second criterion is met; there are several bars closing lower and lower to the left of the 0 bar, more than is sufficient to represent overexertion by sellers. The sellers may have become exhausted.

fig. 89

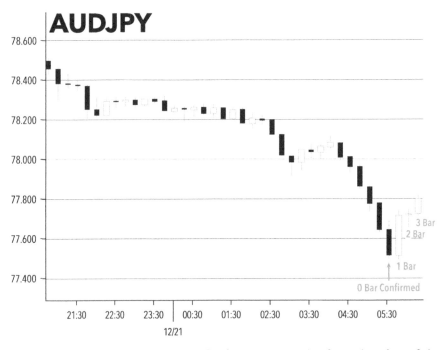

Let's look at another example. In figure 90, on the far right edge of the chart, we can see a bar that closes lower than the bar to its left.

In figure 91, we see the pattern has developed: three consecutive bars with lower closes than that of the 0 bar. Please note as well that though there is a down bar immediately to the left of the 0 bar on this chart, we still see a clear march upward, with at least three bars closing higher and higher (they need not be successive), culminating with the 0 bar. We can thus still infer that there is overexertion from buyers in the lead-up to the 0 bar.

Figures 88 through 91 are actually all pieces of the same 15-minute chart. Within this chart, we've identified what appears to be an oncoming seller exhaustion, and, elsewhere on the chart (later, actually), we've identified what appears to be an oncoming buyer exhaustion. As a trader, you naturally want to know how things played out. If you look at figure 92 you can more clearly see the aftermath of our efforts to identify seller exhaustion. The sellers ran out of gas and the buyers took charge, pushing the market into a strong rally upward. And we can see where this rally might end, as it pushed right up into our second example that marked where the buyers might have become exhausted.

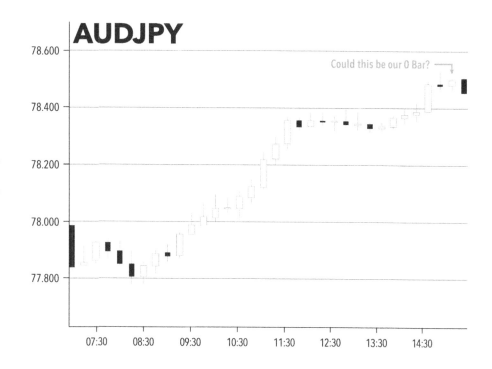

AUDJPY

Could this be our 0 Bar?

fig. 90

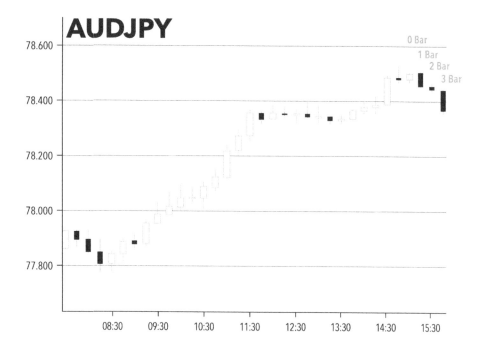

AUDJPY

0 Bar
1 Bar
2 Bar
3 Bar

fig. 91

fig. 92

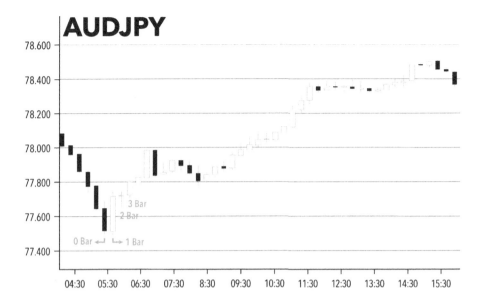

Figure 93 shows what happened after the buyers became exhausted and the sellers grabbed back the reins. The price began a steady march lower.

fig. 93

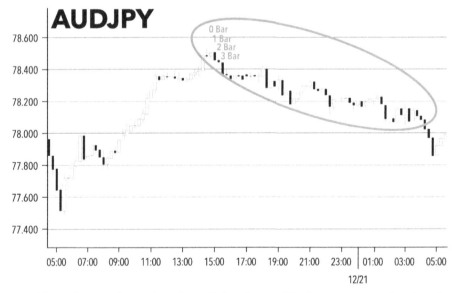

Note that at the right edge of the figure 93 chart, we see the signals forming again, cluing us in to the possibility that the sellers have become exhausted once more. Figure 94 confirms that that is indeed the case.

You may have noticed other places on these charts (besides those specified) where evidence of exhaustion might have been perceived. You may also be wondering how the dynamics of identifying exhaustion might change if we were using faster, lower time frames—that is, 5-minute or 15-minute charts.

GRAPHIC

fig. 94

I chose these particular examples to provide a clear, big-picture illustration of this important phenomenon. Unlike other price action predictors we've discussed thus far, evidence of exhaustion manifests quite similarly across all markets and time frames.

As always, we are using the idea that the immediate past predicts the immediate future. The immediate past is the fact that three bars closed higher (to indicate tired sellers) or lower (to indicate tired buyers) than the prior bar, the 0 bar. The prevailing force that led into the 0 bar (lower bars to represent seller exertion and higher bars to represent buyer exertion) is exhausted, which then predicts the immediate future: the opposing force has a good chance of taking charge, and the market could head in the opposite direction.

It's important to recognize that no indicators thus far have been used with this idea; we have used only the price action itself. We still have more fine-tuning to do before arriving at a real tradeable scenario.

Adding an indicator can increase the three-bar signal's power to identify good trades. The buyers and sellers are engaged in a tug-of-war. What we'd like to see is the line in the sand that marks where the power between the two is perfectly balanced. I like to think of this line as demarcating a pit full of starving, snapping crocodiles, waiting to devour the side that loses and gets pulled in. You can hear their growls, see their sharp teeth and powerful jaws pointing upward, all waiting for the weaker side to get pulled in, torn to shreds, and devoured. After all, that's what happens to your trading account if you find yourself on the wrong side of this ongoing tug-of-war.

This line in the sand we're looking for is a dynamic line that I like to call the croc pit line (CPL), and it is not static. It constantly moves with the terrain of the trading battlefield and with the strength or weakness of each side. To mark it, I use an indicator known as the Donchian channel. This is not one of the more common indicators, but most trading platforms carry it or support third-party versions of it. The indicator was developed by Richard Donchian, who established the first managed futures fund. The channel is the area bounded by the highest high and the lowest low of the last "n" periods. I usually use nine periods to form the channel.

After I plot the channel lines (see the solid lines in figure 95), I plot the average of the outer bands (see the dashed line in figure 95), forming the part of the indicator that I am most interested in. The average of the Donchian channel bands (the dashed line in the middle) is the line that marks our ever-shifting crocodile pit. We want to place our trades on the correct side of the crocodile pit, the side that has the strength. In short, we want to be above the line for long trades and below the line for short trades.

GRAPHIC

fig. 95

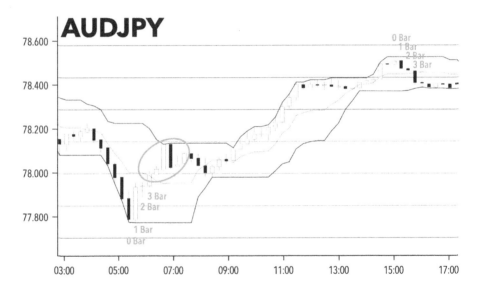

In figure 95, we return to the scenarios we've described earlier in this section, but this time we're going to put our Donchian channel and its average line to work for us. Notice how a majority of the bars began closing above the croc pit line (CPL) once our three higher closing bars occurred (see circled portion of figure 95), marking our exhausted sellers. Then look at how the bulk of the rally lived on the long side of the CPL as sellers continued to be pulled into the pit, devoured by the ever-famished crocodiles below. The crocodiles are grateful to the buyers and reward them by lining their pockets with newly found riches, the plunder left behind by the devoured sellers.

On any given chart, there are many places where an exhaustion trade setup will occur according to the parameters we've defined thus far: three bars closing lower (or higher) than the 0 bar, with three or more bars to the left of (or including) the 0 bar closing higher (or lower). Not all exhaustion setups, however, will lead to profitable trades.

Study the rightmost bars circled in the preceding chart (figure 95). You should be able to identify the criteria for a possible buyer-side exhaustion signal (for instance, a possible short trade forthcoming). The new 0 bar could be that long up bar (just two bars to the right of bar 3 from the previous setup, followed by bars 1, 2, and 3, all of which technically close lower than the 0 bar). In adherence to the rules we've established explicitly thus far, we would place an order to go short after that third down bar (see the leftmost bar circled in figure 95) broke through our CPL.

Sometimes the exhausted side just needs to catch its breath. In the case of the short (buyer exhaustion) signals that we just identified in the preceding example, we will need another degree of confirmation before reversing out of our existing long position to get short.

Imagine yourself experiencing this trade at the right edge of the chart, just as that first down bar broke through the CPL at around 8:15 or so. It's important to remain skeptical and allow the price action itself to continue to tell the story of the trade. In this scenario, we would have gone ahead and placed our order to get short, but we would have done so using the adjustments and price action confirmation techniques that we've detailed in our previous "In the Trade Room" scenarios. In other words, we'd have placed our entry order a few pips below the setup bar.

From the perspective of our initial long position, this new short setup is but a caution flag. We have to pay attention to it, but we must do so in accordance with our established set of mechanical rules. Price action confirmation is our ace in the hole. If the short setup is a true opportunity, then the entry will be hit, and we will stop out of our long position and go short. If the entry is not hit, then the buyers were just catching their breath, and the dangers represented by the caution flag never materialized. As you can see in figure 96, the entry to go short was never hit and the setup was canceled.

It's important to note, too, how we respond to the often volatile and often opposing currents of price action. Notice how when our short setup is forming, breaking downward through the CPL, it comprises another signal of seller-side exhaustion (circled in figure 96). Sure, we won't have another viable long setup bar until a few bars later, but what about the bigger question: How do we know what signals to act on and what signals to pass on?

The answer is our ace in the hole: price action confirmation, the mechanical rules that govern our trade entry that we have already discussed in previous "In the Trade Room" scenarios and will continue to define and expand upon as we proceed in our study of exhaustion signals.

To summarize, the short setup circled in figure 96 needed to be heeded and taken seriously, but it proved to be just a sign of the bulls catching their breath in front of another strong pull of the rope that propelled the price higher (and promptly back to the long side of the CPL!) to fatten those gluttonous crocodiles—as well as the pocketbooks of the buyers—with misfortunate sellers and the wealth from which they were just separated.

fig. 96

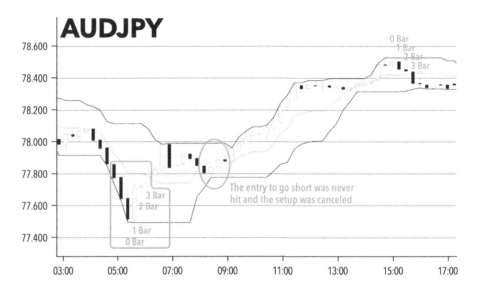

It's easy to see how one might find themselves adrift, being tossed about by violent riptides and the ever-changing direction of currents as price action pulls everyone but the most skilled traders into the crocodile pit. No one wants to be getting long, flipping to short, flipping back to long again, etc., yet without a clear objective mechanical approach to deal with this situation (which is quite common), that's exactly what might have happened to us. This is where the power and benefit of mechanical trade setup and tradeplan rules come to our aid, to guide us through the dangerous waters we often find ourselves in.

The three factors we've used thus far to stack the odds in our favor are (1) identifying signs of exhaustion by following the method outlined earlier in this section, (2) using the CPL to confirm our assumptions, and (3) looking for compelling price action confirmation (this is crucial, and we will dig even deeper into it shortly).

Keep in mind that even if you think you can see a trend forming as plain as day, there is never a guarantee that any trade will win—there never is. But if you're beginning to see things with clarity and confidence, then you're off to a good start. Remember, the goal is simply to be right more than you're wrong, which is what "stacking the odds on our side" means.

Now we need to begin talking about how we're going to apply our growing knowledge of the exhaustion trade into the creation of actual, actionable trade setups. In our prior trade setup example, the 20 SMA pullback, we first identified a setup bar and then looked for the price to push past it by at least 2 pips (and possibly more due to key-level adjustments) before triggering into the trade. If the price failed to break out enough to hit our entry price, then the trade setup would cancel itself. We need to apply this power of price action confirmation to our exhaustion setup as well. But how?

I'll answer that question in a moment. But first, let's examine a unique challenge with this setup that you may have already begun to pick up on. We can drive ourselves nuts identifying prospective 0 bars and looking to see if we have the three required "opposite closes" (on the far side of the 0 bar) to justify our initial interest in the possibility of exhaustion. The signals can stack up on top of each other, intermingle, and, as we've seen, contradict. We need to simplify the landscape, so we're not using all of our energy to spot these signals.

fig. 97

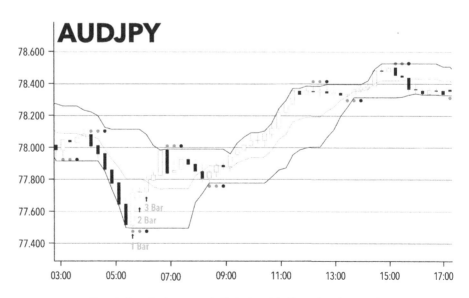

Dots below the bars are a bullish signal (seller-side exhaustion).
Dots above the bars are bearish (buyer-side exhaustion).

In an effort to reserve more of my mental capacity for the finer points of the exhaustion trade, I decided to hire a programmer to create a custom indicator that would show me when these "opposite close" exhaustion level signals occurred. The program marks the three opposite closing bars by placing a dot below each of the three bars closing higher than the 0 bar, or above each of the three bars closing lower.

Let's look at the initial signal we discussed in this section (see where the bars are labeled 1, 2, and 3 in figure 97). Were we witnessing this signal form in real time, at the right edge of the chart, we would see our bullish dots plotted once the 3 bar appears, and we'd note that the 3 bar closes above our CPL.

Our next step is to look for the setup bar on the long side of (above) our CPL. Ideally, we want our setup bar to be the first bar that breaks through the CPL and closes on its opposite side, in the direction of our trade. This could be our 3 bar (as it is in our current scenario) or it could be another bar that forms after our 3 bar. I allow for as many as four bars to the right of the 3 bar to be considered for the setup bar, as long as it is the first bar to close up and above the CPL.

For the record, I do count dojis when scouting for the right setup bar (up to four bars to the right of the 3 bar). Dojis are bars with the same open and close, considered neutral in this case (they are neither down bars nor up bars), and I will accept them as a setup bar when they occur.

fig. 98

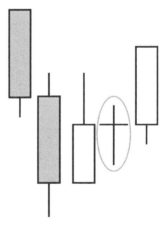

An example of a doji

We'll use our setup bar to set our entry; let's do that now. In our current scenario, our setup bar is our 3 bar, because it was the first bar to close up and above our CPL, as I just explained. Remember—and this is important—it can occur on the 3 bar or up to four bars after the 3 bar. Using an approach similar to our 20 SMA pullback setup, we'll place our entry 2 pips higher than the high of our setup bar, using the same key-level adjustment and spread considerations.

Had this been a slower, higher-time-frame chart, like an end-of-day chart where each price bar represents a full day's worth of price action, I might have used a 10- to 20-pip entry above or below our setup bar. What's important is that we get our additional price action confirmation to get triggered into a trade. In the swing trading scenario that follows this one, we will be working with a slower, higher-time-frame chart, and you will see why it often makes sense to place our entries 20 pips off of the setup bar rather than 2 pips off.

Returning to our current scenario, the high of our setup bar is at 77.818 (77.82); 2 pips higher is 77.84. Let's adjust upward by two more pips. We don't want to bounce off the key level of 85. Even though 85 is not technically a round number, it's still what we refer to in trading as a "nickel," halfway between round number key levels; I want the price to push past 85 before I commit to the trade. We'll enter at 77.86 plus spread (see figure 99).

In chapter 3 we discussed the unique attribute of the JPY when it comes to pips. For any pair that includes the JPY, "1 pip" does not refer to the fourth decimal place, but the second decimal place. For example, the difference between 77.82 and 77.86 is a 4-pip difference.

Our trade setup will also need a stop and targets. Let's continue this setup by identifying our stop. As always, we want to put our stop where it is unlikely to be hit while protecting our position, unless the odds change and the price moves against us. Remember, price action is always in charge, and the power and effectiveness of this setup is that it is based on the pure price action itself, including where we place our stop. Our three higher closing bars that form the basis of this setup do a great job of revealing near-term support. We can strategically place our three exhaustion dots in a way that quickly shows us where our stops should go, 2 pips below the lowest price reached by bars 1–3. (If going short, I'd place it 2 pips above the highest point reached.) And yes, as a habit, I also factor in key level and spread considerations when placing my stop.

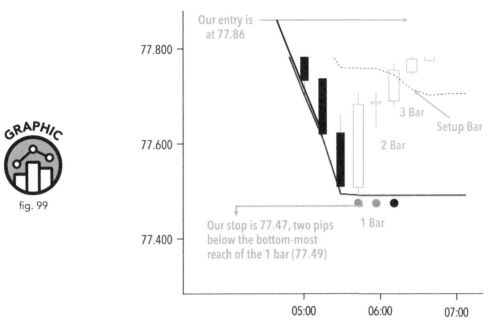

Our entry is at 77.86

77.800

77.600

77.400

3 Bar

Setup Bar

2 Bar

1 Bar

Our stop is 77.47, two pips below the bottom-most reach of the 1 bar (77.49)

05:00   06:00   07:00

GRAPHIC

fig. 99

MY TAKE

Your stops in these setups can generally be visualized by the exhaustion dots themselves; it's the simplest way to think about it and visualize your stop. You can look at the chart and easily see the support and resistance levels as revealed by nothing more than the price action itself. As an added and valuable benefit, this allows for much easier testing and proof of concept. Keep in mind, as always, that if you're at a key level, you should always "hide the stop" on the opposite side of the key level so as to force the price to break through the key level before you stop out of the trade. Our goal is to stay in the trade, so let's make the stop harder to get to whenever we can with small adjustments.

To determine our targets, we will use our "x factor" idea. You'll recall that the x factor is simply a multiplier derived from the trade setup that helps us project where the price is likely to be in the immediate future. We'll establish a multiplier that will give us a range of adjustable targets and will tune itself to the current condition of the market, based on the setup itself, while keeping the risk-to-reward ratio firmly on our side.

In our current setup, to find our x factor for a long trade, we are going to measure the vertical distance from the lowest point of the three bars on top of our three exhaustion dots to the high of the actual setup bar (figure 100). The same method can be applied to shorts.

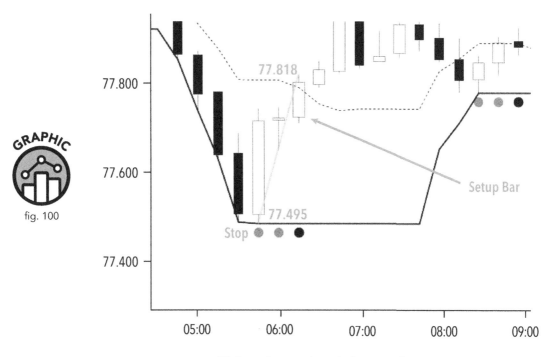

We have all we need to calculate our x factor.

Notice how handily the exhaustion dots mark where the lowest of the three bars takes place. Notice also how easy it is to spot the first bar to close long, above the CPL. The lowest point of our three bars is 77.495, which we will round down to 77.49. The high of our setup bar is 77.818, which we will round up to 77.82. Our x factor is 77.82 − 77.49 = 33 pips.

Once you get your feet wet with real trading (and hopefully superior charting, as I have suggested earlier), you will be able to configure your tools to project the targets by merely drawing them on your chart, bypassing the need to manually do the math. The tool I quickly turn to is the Fibonacci price retracement lines tool, reprogrammed similarly to how we did the Fibonacci price lines extension tool described in our 1-2-3 trade setup examples in chapter 12. I combine this with the use of fast action hot keys. I should note, though, that not all trading platforms have such a tool, so learning the simple math is a good idea. The math is rather easy, and not having the perfect tool shouldn't dissuade you from taking advantage of these excellent trade setups. Of course, having the best tools is still what I would always advise, but it's a decision that traders have to make for themselves.

The next step is to use our *x* factor to project our likely targets. We are going to build upon the same concepts I taught in the earlier trade setups.

We are going to add our *x* factor to the high of our setup bar:

» Target 1 (**T1**) is 1x higher than 77.82 = **78.15**
» **T2** is 1.5x higher than 77.82 = **78.32**
» **T3** is 2x higher than 77.82 = **78.48**
» **T4** is 2.5x higher than 77.82 = **78.65**
» **T5** is 3x higher than 77.82 = **78.81**

A good starting point is to use the 1.5x level, our T2, as our "primary target objective." This target typically gives us a favorable risk-to-reward ratio (exactly 3:5 in our current scenario). When determined correctly, our T2 target should be winning about 60 to 70 percent of the time; our preproduction work should establish the tradeplans and win percentages in advance (see chapter 15).

Stacking a favorable winning percentage with a favorable risk-to-reward ratio is a recipe for success.

fig. 101

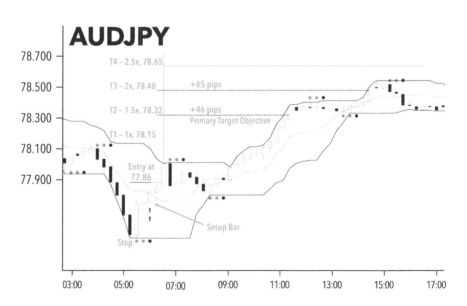

As we did with our previous setups, we will look to scale out at our various targets while also employing the use of a trailing stop, so that we can at once limit our risk and capture any explosive moves that may occur. Our trade will be deemed successful if we hit our primary target objective (T2); any money we make hitting the larger targets will sweeten the deal. Let's take a look at our setup and how it panned out (figure 101).

In figure 101 you'll note that I used my handy Fibonacci retracement tool to project the targets. I've removed the grid lines from this chart, though, drawing horizontal-only lines instead to show where the targets are hit as this trade progresses.

If your trading platform doesn't have the Fibonacci retracement tool or a similar one, don't panic; the math involved in this setup is simple, and even if you have to make manual calculations, the process should become routine with practice.

To recap our setup:

» **Entry:** 77.86 (2 pips above the high of our setup bar plus 2 pips to adjust off the "nickel," .84 adjusted to .86)

» **Stop:** 77.47 (2 pips below the lowest bar associated with the three higher closing bars)

» *x* **factor:** .33 (the distance between the lowest point of bars 1–3 and the high of the setup bar)

» **T1:** 78.15 (We will move our stop to break-even if the price gets to this level and has gone a full 12 pips, a little less or more depending on the pair's average spread. We want to see a minimum of T1 and 10 pips after accounting for the pair's spread.)

» **T2:** 78.32 (At a minimum, we have to hit this "primary target objective" if we are to consider the trade a true success, achieving the goals of the tradeplan and allowing us to quit the session with a positive result. For swing traders, this concept wouldn't really apply.)

» **T3:** 78.48

» **T4:** 78.65

I'd like to circle back now to the possible short setup that appeared between the hours of 7:00 and 9:00, while this long trade was in progress. If you'll recall higher up in this section, we were faced with the unpleasant prospect of perhaps needing to reverse our position to short. I mentioned that we had an ace up our sleeve that would help us with this very difficult, right-edge-of-the-chart decision. Now that I have explained the components of this setup, do you recognize what the ace in the hole actually is? Think about it.

If you think through this trade setup, you should be able to see that our ace in the hole is the price action itself. Following the trade setup rules just described, when considering this potential short trade (threatening to derail our current long position), we would need to place a short entry two pips below the short setup bar (minus adjustments). This short setup bar is the first bar that closed below the CPL, three bars to the right of the buyer exhaustion dots that formed around 7:00 a.m. The entry, per this trade setup's rules as described above, asks for additional price action confirmation that never came and was enough to keep us in our long trade and protect us from getting short. The threatening short setup was self-mitigated by the price action, canceling as the price moved higher, and two bars closed above the CPL.

That leads me to this important rule: once we establish a trade setup, if two bars close on the opposite side of the CPL prior to our hitting the entry price, the setup is immediately canceled.

By design, this important rule is also based on pure price action (in fact, this entire trade setup is, from start to finish). Remember, the CPL marks the balance of power between buyers and sellers. In this situation, to get short, we need price action pushing lower, below the CPL, and hitting our entry. We were presented with a valid short setup bar, but our entry rules protected us. The price failed to move lower and instead moved higher. Once the price moves up and two bars close above the CPL, this is evidence enough that the short setup has lost its validity. Cancel the short and put it in the rearview mirror. We still have a long trade to manage to its natural end, which, as you can see, rewarded us in a most spectacular way, hitting two of its three profit targets for attractive gains.

I've used this setup for many years, and to this day it still amazes me how simple ideas, like letting the price action itself be your leading indicator, continue to work so well—and always will!

Repetition is key, so let's continue. Later in the day, the buyers that pushed this market higher appeared to become exhausted again, setting up the next trade in this sequence. We were alerted to this by the three bars closing lower. Now we need to keep our ears pressed against the ground, listening to what the price action itself is saying, to confirm that the buyers have indeed become exhausted. We want to hear if the additional ingredients for this setup arrive. Namely, we want a bar that closes lower on the short side of our CPL, either on the third dot or up to four bars to the right of that dot. Then we want to see the price move lower to hit the level that we would use as our short entry, 2 pips below our setup bar and adjusted for any key levels.

MY TAKE

This process may seem to have a lot to consider, but if you think it through and follow it a few times, it soon becomes second nature. It's like riding a bike. Practice and repetition pay off.

As we continue to listen to the price action, we finally hear the necessary short trade setup ingredients, and the trade should be placed immediately. Figure 102 shows us the next trade in the sequence.

GRAPHIC

fig. 102

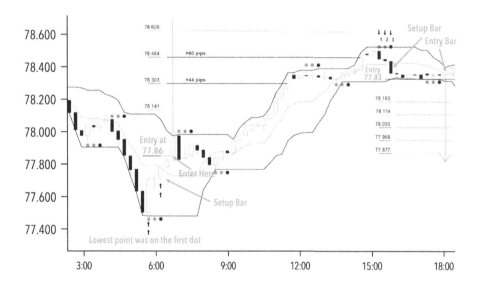

I drew the entry, stop, and targets as well as the bar that finally stabbed down to trigger us into the trade. The setup bar is the first bar that closes below the CPL, either on the third exhaustion dot or up to four bars to the right of that dot. In this case, it was the bar on our third dot. Notice that the bar that triggered us into the trade happened nine bars later. That doesn't matter. What matters is remaining true to what this setup is all about: the price action is in charge. A trade will take as long as it needs to develop. As long as we don't get two bars that close above the CPL prior to the trade hitting its entry, this short trade setup remains valid and should be allowed to trigger in if the price pushes down to hit the entry. That number *two*, as in two bars closing on the opposite side of the CPL, didn't magically appear. It was discovered as a result of extensive testing (backtesting, forward testing)

and lots of actual live trading. The result of such time-intensive work is our knowledge that canceling the setup is the best approach if and when two bars close on the opposite side of the CPL before we hit the entry price; therefore, it is now an important part of this trade setup's rule set.

There are two additional cancel rules: (1) If a bar closes at or beyond the stop, even if it is only the first bar to close on the other side of the CPL, then that too would cancel the setup. (2) If a new setup in the opposite direction appears and triggers in, the prior setup should be canceled. These two additional cancellation rules are the final ingredients of our exhaustion trade setup.

Figure 103 shows how well this trade worked out, hitting a perfect fifth target.

fig. 103

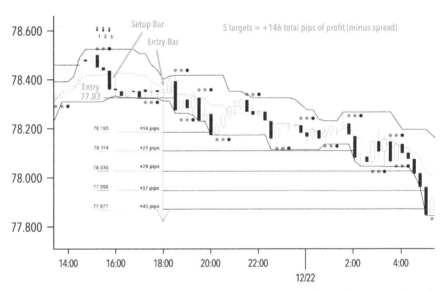

Notice how our exhaustion dots show us a number of potential trade setups where both the buyers and the sellers appear to be tired or exhausted. Remember that these potential setups appear at the right edge of the chart only after the third qualifying bar closes higher when the buyers are taking charge, or lower when the sellers are taking charge. We can ignore the short setup opportunities because we are already in a short trade.

In theory, we could scale in more short positions in concert with our initial short trade, but it opens up a can of worms known as FIFO (first in, first out) regulations, making a trade with multiple scaled-in positions very difficult to manage.

But how do we react to the long setup opportunities? This is a seller's market, and the sellers will get exhausted at some point. In figure 103, dots appear under the bars at possible areas of seller exhaustion while we are in our short trade. Notice there are two places where we have tired sellers and the price bar closing on the long side of our CPL. In every other instance, the price remained on the short side of our CPL, illuminating the self-mitigating aspect of this dynamic setup, allowing for trade setups or a lack thereof to dictate what we do or don't do.

Let's examine the two situations where the price bar actually closed above the CPL, possibly giving us long setup bars while we were still in our short trade. In figure 104 I have put arrows under each of the bars that closed above the CPL with the associated three higher closing bars (exhaustion dots) to show you exactly where this occurred.

fig. 104

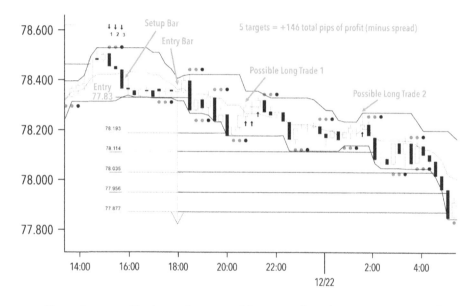

I'm going to talk about the second instance first, because it requires less explanation (see "possible long trade 2" in figure 104). There was a qualifying long setup bar that happened one bar to the right of the third dot. There is a doji on the third dot that closes directly on the CPL, but closing on the CPL doesn't meet the requirement of closing *above* it for a long setup. At around 1:30, though, there was a legitimate long setup bar. However, to give us our price action confirmation and trigger us into the trade, our entry would need to be placed 2 pips above the high of that bar. A long trade could have been placed at this point, but the price was never able to break out up and above our setup bar. It never triggered in, and after the two closing bars below the CPL, the long trade would have needed to be immediately canceled.

Now let's examine the earlier example, between 20:00 and 21:30. You will notice that there were three bars that closed up and above our CPL, the first one being on our third dot, making it the qualifying long setup bar. At that point a long trade should have been placed, as we would have no idea what would happen next. We'll talk about that, but first, if you'll indulge me for a moment, I want to illustrate a very important concept in trading. At any point, even when we're already in a trade, the market can threaten to change direction and give us a new signal that requires us to reverse our position. This is very frustrating to many traders, but I have devised a way to deal with this situation and avoid that anxiety. Let's control what we *can* control with smart tradeplan rules. Let me break it down, step by step.

The setup bar's high is 78.304, which we will round to 78.31. The entry would be placed 2 pips above that, at 78.33. Our short trade's stop would also need to be moved to 78.33. Two bars later, the price stabbed up to 78.331 and would have stopped us out of our short trade while also triggering us into the reversing long trade. We would have placed our order at 78.35 to accommodate the spread (assuming that the pair had an average 2-pip spread), so when the bid came up to hit 78.33, we would have been filled at 78.35, the ask. This would have bumped us out of our winning short trade and into a fast-losing long trade, because the sellers remained in complete control, as we would have quickly discovered. Perhaps now you can see why this situation gives so many traders fits! As previously stated, it's not uncommon for a reversing trade setup to occur when we are already in a trade. In the figure 104 chart, we would have been in a short trade when a long trade showed up in the price action, at the right edge of the chart. Examining this situation now, we have the benefit of hindsight, but when it actually happens, it will be in real time at the right edge. Perhaps you can sense your own anxiety beginning to take hold?

This is the classic "stop and reverse," and, as I will show you shortly, it doesn't have to give you ulcers and in fact can actually be used to your advantage. The entry for the new long trade becomes the stop for the current short trade. Do we really want to get out of our short and reverse to long? We won't know for sure until the market continues to move forward and bars continue to close and print on the chart. Sometimes we would want to exit the short trade and reverse to long. If the market were to continue higher, we would have a clean way to cut our losses quicker on the short trade and jump on the winning side of the price action, creating a very profitable two-trade sequence. Of course, we'd rather just stay in our original short trade, if possible. How do we navigate these treacherous waters? Remember, the market will do what it does, unconcerned about what we want. The answer is found in a common-sense approach: mechanical rules that allow us to remain completely objective.

The dilemma here is that sometimes it is better to flip our position and other times it's best to remain in our original trade. How do we make the right decision? To answer this question in the best way, we will stick to what we know. While we can never know for sure what will happen next, we can improve our odds in these situations by leaning on our philosophy, surrendering to the price action and allowing it to tell us what to do, yet again. We do so by asking for additional price action confirmation. So we let the price confirm, just a little bit more, what it most likely wants to do. We use this technique, in a possible stop and reverse situation like this, in an attempt to "protect our current position" (remain in our short trade, in other words), while also recognizing the fact that the market could actually be changing direction, forcing us to flip our position to the other side, which we also must be willing to do. This decision has to be made at the right edge, in real time—but don't worry. I have the perfect prescription to prevent any ill-timed unpleasant acid reflux episodes. This situation is going to happen quite often after you embark on your trading journey, so let's solve it now.

The technique I like to employ in a stop and reverse situation like this, as I said, is asking for additional price action confirmation. I do this by adding *2 more pips* to our adjusted long entry so that the price has to move *further up* to trigger in. I want the price action itself to offer more of a clue that it really wants to head higher before I ditch my short trade and jump into the reversing long trade. There is no way to know for sure what will happen, but often enough, this maneuver will keep me in the original trade. I call this my "insurance policy." I simply refer to this maneuver as a "stop and reverse adjustment." In the figure 104 example, instead of the long entry being 78.33, we would move it up 2 pips to 78.35, plus 1 more pip to get it off the .35 key level and up to 78.36. Then we would place the new long order at 78.38 to accommodate 2 pips of spread. We would also move the stop on our short trade to the same location, 78.38, so that we would exit our short position at the same place we entered our new reversing long position.

Sometimes the stop and reverse leads to a smaller loss than the original risk allowed for. If it's followed by a winning reversal trade, then the end result is a profitable two-trade sequence.

Other times, the reversing trade will prove to be a false alarm. Our stop and reverse adjustment (the additional pips we added to our setup) will often be just enough "protection" to keep us in the original trade. That's what happened here. The price was never able to get to 78.36. A reversing long trade never would have triggered in, nor would the short stop have been hit. The reversing long trade was canceled and our original short trade then proceeded to hit its targets for a very profitable move.

We take the pressure off of ourselves and let the price action dictate what to do. There is no perfect method, but we don't need perfect to make money. Those who never learn this technique will continue to struggle with stress, ulcers, and acid reflux, but you can rest assured that you will never again suffer those problems—at least not when faced with trying to figure out what to do with stop and reverses!

There will be times when our insurance policy ends up costing us. Every now and then, we will get triggered into our adjusted reversing position only to see the market do another about-face. It's common to have two losses in a row. You should not get upset over this (see the "Drawdown and Losing Streaks" section in chapter 13). Sometimes the fish gets away.

Success in trading depends on one's ability to establish and follow a proven tradeplan. As much as possible, one's trading behaviors should be reduced to mechanical rules, so that they can be done the same way every time. Trading involves developing rules and backtesting them to obtain positive measurable results. Prove it to yourself first. Only then should you add a rule to your tradeplan.

fig. 105

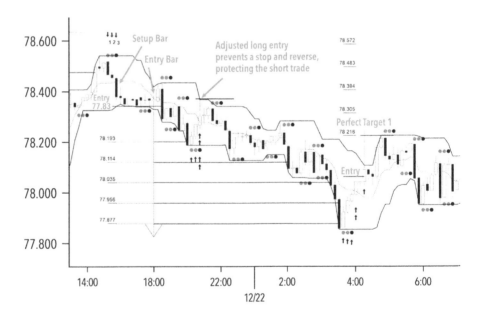

Figure 105 shows us the next trade in the sequence (see the rightward area of the chart). It is another long setup. What makes this trade different is that we have already hit our target objectives with the prior short trade, so no stop and reverse adjustment is needed. The first bar to close above our CPL is the first bar to the right of our third dot. Its high is 78.038, rounded to 78.04. The entry is placed 2 pips above at 78.06, but the actual order is placed at 78.08 to accommodate for 2 pips of spread.

The price comes up and the bid hits 78.06, which would fill us on the ask at 78.08. I have placed the targets based on our x factor formula that we've now used several times. We can visualize the stop, as we often can, by using the exhaustion dots themselves as the marker. The lower line of the Donchian channel is a convenient indicator, marking where near-term support is. We are "hiding our stop" 2 pips below it.

Target 1 (T1) is at 78.216, but we will round that down to 78.21. I always round my entries and stops further out, making it harder to hit those levels, as part of my price action confirmation process and to give extra protection in the case of my stops. For targets, I round them closer to my entry so that they are easier to achieve. Such an approach would have served us perfectly in this example, as the price stabbed up to 78.217, hitting T1 perfectly. And while T2 is our primary target objective, I like to take advantage of the flexibility of forex position-sizing capabilities by scaling out part of my position at T1 if the T1 target is 10 pips or greater in value. In this case, it was 15 pips, 13 pips after spread. Moreover, once I take profit on a trade, or the price has hit T1 and has gone 12 pips, I feel that I have earned the right to move my stop to the break-even point.

In this case the price ended up working lower and would have stopped out the remainder of the position at break-even. It would have been a modest winner. This is a trade setup strategy that takes what the market wants to give. It should be noted that if we'd used this break-even tradeplan rule, the prior short trade would also have stopped out at break-even after hitting its T1. We then would have had a new short setup shortly thereafter, which would have resulted in a winner.

Each trader has to settle on their own personal style of trading. I like to move my stop to break-even once I hit a profit objective. Some traders prefer waiting until the price has moved halfway between T1 and T2, giving the trade more room to breathe. Others prefer to cut risk but not go all the way to break-even. The rule should be developed in preproduction work. This trade would have ended up losing if the stop had not been moved to break-even after hitting the T1. The prior trade would have been only a modest winner and we would have missed out on larger targets if the same stop approach had been used, but then subsequent short setups would have been available. If it were easy, everyone would do it, but this is a resilient trade idea, and there are many ways to get it right, regardless of one's personal trading style. The reason this setup works is because it is based on pure price action and patterns that happen on all charts and time frames over and over again. These patterns result in a predictable outcome and there are rules that take advantage of such an outcome, stacking superior odds on our side from start to finish.

Swing Trading Using the Exhaustion Trade

If you have a keen interest in swing trading and have skipped ahead to this scenario, please do review the preceding section, "Exhaustion Trades," before proceeding into this next lesson. You will be better served if you have a clear and general understanding of exhaustion trade dynamics, tools, and setups.

One of my favorite ways to trade forex is swing trading using daily charts. Once I have my tradeplan established, it only takes five to ten minutes per day to follow the charts. I can literally follow a dozen different pairs while maintaining my "backpack trader" philosophy of freedom through successful trading. I spend a few minutes a day perusing charts, placing trades, canceling trades, and managing trades, usually in the evening right before I begin preparing dinner for the family. I check these trades again in the morning to see if I need to adjust my stop to reduce or eliminate risk. I let my trading tools do the rest for me. When I hit targets, my trading software knows what percentage to liquidate, because I preset it when I place the trade in the first place.

There are pros and cons to swing trading with daily charts. One of the pros is that you don't have to sit and watch the trade play out in real time; this prevents many traders from overreacting and taking impulsive action—that is, getting in their own way. On the con side, these trades are very slow and often it feels like you're not making any progress. It requires a lot of patience. The moves happen when they happen. Another perceived con—which, as you will see in a moment, isn't really a con at all—is the fact that when you're trading off a daily chart, you're going to see some very, very large trades, which many traders will bristle at if they're not yet ready for that level of risk. With forex, however, we have great flexibility in determining the size of our trade. All we need to do with larger size trades is lower our lot size (see chapter 3) and trade with smaller positions. We can use any combination of micro, mini, and full-size lots to maintain our 2% risk limit. Some brokers even allow you to use nano lots, which are fractions of a penny per pip. Don't be intimidated by large trades.

Which trade is riskier: a trade with 10 pips of risk with 2 full-size lots, where 1 pip = $20, or a trade with 100 pips of risk using 2 micro lots, where each pip is worth 20 cents? Do the math: 10 pips x $20 per pip = $200 and 100 pips x $0.20 = $20. The 100-pip trade may have looked scarier initially, but in reality, it's all relative to the size of your actual position.

Some traders might argue that their tradeplan wins a very high percentage of the time and can thus justify higher risk levels, like 3% for example, or even as high as 5% if the trader is using money they can afford to permanently lose. Going from 2% to 3% might not seem like much, but over time, and when factoring in the power of compounding, it can result in huge differences, both on the positive side and the negative. Changes to your plan should be thoroughly analyzed before being executed with real money.

One of the best pieces of advice I've heard is "If it ain't broke, don't fix it." I say that tongue-in-cheek because I'm sure you've heard it too, but if you have a plan that is already making money, then be slow to make changes. Prove that the changes will help and not hurt. You could be surprised, and not in a good way, to learn that your money-making tradeplan, while not perfect, now no longer works because of something you changed or started doing differently. I have found that the pursuit of perfection usually leads to losses.

In the next trading examples, we will use our exhaustion concept, looking for three higher closing bars for a long trade (three lower closing bars for shorts) with another indicator, the high trend chop (HTChop) histogram.

The HTChop histogram is included with your Digital Assets that accompany this book. You can use it with TradeStation, NinjaTrader, MT4, or thinkorswim (TOS). To get access, go to go.quickstartguides.com/forex.

Think of trends (chapter 8) in terms of three categories: there's the fast trend, the intermediate trend, and the long-term or "slow" trend. Seems simple enough, right? On any given chart, the fast trend, as you might imagine, is the movement of the price action in the short term. Even if there is a clear long-term/slow trend movement down, you will almost always observe various fast trends that move upward within a given period in opposition to the persistent slow trend downward. And the intermediate trend is simply faster than the slow trend and slower than the fast trend. It's not that complicated, it's just a convenient way of categorizing various trends on various charts relative to their duration. The high trend chop indicator provides us with a means to visualize trends that are relevant to our trading but are too slow to be perceived on the chart that we're currently using to trade. With this indicator, you can sync the chart you're trading with the slower trend that's also in play, thereby stacking more odds in your favor by trading in sync with the larger waves of price action. That's the edge that the HTChop histogram allows us to exploit.

The HTChop histogram lets us see what the fast trend looks like on a chart that is approximately five times higher (slower) than the chart we're using for our trades. For example, if we are trading a five-minute chart, then the HTChop histogram will describe for us the fast trend on, say, a 25-minute chart.

The fast trend on the higher-time-frame chart will in all likelihood subsume within it a great number of opposing fast trends that could be visible in lower-time-frame charts.

The information about this higher-time-frame fast trend is contained in the histogram itself, which we can easily and conveniently view in real time at the bottom of our candlestick chart (see figure 106). It's convenient in that we don't have to pull our eyes off the chart we're trading to look at another, slower chart. The HTChop histogram puts this information all on one chart. This also makes backtesting the idea much easier.

If we are trading a daily chart, the HTChop histogram will show us the fast trend on a five-day chart, which is about the same as a weekly chart. We can also use the HTChop histogram to help us select an ideal setup bar after we observe the three reversing bars that mark a potential exhaustion. Here are the steps you need to know for this technique:

For Long Trades

First, look for the vertical histogram bars that appear below the zero line. The histogram bars on our HTChop histogram correspond exactly to the candlestick bars directly above them in the main section of the chart. Both types of bars indicate the same increment of time.

In figure 106, you'll see that all the histogram bars, whether they go up from the zero line or down from it, are rendered in black. On your trading platform, however, the bars going up from the zero line will render in blue and the bars going down from the zero line will render in red.

We are looking for a strong clue that the fast trend on a higher-time-frame chart might be reversing, so that it corroborates our three-bar exhaustion pattern. We want to see the fast black line cross over the slower, thicker gray line from below to above. And we want to see this happen when the histogram bars are either negative (in the red) or were very recently negative (just coming back into the blue).

NOTE

In addition to the histogram bars, the lines will also render in color on your trading platform. On my charts, the fast line is cyan and the slow line is yellow.

Once we find the signal we're looking for on the HTChop histogram, the next thing we do is look up to see if there have been three bars that have closed higher than the 0 bar. The setup bar we choose must appear at the same time or after the fast black line has crossed over and closed above the slower gray line on the HTChop histogram.

fig. 106

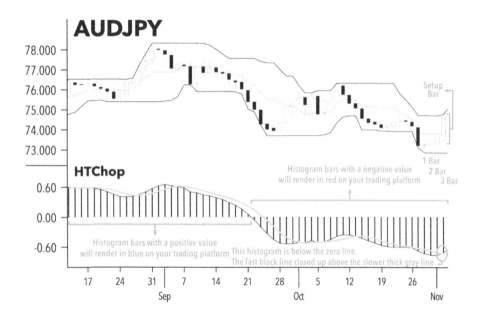

Figure 106 shows the concurrent plotting of the main chart and the histogram. In this approach to the exhaustion trade, I've removed the "exhaustion dots" we used in the previous scenario; we will rely instead on the histogram to trigger our attention, and then we will look for the three reversing closing bars.

It's very important to note that even though we're walking through a swing trade on a daily chart, this approach works just as well with faster time frames. And although we're working with AUD/JPY, this technique can be used with any pair.

As you can see in figure 106, the histogram is below the zero line and has been for over a month. The fast black line has closed above the slower thicker gray line. The top chart shows that three consecutive bars have closed higher than the preceding bar, our 0 bar. Notice also that the next bar, the fourth bar, closed up and above our croc pit line. This is our setup bar.

Let's calculate this long trade. On the faster day trading charts in our earlier examples, we used a 2-pip breakout above the high of the setup bar for the entry (plus any necessary key-level adjustments). Because a daily chart shows a much longer time frame, these trades will scale accordingly. The setup bar itself shows 140 pips of range. Because of the larger scale of the daily chart, I like to see more price action confirmation to establish my entry and stop levels. I typically put my entry 20 pips above the setup bar. You could try something different—but, as always, test it first.

For stops, I use 10 pips below the lowest point of our three higher closing bars. Take a look at figure 107, which shows the same chart as in figure 106 but with the trade setup and targets marked.

fig. 107

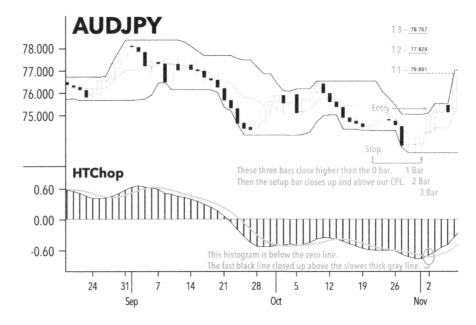

» The high of the setup bar is 75.015, which we will round to 75.02.
» The entry is 20 pips above that, at 75.22 plus spread.
» The lowest point of our three higher closing bars is 73.139, which we will round to 73.14. The stop is 10 pips below, at 73.04.

Just as in our previous examples, we derived our targets from our *x* factor. We obtain the *x* factor in this setup by measuring the distance between the high of our setup bar and the lowest point of bars 1 through 3, and then we add that value of *x* to the high of the setup bar at factors of 1x, 1.5x, and 2x to give us our respective targets of T1, T2, and T3.

T4 and T5 are off the chart due to the scaling of the chart itself, but they have been calculated at 2.5x and 3x.

With large daily charts like this, I like to scale out part of my position at T1. In figure 107, look at how just four bars later (that is, four days later), the bar stabbed right up and through our T1.

T1 = 167 pips of profit. Notice how accurate the bar was that stabbed up to this target level. At this point, it is time to move our stop to break-even and take the risk off the trade. We now have the rest of our position free of any risk, with the potential to make much more should the rally continue.

The move to T1 could have happened at any time, including in the middle of the night. This is why I use my trading platform tools to handle the trading for me. My FX Synergy Trade Manager Interface plugs into MT4, which is connected to my broker. It handles all of this for me. Go to go.quickstartguides.com/forex to find out how to acquire this tool.

We have no reason to think the bullish rally won't continue. The histogram on our HTChop is rising, indicating bullish activity on the "fast trend" of a chart that is five times higher than our chart. We are in sync. We have already banked 167-plus pips of profit minus a tiny spread. The remainder of our position has no risk. Life is good! Best of all, we only have to spend a few minutes per day to check the chart and track our progress as this trade continues. That is the way of the Backpack Trader!

Figure 108 shows how this trade progressed. The price did come down but not quite low enough to hit our break-even stop. Then it turned and proceeded higher. Notice how perfectly each bar stabbed right up to its projected target. The immediate past certainly did a great job of predicting the immediate future, didn't it? One of the best secrets of successful trading is being able to identify price patterns that repeat often and resolve in a way that is predictable most of the time. That's what makes this trading idea so powerful. It checks all the boxes we need to succeed.

GRAPHIC

fig. 108

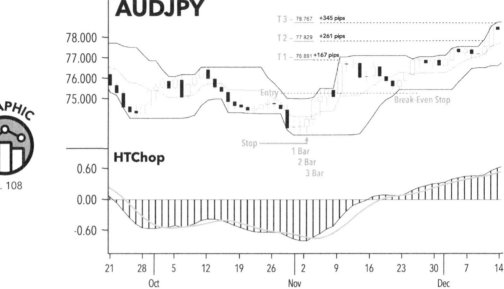

T2 was hit, giving us more than 261 pips. Then two days later, look how perfectly T3 was hit, banking another 345-plus pips. While we shouldn't be surprised at the accuracy of our trade setup targets, it's still gratifying to see that T3 was at 78.77 (rounded) and the high of the bar that hit the target was 78.78! We don't need to squeeze every pip out of a trade, but it's marvelous to capture the entire potential of a trade when the targets prove to be as accurate as these are. More important, it serves to strengthen our foundation of belief in our trade method.

Now look at figure 109; you can see that the next two targets (T4 and T5) were also hit. The gain thus far is 1,763 total pips. The only question is, do we continue to hold out for more, or close out the remainder of our position at the T5 level? There is no right or wrong answer. It's a question of style and preference.

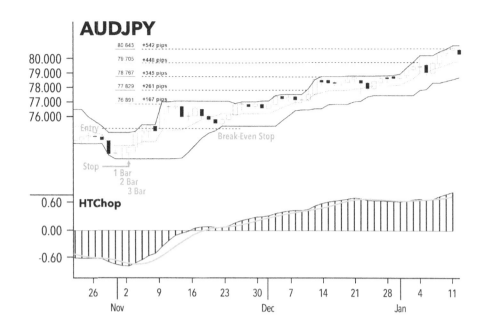

fig. 109

This example gives me a perfect opportunity to point out some trailing stop techniques. First, you can trail a few pips below the CPL. As each bar closes above the CPL, move your stop to a few pips below it. With a larger daily chart like this, 10 to 20 pips below the CPL works pretty well. Notice that this technique would have stopped us out after T3, so we would not have captured the remainder of the larger move higher. In fact, we might have been stopped out after T1, depending on when we activated this technique. While you might sometimes cut your potential too soon with a trailing stop, this strategy can save you if the market turns lower instead of continuing its upward trajectory. It's easy to see after the fact, but that doesn't help. What does help is backtesting, which aids in determining the best course of action. Using your Ultimate Trade Analyzer (UTA) spreadsheet to log your trades and track the various targets and trailing techniques, you can discover (with a large enough sample set of trades for a given pair) the exit locations with the highest average net profit when factoring in all wins and losses over the sample. I think a sample of 75 to 125 trades would be adequate to get the answers you need.

Or you can trail the lower line of the channel. Sometimes this will give back more profit than the aforementioned technique; in our example trade, using this would have kept us in for its full potential while continually locking in profit along the way. Proper backtesting of both trailing techniques would reveal the data you need to make the best decision.

You can also split your trailing position by exiting part of your position just below the croc pit line (CPL) and the rest below the lower channel line. Using a three-bar stop is another popular technique. You merely place your stop 1 or 2 pips below the lowest point of the last three closed bars.

We can also use our HTChop indicator to show what the faster trend on the higher-time-frame chart is doing. If our faster black line is rising above the slower gray line, it indicates we should stay with the trend, especially when the space between the two is widening as the trend accelerates. Alternatively, if the price action begins to diverge from the histogram, that is, the price action is making new higher highs but the histogram is making lower highs, then it's time to start looking for the exit. This is a concept called "divergence." We respond by tightening our stop with a more conservative technique, such as using the CPL as the basis for our trailing stop, or we may even take off all our profits following the gift of a higher price spike.

In the next example, we are looking at another JPY pair, the GBP/JPY. This is an explosive pair that can generate large gains.

GRAPHIC

fig. 110

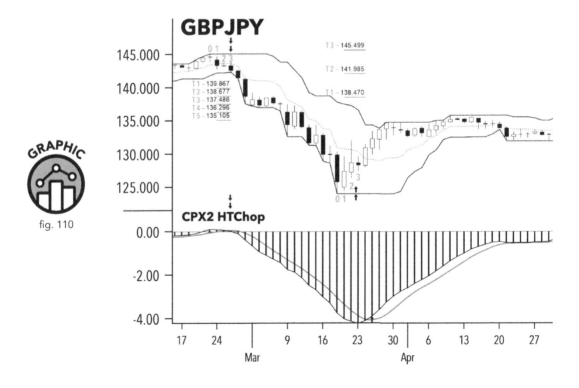

Figure 110 displays two great trades. Notice the short trade shown on the left. The HTChop histogram barely got above the zero line and then the fast black line crossed below the slower gray line. Right at that point in time we can see the third of the three lower closing bars as well as the setup bar (just to the right of bar 3) and the ensuing trade. This trade was a big winner on the short side, leading into the subsequent long trade in the last week of March.

In figure 111, I have added some additional markup that will help us to better understand these trades.

On the short trade, now that we've identified the three lower closing bars and their 0 bar, note that bar 3 closes below our croc pit line. Because it does so, it is our setup bar.

In a short trade, the setup bar is the first bar to close below the CPL, on either the third lower closing bar (bar 3) or up to four bars to the right of bar 3.

fig. 111

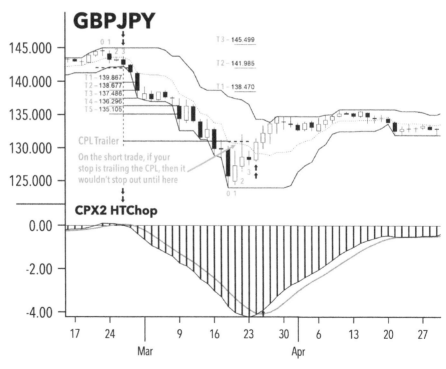

With respect to how we arrived at our targets on the short trade, you should know by now how to set this trade up. But let's walk through it again. The low of the setup bar is 142.248, which we will round down to 142.24. In our day trading examples, we would typically configure our entry 2 pips below the setup bar when going short, but for swing trading purposes, let's expand that to 20 pips, making 142.04 our entry on this trade. And since 142.04 is only 4 pips in front of the major key level of 142.00, I'd like to move my entry down a little bit further to 141.98 or even a bit lower, 141.94. I want to make sure the price action has the necessary selling juice to push lower before triggering me into the trade.

Regardless of the entry adjustment, the trade easily triggers short and proceeds to move through all its targets. As depicted in figure 111, we can also see how well the CPL would have served as the trailing stop. Had we set our trailing stop using the opposite channel line, we would have given back too much in this case.

>   T1 = 139.87 = +207 pips
>   T2 = 138.68 = +326 pips
>   T3 = 137.49 = +445 pips
>   T4 = 136.30 = +564 pips
>   T5 = 135.11 = +683 pips

If we had just let the trade run until it stopped out, using the CPL as an ongoing trailing stop, the trade would have moved 1,104 pips in our favor before stopping out.

While this short trade seems like a relatively small one compared to the long trade that follows, you can see that our approach would have resulted in significant profit. Best of all, trades like this take just a few minutes per day to discover, place, and manage from start to finish.

Now let's look at the long trade that follows, in figure 112. There are a couple of interesting comparisons between this example and the preceding short trade.

First, the HTChop histogram doesn't necessarily reflect the magnitude of its corresponding price action. The short trade just barely had the histogram popping up above the zero line (figure 111). I don't care about the magnitude of the pop, only that it got above the zero. This long trade shows the histogram going very deep and low. I don't care about that either, only that it is below the zero line. The depth doesn't give us additional useful information for this trade.

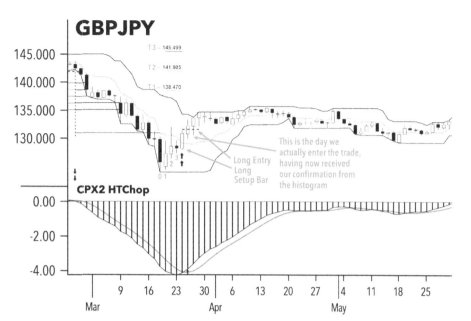

GBPJPY

T 3 – 145.499
T 2 – 141.985
T 1 – 138.470

CPX2 HTChop

This is the day we actually enter the trade, having now received our confirmation from the histogram

Long Entry
Long Setup Bar

fig. 112

In this case, the setup bar occurs one bar after our three-bar exhaustion reversal. As you know, the setup bar in a long setup is the first bar to close above the CPL on either bar 3 or up to four bars to the right of bar 3. Also, notice how the faster black line in our histogram crosses over and closes on the next bar (see the single up arrow near the bottom center of the histogram), one bar after our setup bar. We are keeping our powder dry even though, had we entered immediately prior to the histogram confirmation, we would already be in the trade. Can we take the trade now? Yes! The purpose of our histogram is to offer additional confirmation for this trade setup, and it has done so.

It is certainly possible that a tradeable setup will occur before the histogram confirms our assumption. The histogram can be a little late to the party sometimes, but even if it delays our entry by a day (a bar), the setup remains valid. Notice how the bar that follows after our histogram confirmation would have stabbed down and gone back through our entry from above on a pullback. As long as the price hasn't hit our T1 or gone most of the way toward it (say, 95% of the way), it is okay to take this trade on a pullback. The high of the setup bar is 131.44, making our entry 131.64. Normally I would move my entry a couple of pips above to 131.66 and then add the spread, 131.68.

Notice how the prior short trade only took one bar to blast through the first three targets, just two days after the trade triggered in. This subsequent long trade, however, took much longer. The stop is 10 pips below our setup bar, and, as you can see, nearly two months after triggering long, the trade was still in the doldrums, or what I like to call "no-man's-land." That's the place a trade lives once it triggers in, between its stop and its break-even target. It's also the place that tests most traders' resolve. Inexperienced traders will meddle with their trade while it's in no-man's-land, trying to impact the outcome in their favor. That is the worst thing a trader can do; it leads to the slippery slope of destroying a perfectly good trading method. This is the typical self-sabotaging pattern I see time and again. Experienced traders know that the market has its own rhythm. It's the leader of the dance. We need to go with the flow and let the market lead. The price action itself will tell us what to do. We have our tradeplan, we have our rules. As traders, it is up to us to just lean on the system and let the strategy do its thing. No-man's-land often represents the space and time that the trade needs to develop before launching to our anticipated targets. After all, if we have done our preproduction work correctly, we know the odds are stacked in our favor with every trade we take, as long as we stay out of our own way. When a trade is in no-man's-land, the best thing we can do is nothing at all. Sit on our hands. That proved to be the best thing one could have done for this trade. Patience is often the best tool a trader has.

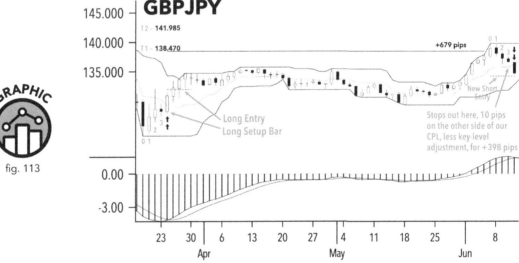

fig. 113

I compressed the chart (figure 113) to show you how, in early June, T1 was finally hit at 138.47 for +679 pips. Again, the target level, tuned to this specific trade, was perfect. Then the buyers became exhausted and the price fell hard. Our CPL would have stopped us out for an additional

398 pips on the remaining three fourths of the position, while also giving us a new short setup bar (see the double down arrows on the right side of figure 113 and in the center of figure 114).

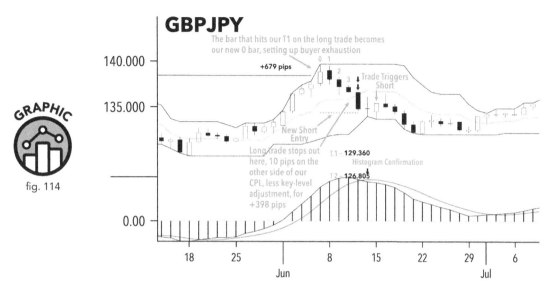

fig. 114

In this short trade setup, the histogram didn't give us our confirmation until one bar past our setup bar. In other words, we wouldn't have placed our order to enter the trade until that bar had closed, in agreement with our histogram confirmation (see where the "trade triggers short" in figure 114). Again, it may seem as if the histogram confirmation is delaying our entry, but we should wait for this important signal to materialize. Two bars after the initial setup and one bar after our histogram confirmation, the price moved down to trigger in this trade.

This short trade, which followed our long T1 winner, was a loser.

This is what a losing trade looks like. The price couldn't get close to its T1 objective (129.36), and instead we notice that the sellers have become tired and the buyers are taking over again (see the seller exhaustion signals labeled in figure 115). In fact, an interesting thing happens. We actually see two seller exhaustion patterns occur one after the other. The first occurrence isn't followed up with a valid setup bar until the fourth bar to the right of bar 3. By that time another seller exhaustion pattern is nearly complete. The price was unable to move high enough to hit the entry of the first setup by the time the new setup formed. When something like this happens, I always like to go with the newer setup, so the first setup should be canceled.

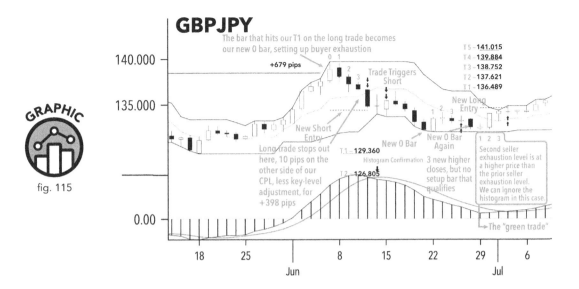

fig. 115

Our pair of actionable seller exhaustion levels occurred before our short trade could reach its full stop-out. Remember, price action is in charge. As explained earlier in this section, we typically want to see our histogram visit the negative side of the zero line before we watch for our long trade confirmation (with the fast black line crossing up and over the slower gray line), but sometimes a longer-term trend is just too strong. Luckily, I have a great rule for dealing with this. I call it the "green trade." It's easy to understand, and I'll explain it to you here.

When you get a seller exhaustion level equal to or at a higher price level than one seller exhaustion level prior (to the left), you can ignore the histogram altogether. This is easy to visualize if you think of our basic definition of an uptrend: when price action is marking higher swing highs and higher swing lows. In figure 115, the second seller exhaustion level is marking a higher swing low than did the first. I have found these trades to be incredibly effective, especially early in a new trend, as is the case in our current example (figure 115).

Sometimes the first exhaustion setup will have a setup bar but will be unable to break out enough to hit our entry level, as in our current example. We can place a trade using the new setup and without the need of a histogram. We are using basic trend analysis (rather than the histogram) as our confirming information. The new exhaustion level coming at a higher level than the prior exhaustion level is all the confirmation we need.

Remember, the exhaustion level is a simple pattern where we have three higher-closing bars to the right of a 0 bar, as we defined earlier for this setup. Then we need a bar to close up and above our CPL, on either the third bar that finishes our exhaustion pattern or up to four bars to the right. In figure 115, you can see that the price was unable to push up and hit the entry on the first setup, with the setup bar coming on the fourth bar following our bar 3. The entry would have been hit on the very next bar, but a new setup, a "green trade," occurs, which immediately cancels the prior setup, and that trade does move the needed 20 pips above its setup bar (because this is a daily swing trade chart, we're using a 20-pip entry offset, adjusting if needed around key levels) and triggers into a new long trade.

But what happens if this pattern occurs when we are already in an opposite trade (we're still going short, for instance, in figure 116 when the green trade manifests). This is actually quite a common occurrence. As traders, all we can do is just let the market take the lead. We use our well-defined and tested mechanical rules to guide us through this ever-changing dance.

The dance changes when our short position is called into question amid the new seller exhaustion patterns. This sets up the dreaded (though it shouldn't be) and often misunderstood stop and reverse technique, which was explained at great length a little while ago. I say "dreaded" because inexperienced traders tend to view losing trades as a bad thing. Not all losing trades are created equal, however, and if you are following your proven tradeplan, then a losing trade is just another necessary business transaction along the pathway to ultimate success. We have to follow the dance.

Stop and reverses happen all the time. They are inextricable from routine trading.

I don't mind a stop and reverse and, actually, with the techniques that I like to use, they often prove beneficial, cutting the loss on the trade I'm in and flipping me over to the setup with the better odds of succeeding. After all, as in this case, we were short, the sellers became exhausted, and the buyers started pulling sellers into the crocodile pit. I'd rather get out before being pulled in and join the winning side. Wouldn't you?

With our stop and reverse technique, we want to ask for a little more confirmation before "crying uncle" on the short trade and jumping ship to join the buyers with our new long setup. I will therefore add an additional 10 to 20 pips to the long entry, depending on the size of the new long trade. In this case (figure 116) it is quite large, with hundreds of pips between the current price and my long targets. I am very comfortable adding another 20 pips to the entry. *This entry will then become my new stop for the short.* The short trade stops and reverses into a long trade at this price, giving me the additional price action confirmation I need.

The result is that the losing short trade's losses are greatly reduced while the price is being swung around by our powerful dance partner into a new long trade that ends up winning big (see figure 116).

Nothing is ever perfect in trading, as we just witnessed firsthand with the losing short trade. However, we were able to quickly identify the change in market direction to avoid what would have been a much larger loss. Take a close look at the first three targets in the next long trade, figure 116. While nothing is 100% perfect in trading, these targets were well tuned, each one being hit with near perfection.

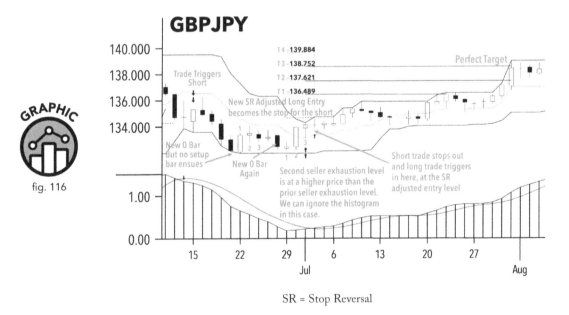

fig. 116

SR = Stop Reversal

The setup bar's high was 134.226 rounded to 134.23. The unadjusted entry would therefore be 20 pips above, at 134.43. We will add another 20-pip adjustment to help convince us it's time to bail out of our losing short trade and jump onto the winning long trade, 134.63 + 2 pips of spread, 134.65. Remember, we do not make key-level adjustments after we apply our spread. There are no key-level or chart-level adjustments needed in this case.

Sometimes the price isn't able to push high enough to cause us to reverse, which is why we make the additional adjustment. When it can't push through, it gives us the opportunity to stay in the original trade, which still has a chance of winning. In this case, however, the adjustment did its job, insisting that the buyers had enough energy to push the price high enough to reverse our position. We ended up paying an additional premium for this added price action confirmation—40 more pips, 20 extra on the stop and 20 more on the reversing entry. (We're not counting the spread as part of this additional premium because we would have to pay that on the exit of our short in any case.) However, this premium gives us unique value. If the price had been unable to rise high enough to hit our adjusted stop and reverse entry, we would have been able to stay with the short trade. Earlier, I referred to this as an "insurance policy." It could keep us in our original trade, or, as in this scenario, we pay a small premium but we gain the additional price action confirmation we need to convince us to jump off the sinking ship and onto the winning side. It's a price worth paying, in other words, because of the unique value it gives.

The trade flips over to long and runs to big profits, hitting not three, but four perfect targets (figure 117).

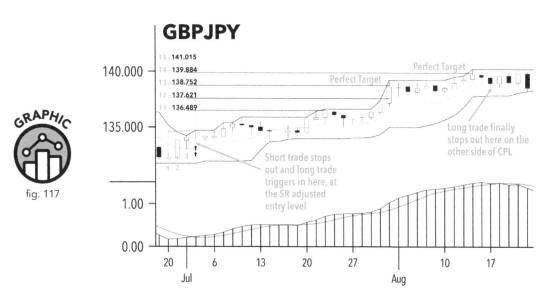

fig. 117

Let's look at our costs and our gains on this stop and reverse:

Loss on the short trade:
- » Entry was 134.27
- » Reversing stop was 134.65
- » Loss = -38 pips x 100% of the position

The original stop on this short trade was 139.78 after a minor chart adjustment, plus 2 pips of spread, making the total initial risk 551 pips. Our stop and reverse got us out of a trade in which we would have lost 551 pips on the entire position—for only 38 pips!

Profit on the long trade:
- » T1 = 136.49 = +184 pips
- » T2 = 137.62 = +297 pips
- » T3 = 138.75 = +410 pips
- » T4 = 139.88 = +523 pips
- » CPL trailer = 138.81 = +416 pips

The prior short had an original trade with 551 pips of risk from entry to stop, including the spread. Due to our stop and reverse, we were able to escape with just a 38-pip loss instead of a full loss on the trade. We moved our stop from the original location of 139.78 to the adjusted entry of the new long trade, the "reversing long entry" location.

Don't be afraid of stop and reverses. Being able to cut our full risk of 551 pips down to a loss of just 38 pips is money in the bank. It saved us 513 pips. Then we flipped over to a winning trade that hit four large targets while also capturing a nice trailing stop. The reversing trade gained 1,830 total pips with a five-position trade.

- » The loss was 38 pips x 5 positions = -190 pips instead of -2,755 pips!
- » The reversing long trade made +1,830 pips.
- » Net of the two-trade sequence = +1,640 pips of profit. Not bad.

Though we ended up winning on this stop and reverse, it's important to keep in mind that you will inevitably encounter some stop and reverses that lose on both sides of the trade. Nothing is perfect in trading. Don't lose your cool. Stick to your trade plan.

The exhaustion trade setup has served me well over the years and is one of my best trade setups. I want to give you plenty of examples so you can learn it well and hopefully employ it in your own forex trading. In fact, this setup works so well that it's the primary one I use to this day, with my Spotlight FX Swing Trade Alert service. Using this setup on slow-moving swing trade charts, we tie everything together, sending out live alerts in real time to subscribers as exhaustion setups occur and progress from start to finish. Using our "snapshot" techniques as taught earlier, subscribers enjoy the fact that they can place and manage their trades at times that are most convenient for them. Best of all, this style of trading requires only about 10 minutes, on average, per day. I have worked out a special arrangement with Clydebank Media to offer this service at a special discount to any reader of this book who wishes to subscribe.

Chapter Recap

» An understanding of the exhaustion trade is an invaluable tool for traders looking to cultivate their edge. You should locate and use the tools available to help you visualize possible exhaustion scenarios.

» Don't lose your nerve when your tradeplan faces a stop and reverse scenario. It's common in trading, and if you relax and let the market lead the dance, you can reduce your losses from the stop while making big gains on the reversal, all while gaining additional protection with your "insurance policy."

| 15 |

Trading and Digging Ditches

Chapter Overview

» Building a strong foundation
» Understanding your trading psychology
» Following a "rites of passage" action plan

Trading is a business, and you are the CEO. It is also a profound psychological test. Even the best trading system will fail due to poor money management, panicky trading, greed, or simply not following your proven tradeplan rules, which violates the system in the first place.

New traders always ask me what the best system is, which patterns and pairs are sure things, and what tips I have to give them an edge. I always tell them to concentrate on the foundation first. Until a trader digs the ditches necessary to create a strong foundation, all the rest is moot.

A strong trading foundation has three components. The first is a coherent trading methodology. You need a methodology that you understand and have tested enough to ensure it works. The second component is the building of sound risk and money management habits—your trade strategy, in other words. The third component, and the one that is arguably the most difficult to master, is an understanding of your own psychological makeup in order to overcome fear and other emotions that will try to get in your way. Let's take a look at those three components in greater detail.

Trade Methodology

Trade methodology is the logic used in placing and closing trades. It shapes the edge that the trader has over the market. It is honed through practice. As you see how your plan works, you will grow in confidence and believe in it. Your strategy is your starting point. You prove it through backtesting (testing your plan against data from the past) and forward testing (reviewing and tracking your ongoing results). You should also apply your plan in simulated trading, which allows you to practice your trade executions without real money at stake. You should continue to track your trades with sim trading and evaluate your results before you earn the rite of passage to trade with real money.

The edge puts the odds in your favor. But what is this edge? Your edge is your empirically proven results, showing that your trading plan is going to generate gains for you over time. Good methodology allows you to control what you can control—things like key-level adjustments, accounting for spread, selecting and using setup bars to define stops and targets—all with the goal of building consistent tradeplans with a testable, provable winning edge. The winning plans—the ones that you will put real money behind—will emerge through that testing and refinement. You'll move from a carefully tested plan, measurable results, and a long series of sim trades into real trading with confidence.

But before we proceed, let's return to the question "What is the edge?" The edge is the statistical advantage of your tradeplan over the market, an advantage that you prove to yourself in every respect through disciplined testing, live sim trading, and continual tracking and monitoring of your results.

It is important not to overlook the fact that all this preproduction work, testing, sim account trading, etc., (what I call ditch digging) allows you to build a personal conviction regarding the value of your methodology. This conviction will help you execute with confidence and accuracy and will steel you against the intrusion of destructive emotions. Without that confidence in a solid trading foundation, most people quit at the exact wrong time.

Tracking Your Trades

An essential part of developing and using a trade methodology is keeping track of your trades. A notebook or regular spreadsheet can work, but the UTA (Ultimate Trade Analyzer) spreadsheet is a valuable power tool for this process. For each trade placed, take note of the following:

- » The date
- » The time of entry
- » The pair, the price, and the trade (long or short)
- » The position size
- » The stop
- » The exit price

The Ultimate Trade Analyzer (UTA) spreadsheet allows for simple, convenient trade tracking. It be accessed for free at go.quickstartguides.com/forex.

The trade log has two benefits. First, it forces you to think about every trade that you place. Second, it gives you data you can use to refine your trading methodology. Make changes slowly and carefully (or not at all if it's working). When you have a system that works, lean on that system.

As you witness the fruits of your preproduction work manifest in the form of your winners overtaking your losers, you should continually build more and more belief in the system you've been researching. Working with a power tool like the UTA gives you the ability to create a win/loss column that makes clear the random distribution of wins and losses; in this way you can experience the good, the bad, the ugly, and the great, while also witnessing your equity curve grow despite the ugly. It is the repeated experience of this exercise that builds the foundation of belief and transforms someone into a trader rather than just someone trying to trade. It is the most important thing you can do—and those that don't usually struggle endlessly. You can't control the random distribution of trade results, but you can control the plan that grows your equity, despite said random results. A proven tradeplan is your valuable edge.

Risk and Money Management

Risk is an essential tool that we as traders need in order to make money. It's also a dangerous tool, and the way a trader deploys it will determine their degree of success or failure. If you don't risk enough, there is no way to make money, even if you win a lot. If you risk too much, there's no way you can win either, because when losing trades happen (and they will), you will lose a lot of money, even with the winningest strategies and tradeplans.

Risk tolerance is something that each trader must come to grips with. We are all different. But even if you believe your risk tolerance to be sufficient for trading, you might be surprised when you actually have real money at stake.

Having real money at risk can cause people to do all kinds of strange and misguided things to influence the outcome of their trade—which typically leads to the unpleasant and ironic self-fulfilling prophecy of losing. They expend pointless energy attempting to control something that they ultimately cannot control—the market itself. This happens over and over again with traders who have not built up their foundation. They don't believe in what they're doing and are destined to fail. This is what I call risk aversion, rather than risk tolerance. When a trader is overtrading their account with too large of a position size or too many trades, not knowing when to quit their session, the way they feel, behave, and react to the risk they are experiencing will reveal much about them. If they pay attention, these reactions can instruct them in what they need to focus on in order to solve these issues—usually pointing to the need to go back and put more work and effort into their foundation.

In general, successful traders have more risk tolerance than the average person, because they have built their foundation to the point where they have established an unwavering belief in their entire trade strategy and tradeplan.

For whatever reason, some people love risk so much that they cannot manage it. These people are gamblers, not traders. Trading is a poor substitute for gambling, and a desire to gamble is one of many wrong reasons to explore trading. In gambling, the house has the edge. In trading, you should have the edge, and the time and effort you put into your preproduction work, building your foundation, is how you prove it and believe in it. You want to trade with the house odds on your side.

Risk tolerance comes from understanding what you can actually risk without putting yourself in a bad place should you lose. In other words, risk no more than you can afford to lose. Otherwise, you're putting too much pressure on yourself. Your tradeplan should have risk management rules, like my recommendation of 2% of your trading capital on a proven tradeplan trade, for example. If you overtrade your account, you will become the person afraid of the trade. This will lead to bad decisions and losses. Human beings are not wired for trading and will do anything they can to avoid losses—which, ironically, leads straight to losses.

Here's the reality: all successful trading systems are about stacking the odds on your side. With proper risk and money management, the odds do all the heavy lifting for us. We work through some losing trades so that we can get to the winners and thus grow our accounts. In fact, in trying to avoid the losing trades that result inside of a winning tradeplan, we will avoid the winning trades too and be left without a tradeplan at all! It's a pure numbers game. That's why we need proven tradeplans that show positive measurable results. With this proof, we can take ownership of our trading, because we develop belief in our tradeplan and what it will produce if we just stick with it. That makes all the difference.

The power of the tradeplan is in its cumulative effect. It is not concerned with the result of a single trade or series of trades. It's built on a large enough sample set that allows us to survive the random distribution of wins and losses as the overall equity curve grows.

Your goal is to make money. You need to put money at risk to do so but not without a sensible risk management method. Position sizing, as was discussed in chapter 13, and trading with predefined stop losses, are nonnegotiable. These are rules that must be defined by your proven tradeplan and then consistently executed trade after trade, per the tradeplan rules.

You may be thinking, What happens when I see a sure thing, a can't-miss trading opportunity that doesn't come along every day? Shouldn't I place everything on that trade (and more, with leverage) and make a boatload of money?" No. You shouldn't. That's what gamblers do, not successful traders. "Sure things" rarely are. People lose money on sure things all the time. And one lost sure thing can end your trading career. Nonetheless, as you gain experience as a trader, it is okay to take a flyer on a "trade of opportunity" that you have learned to identify, using the proper risk management we've been talking about. Trades of opportunity present themselves sometimes, offering superior odds, but the idea of superior odds is not the equivalent of a sure thing. Good trades still lose sometimes.

The market can remain irrational longer than you can remain solvent.
— A. GARY SCHILLING

With good risk management, a very small edge can pay off through the power of compounding. Your small gains, bit by bit, steadily grow your account while controlling drawdown, eventually allowing you to safely increase your position size. That's what trading with an edge does for you.

The Importance of Trading Psychology

Traders work alone against a market that does not know and does not care who they are or what they are doing. Trading is thus very different from most businesses. Even people working remotely check in with coworkers and clients over the phone or online during the day; traders, meanwhile, are alone in the purest sense.

This makes trading a lonely business, one where traders find it easy to become distracted. Maintaining one's attention on price movement—or worse, the lack thereof—proves far more challenging than most new traders imagine. Waiting, watching, hoping, and trying to maintain focus while the markets seem to have fallen asleep can be exhausting, stretching your attention span to the brink. Faster-moving markets present their own set of challenges, with prices moving at head-spinning rates. When it comes to building your focal abilities and coping with the loneliness of the work environment, these are skills that neither I nor anyone else can teach you. You have to live through it yourself and acquire such skills. Well-tested, tight tradeplans that are designed to account for these challenges as they relate to a trader's personal situation are the key to solving this common trader dilemma.

The survival impulse, a very basic element of the human psyche, is another factor that makes trading challenging on a mental level. Simply put, humans are not wired to be traders. It is an entirely unnatural act. To be successful, you must fail on a regular basis, enduring some random losses courtesy of a winning tradeplan you spent weeks or months creating and testing. Humans are evolved to avoid pain, and losing trades equates to pain for inexperienced traders. And in their efforts to avoid pain, human beings are prone to doing things that are detrimental and even fatal to their trading, such as amending or throwing out their proven tradeplans on the fly after a string of losses (see figure 84 from chapter 13).

Luckily, there are techniques you can use to achieve a trader's mentality. It will take work, but that work will help you overcome the psychological hurdles that prevent so many people from becoming true traders. You must be committed to the process and do each step, earning the right to pass on to the next step (see the Rites of Passage Action Plan later in this chapter). If you follow these steps while maintaining a high level of self-awareness (see below), you will emerge in the strongest, most advantageous position you can possibly be in, with the best chances of succeeding.

Would-be traders who fail to master their psychology will not be traders for long.

Know Why You Are Trading

Let's face it: traders trade to make money—or at least they should. You might think that's a given, but I often encounter would-be traders who are doing it for other reasons. They may not be aware of these reasons, but I see them as clear as day. Trading represents something else to them, beyond just a vehicle for making money: they're trying to trade to prove that they're smart or that they're capable. Sounds innocent enough, but I'm telling you, that's a problem. Your only reason for trading should be to make money, not for self-validation.

The two traders that we have been following illustrate the point. Harvey is driven by ego. He gets upset by what he cannot control. For him, trading is about validating his ego. This is why his emotions so often get the better of him and derail his trading. Trish, on the other hand, is humble. She knows that trading is about making money. Not proving your genius, not curing cancer, not making happy family memories, just making money. This attitude allows her to accept that the market is in control, and if she pays attention and executes on her proven tradeplan, she can profit from it. She puts her entire focus and energy into what she can control, the planning and execution of trades. She quickly casts aside the agony and the ecstasy of the losses and the wins, because dwelling on them (either of them) will only bring trouble.

Q: What's wrong with celebrating a big trading win?

Nothing—so long as you know that you're not there to win on a trade. You're there to make money. Do you recognize the difference? Your wins are a part of that, but so are your losses. This is the cold hard truth known by every successful trader.

Like anything in life, your actions matter more than your words. You can put all the powerful indicators you want onto a chart, and it won't amount to anything until you're ready to take full ownership of why you are trading in the first place. The things you think, the things you say to yourself under your breath, are meaningless. It's what you do that matters. That is your most relevant indicator, far more valuable than anything you put on your charts. Is your reason for trading truly to make money? And are your actions congruent with that reason? This is the starting point for fixing all trading problems and from which to launch a successful trading business.

If your reason is the right one, and the only one, then prove it with your actions. Get your preproduction right, lay your foundation, prove your plan works, practice it until it becomes a reflex, and then execute your plan per your proven rules.

And on any given day, if you start thinking that this next trade is going to be the one that will make you feel better, that will make you cash-positive for the day, that will prove you right, that will impress the people you knew in high school, that will make your dad respect your lifestyle choices… if you find yourself thinking these or similar things, then it's time to quit trading for the day. Maybe even forever, unless you can move beyond those thoughts. The more emotion that gets into the mix, the greater the likelihood of failure. Traders working from emotion ignore their risk limits and ignore what the charts are telling them. They make terrible trading decisions. They will not be trading for long. It would be so much easier and far less painful if they would just send me the money directly!

GRAPHIC

fig. 118

REMEMBER WHAT YOU...	
CAN'T CONTROL	**CAN CONTROL**
You **can't** control the rhythm of price action or the market.	You **can** control how you dance with said rhythm, and this is where you want to place your focus.

Self-Awareness Pays Off

The goal is to be the trader, not the person trying to trade. How do you get there?

Usually, if a trader is afraid of trading it means they are uncomfortable with their anticipated risk levels. They are risking too much, often because they have not done any of the preproduction work needed to demonstrate that their tradeplan will make money. To have any hope of succeeding, a trader needs to trust the tradeplan. I find that the best way to deal with doubt, fear, and greed is to trade smaller and set smaller goals that are easier to achieve. Take note of the feeling, and then put it aside to concentrate on executing the tradeplan in a sim account or with smaller positions. The more work you do to test your tradeplan, the easier this will be. Keep working on practicing and building proof. In the end, your strong trader foundation is really the belief you build in your tradeplan. You have to believe in it to execute it and benefit from it. You can't talk yourself into this belief. You have to follow the steps if you truly hope to build a strong foundation that you can rely on.

The 5-Point Rites of Passage Action Plan

We are nearing the end of the book, so it's time to summarize what I like to call the 5-Point Rites of Passage Action Plan. It is designed to help you learn to trade and start trading effectively. There are never any guarantees with trading, but it will set you up to be in the most advantageous position you can be in for ongoing success, which puts you in a better place than a majority of traders. Are you ready to do this? If so, read on.

Master Your Method

The first step is to master the method. There are a lot of trading systems out there. Whichever method you choose, you will need to commit to learning its techniques. In this book we've reviewed several sample trades that illustrate some excellent price action patterns that set up outstanding trade opportunities. Those particular setups present a great starting point, and for some of you, it might be all you need. The exhaustion trade setup I taught you in the last chapter, for example, could be the foundation of a full-fledged trade methodology and tradeplan. Learning and using my ideas can help you get started, but with more experience you'll eventually come up with ideas of your own (as you should). With your money at stake, you shouldn't just take my word for it that these setups work. You need to test them for yourself, so that you develop your own belief and conviction. Don't try to do too much too fast. Keep things simple. I would rather see you master one effective technique than jump around from one method to the next, as so many people do, in search of perfection—which doesn't exist anyway. Most would-be traders fall into that trap, and I want you to avoid it from the start. Like Rome, a successful trading business isn't built in a day. Focus on building your foundation first. Choose your method and then set out to prove it to yourself. You may learn it's not the one for you, but through a process of elimination you will arrive at the method that best suits your needs.

Using Manual Backtesting to Track Your Trades

Some trading platforms offer automated backtesting tools. These can be helpful for testing many things with various "canned" indicators, trading methods, and strategies, but they are not for beginner traders. They can help us answer big, high-level questions, which can be of benefit, often pointing us in the right direction. But they can also be wolves in sheep's clothing, tricking us into thinking that we can use said automation to backtest a possible method and then have it place trades automatically; thus we fall prey to the dream of pushing a button and having a robot trade for us. But that rarely works. And rather than simplifying things, automation often complicates them.

In fact, automation can be a big distraction and can do more harm than good. When testing and optimizing parameters, there is a significant risk of "curve fitting" of which you should be aware. The algorithm might find a solution that works for a given set of data, but that doesn't mean it's logical or will work in the future, and in all likelihood it won't. Think about trying to use a knitted glove on a number of different-sized hands. You might be able to force it on some hands, some of the time, but it won't be comfortable—and if you stretch it out to fit one hand, it might be too big for the next one. One size does not fit all, even if it sometimes works. The market is that series of hands; the size doesn't stay consistent. I'm sorry if I'm dashing your dreams, but if I don't do it here, the markets will do it, and that won't end well for you.

There are other flaws of automated backtesting that go beyond the scope of this book. But the biggest flaw, for our purposes, is that you lose the opportunity to experience the random distribution of wins and losses while in the trenches, which is where your belief is developed. That's why it's best to build your trader foundation with manual backtesting. This is where you really learn what to expect from your trading method. Studying the attractive results of a performance report generated by automation is not going to give you this important ingredient. Intellectually, you will see nice numbers, but none of the other aspects that would build belief and put your psychology where it needs to be will be present.

Backtesting can be a time-consuming process, and many traders resist doing it for that reason. I was one of those traders. For the longest time I either procrastinated or flat-out refused to do this necessary grunt work, to my great detriment. What changed my way of thinking was hearing a successful trader, whom I respected, say that she would never consider risking a single penny until she had manually entered at least 600 trades in a spreadsheet so that she could, in essence, prove to herself that the method was going to make her money. She had to see that the rules of the tradeplan would survive the ever-changing market conditions that occur day after day, moment after moment, bar after bar.

Hearing that from her left a lasting impression on me. At the time, I was following the rules of a proven method but not finding any success.

The method had been proven by someone else, and whenever there was a trade setup, I would second-guess it and find reasons why the setup was not going to work. Before I knew it, I wasn't trading the method at all. What was I trading? Who knows, but it wasn't working and I was losing. It is nearly impossible to stick to rules that you yourself do not understand. The only way to understand a tradeplan or method, and the edge it gives you, is by manually backtesting it yourself. This is where all the "aha" moments happen.

So, yes, manual backtesting is time-consuming, but it is critically important. You invest your time in hopes of creating something that will make you money in the future. Warren Buffett said the best investment one can make is the investment in oneself. Backtesting falls into that category.

I have developed a simple three-step method that helps you economize your time while also prequalifying what you actually should commit your time to by way of a thorough and more formal backtest. Skipping these three steps is risky, because you might spend many hours backtesting something only to learn what you should not do. I refer to my method as the Three-Step Sniff Test:

1. **Step One – Determine whether the tradeplan you are considering will present enough trades in your selected session**. A great tradeplan isn't going to do you much good if you're never able to fully deploy it. Study the charts that correspond to the trading sessions you will be participating in. Are there enough trades available to make your tradeplan viable?

While you want to ensure that you have an adequate number of trades for a given session, keep in mind that it's also possible for strategies-to-be to trigger into too *many* trades, creating a noisy chart and a lot of costs by way of commissions, slippage, and greater risk of trader errors.

2. **Step Two – Determine whether the trades available in your prospective tradeplan are sized appropriately for your risk management strategy**. If your tradeplan presents ample trading opportunities but requires you to risk way more than your 2% level (chapter 13) or whatever other risk allotment you adhere to,

then it's not viable. Similarly, the risk levels may be too *small*, and deploying the tradeplan may not be worth the time and effort (see previous note).

Risk is calculated by determining the dollar amount lost in the distance from your entry to your stop.

3. **Step Three, the "Fast Test" – Determine whether you can quit your trading session with a positive outcome most of the time.** While steps one and two can be evaluated in a matter of minutes, a good fast test can take several hours. Fast-testing is the prequalifier for your backtesting, which is more extensive. In a nutshell, it is simply analyzing your proposed strategy in your proposed session, tracking your parameters (what pair are you trading, which chart are you trading, start time, stop time, etc.), and determining the rate at which sessions result in a positive (winning) outcome. In the case of swing trading, where the trading session is moot, we can use the fast test to quickly count winning and losing trades.

I recommend fast-testing several tradeplan ideas and letting the best candidates present themselves to you. Check out my other book, *Day Trading QuickStart Guide* from ClydeBank Media, for a detailed walk-through of how I apply the fast test to the crude oil futures market using the same exhaustion setup explained in the previous chapter (see figure 119). The same methodology carries over into forex trading.

Once you have identified the tradeplans most likely to prove viable, then you are ready to begin the work of manually backtesting these plans. The backtesting process is time-consuming, but it's critical to developing belief in your plan and teaching you the random distribution of wins and losses, while also showing you how your equity curve will grow and grow, despite said randomness. Since losing trades are what typically derail traders, despite their being a normal part of a winning tradeplan, this process is one of the most important things you can do if you hope to build a lasting and successful trading business. There are other benefits as well. Backtesting tests and refines your knowledge of your own tradeplan, and it helps you identify where you need to fine-tune your approach. Perhaps most important, it enhances your ability to separate your emotions from your trading as you continue to witness the equity curve in the overall trade results go up. No matter how experienced a trader you are or become, backtesting and forward testing should never cease to be a key part of your repertoire.

Fast-Testing	Example	Notes
Contract symbol	CL	December-Z20
Chart type	8-tick momentum bar	
Start time	10:00 am	EIA report is Wednesday
Stop time	10:59 am	2 ticks above the setup bar
Entry rules	'xyz' strategy	2 ticks above the setup bar
Exit rules	'xyz' strategy	Begin trailing the 'special line' when the price gets 90% to target
Trade management rules	'xyz' strategy	
Min # of trades (per session)	3	
Max # of losses (per session)	2	
Session goals	Target 2 winner	Or two break-even trades
Session win/BE rate	75% – 80% or better	

fig. 119

A sample fast-testing table. For a more detailed breakdown of fast-testing methodology, check out *Day Trading QuickStart Guide.*

I've included the Ultimate Trade Analyzer (UTA) spreadsheet with your Digital Assets. The UTA is one of the most powerful and important tools you can use to become a successful trader. I suggest you use it for all your backtesting, forward testing, and tradeplan development. Go to go.quickstartguides.com/forex for access.

Using Demos to Hit the Perfect 25 Trades

Once your tradeplan is developed and you are confident that it would increase the equity in your account, take it to the next step and start working in a demo account. Most forex brokers allow you to place demo trades, which are like regular trades in every way except that they do not involve actual money. This will allow you to test your ability to properly place trades without error—the primary use of a sim account. You get the added benefit of being able to track your tradeplan results going forward, as you test your method and your plan in actual markets, while proving that you can indeed execute your plan as the CEO, which in my view is the second most significant reason to use a sim account. You will want to see that the results you achieved in your backtest continue to hold up, but also that you can consistently execute your plan without mistakes.

Set a goal of making 25 consecutive perfect trades. Just like with your backtest results, you will experience a random distribution of wins and losses. That's okay. Losing trades that are properly placed according to the rules of your tradeplan are not mistakes. What we are looking for here is whether you can place your tradeplan trades 25 times in a row without making any mistakes. That means adhering to the proper position size, stop loss, entry point and exit points, and managing the trade properly from start to finish.

What constitutes a mistake? Well, if you got a little confused, spilled coffee on the keyboard, or had a "fat finger" error, start back at number one. If something distracts your attention and causes you to do anything but execute your trade perfectly from start to finish, it should be considered a mistake. Getting bored and then attending to emails, answering the door when the UPS man delivers your long-awaited gizmo, or being distracted when your significant other marches into your trading office to remind you to take out the garbage should all be considered mistakes if they keep you from executing your trade perfectly. Even if you're not flustered by external factors, you could be distracted by getting hungry or needing to use the bathroom. Distraction in one way or another will knock at your door every day, if not every five minutes. You need to come up with solutions for anything that prevents you from executing your proven tradeplan trades properly.

Achieving your 25 consecutive perfectly executed trades is going to go a long way in teaching you what you need to know about trading with real money. If you can't do it in a sim account, what makes you think you'll be able to do it with your hard-earned cash on the line?

In the demo account, you are practicing trading as you intend to trade. Analyze the mistakes you make. Do you see any commonalities that you can address? Are your tools adequate? Have you communicated to everyone in your life that you are not to be disturbed when you're running your trading business?

Moving Up to Real Money

After you have placed 25 consecutive mistake-free trades in your demo account, it's time to move up to trading with real money. In theory, this should be exactly the same as trading in a demo account, but some traders find that their psychology is different when working with actual cash. You need to see if and how you're affected when trading with your real money.

When starting with real money, use only the absolute minimum position size. Rather than calculating a position size, trade in minimum lots until you have placed 25 consecutive perfect trades, per the rules of your tradeplan. Again, they do not have to be winners, but they need to be executed correctly from start to finish.

Some traders reach 25 consecutive trades right off the bat. Others find that it takes several months. That's okay. Just keep trading and stay true to your goal of accomplishing 25 consecutive mistake-free real-money trades. This practice will build discipline and help you grow into the successful trader you want to become. And as you do this diligently and persistently, your account value should begin to grow as well.

After executing 25 perfect trades at a minimum size, you will have earned the rite of passage to move up to the varsity team, trading at a risk level that is comfortable for you, 2% for example. Keep tracking your trades in your UTA spreadsheet, building your trade log, and reviewing your performance.

Periodically, take some time to evaluate how your trades have performed. Did you stick to your plan for all of them? What happened when you didn't stick to the plan? Many traders find it useful to actually keep two separate UTA spreadsheets: one that contains all the trades from the tradeplan and another that contains the trades they actually took. You can learn so much from this. Over time, both trade logs should become like carbon copies of one another. Can you do it? Here's how you will hold yourself accountable to truly find out.

Setting Goals to Keep Getting Better

The key to successful long-term trading is to treat it like a business. As with any business, you want to set goals, identify areas for ongoing investment, and make a plan to retire.

As your trading improves, start setting profit goals. As you hit each goal, reward yourself and then commit to investing in your business to reach the next goal. Maybe you want to add a new tradeplan, increase your position size following your risk and money management plan, invest in new training programs or better trading tools. Whatever it is, you should think about your next milestone and how your business is going to progress once you hit that milestone.

As your account grows, pay yourself. It may take a while for your account balance to be large enough for you to do this, but eventually, consider pulling out a salary. A good profit goal is to grow your account to the point where you can pay yourself a $10,000 monthly salary, beginning with $1,000 per month and incrementally giving yourself raises as your account grows, until you hit the $10,000-per-month milestone. Remember, this is best accomplished not by trading more but by using the power of compounding with your tested and proven tradeplan. If trading is a business, then the employees (you) need to be paid. Also set up a "walking away" fund, money kept in other diversified investments. This will allow you to quit trading at a time when you are ready to do so.

Finally, don't forget about the goal of enjoying what you do. Trading suits my lifestyle, and I know it will suit other people as well. That's why I teach and promote it.

Chapter Recap

» A strong trading foundation is based on building belief. We cannot control the outcome of a trade. We can control how we trade, what we trade, and whether or not we go through the proper steps of building a tradeplan we can prove and practicing it until perfect.

» Managing risk and return is critical. Over the long run, being smart beats out being lucky in the market.

» Develop a trading system that works for you with the techniques described in this book. Plan your trade, trade your plan, and then record the results in the UTA.

» Periodically review your UTA results, and refine your system if and when it is necessary to do so. With a great method and tradeplan, you may find that you never need to change anything. Just lean on the system and let it do its thing.

» Remember that trading is a business.

Conclusion

On a basic level, all you have to do to get started in forex is open an account and place a trade. While you may have bought this book to learn about getting started, what you really need to do is learn how to *stay in* trading for the long haul. Otherwise, those first few trades may wipe you out before you know what happened.

That's why I hope you have taken the time to study the material presented in this book, so that you can build a foundation of psychology, risk management, and trade methodology. Take the time to prepare and practice. All this up-front work will pay off down the line.

So yes, open an account. Before you place a trade, analyze charts and look for patterns. Test some ideas for placing trades and then do the work to prove to yourself your method will make money. When you've done your testing, place 25 consecutive perfect demo trades. Then place another 25 consecutive perfect trades using the minimum lot size available. Then and only then should you move up to position sizing that places more risk on your trades. Building this foundation is an investment of time and attention that will place you in the most advantageous position you can be in for ongoing success as a trader.

I want to leave you with my 12 Powers of Successful Trading. I cover these powers in great detail in my day trading book, *Day Trading QuickStart Guide*, and I have touched on them all in some way, shape, or form at various points throughout this book. These 12 powers are all things that you can control and, when utilized, should lead to great success. Here they are all pulled together:

1. **The Power of Why**: Why are you trading? The only reason to trade is to make money. Remind yourself of that as often as you need to, so as not to stray and find yourself trading for other reasons. When your trading results are not what you want them to be, it will usually be due to trading for the wrong reason.

2. **The Power of the Tradeplan**: A proven tradeplan is the key to making money and building equity. It starts with fast-testing, to see if the strategy looks worthwhile; backtesting, which means

looking at past charts to see how the strategy would have worked in the past; and forward testing, which is watching how the strategy would work in real time as you move ahead. Once it is drawn up, with a specific way to trade and exact rules to follow, then you practice until you can execute it perfectly.

3. **The Power of Foundation**: A trader's foundation rests on psychology. You must build a foundation of belief in order to have confidence in your trading system. The only way to do this is to properly test your system until you have proven that it has a legitimate edge in the market. The preproduction work in trading is vital.

4. **The Power of Quitting**: We call it "poq" for short, and it's an integral part of any day trading plan. Poq is a dynamic goal-setting strategy that allows us to take what the market wants to give us (not what we want from the market), and once that occurs, our tradeplan has done its job and we can quit trading for that session. The basic poq plan is to hit our minimum target level, have a positive result, and then quit the session. There are different formulas, but they all accomplish the same goal of taking what the market wants to give us and then quitting our session with our profits in hand and our accounts worth more as a result.

5. **The Power of Numbers**: A trader will make money with a statistical edge. Once a tradeplan that offers an edge has been developed, following it will lead to profits. Trades will win and trades will lose, but the superior odds that our proven tradeplan gives us will let the odds do the heavy lifting as our account steadily grows: two steps forward, one step back, two steps forward, one step back, and so on.

6. **The Power of Compounding**: A small statistical edge can create significant wealth over time. Returns build on returns and create more trading capital. More capital means the trader can place larger trades, generating more cash. Compounding is an awesome power, so much so that Albert Einstein referred to it as the eighth wonder of the world. As we grow our account using our predefined money management strategy, our position size grows as well. The rate of growth increases exponentially until we reach our critical mass: our maximum position size.

7. **The Power of Mechanical Rules**: Mechanical rules keep us objective as traders. We prove our tradeplans based on a set of rules, and, once established, they become mechanical. They are not open for interpretation. They are objective and take all the guesswork out of trading. They include things like when to begin trading; exact entries, targets, and stops; and rules for managing the trade from start to finish. They can be tested and proven, which is essential to achieving and proving our edge and accomplishing our reason for trading. After they have been proven in backtests, the rules can be applied to trades going forward, and they ultimately become our tradeplans.

8. **The Power of Dynamic Setups**: A dynamic trading strategy is one that can adjust to changes in the market. It can "tune" itself in real time, bar after bar, as prices move and market conditions continually change. The trade sizes and targets will vary, based on the price action itself.

9. **The Power of Structure**: This is another way of saying the "Power of the Best Trading Tools," which include a great trading method that can print trades for you right on the chart, eliminating all guesswork and making it much easier to trade in general. A trade setup must have a specific entry and exit and rules to follow from start to finish, as we have learned with the other powers. When these trades are printed directly onto your price charts, it provides a visual structure that makes trading much easier.

10. **The Power of Surrender**: Drawdowns are inevitable. Not all trades are going to be winners. Accepting the certainty of losing trades will reduce your psychological pain. No one can control price action or market risk, but any trader can control the development and testing of their tradeplans. They can practice proper trade execution and risk management. This power teaches us to surrender to what we cannot control and instead focus all our energy on what we can control.

11. **The Power of Lifestyle**: The Backpack Trader philosophy that I mentioned in the introduction is about using trading to give you the kind of lifestyle you have always imagined for yourself and your family. Let that lifestyle guide your trading by trading within the lifestyle you want to lead. Less can be more, as we've seen with

the previous powers. Most of the work of trading happens when you're just starting out. As you develop your plan and practice your trading, the time commitment will decrease as your account grows. If you give your trading what it needs, then your trading will give you the kind of lifestyle you want to live.

12. **The Power of CEO**: As an independent trader, you own your own business—so run it like a business. Establish rules, manage your capital, and insist on operational excellence. Humans make terrible traders, as we have learned. Don't just be that guy or gal trying to trade. Instead, be the CEO of your trading business. That will help you make decisions from the proper point of view and, in turn, help you detach yourself emotionally from the outcome of any trade. And that will take you full circle, because in so doing, you put yourself in a position to achieve your objective, your *WHY*.

Trading has made my life possible. It has helped me design a lifestyle that fits me and my family. While I love the challenge of the market and the satisfaction of developing a new trading strategy or tradeplan, it is not why I trade. I trade for what trading gives me. I am gratified that I have been able to help so many other people learn how to make the benefits of trading work for them.

Develop your plan and test it. Practice your trades. Manage your risk. Over time, you will develop conviction, belief, and confidence in your system. You will master forex. I wish you much success.

REMEMBER TO DOWNLOAD
YOUR FREE DIGITAL ASSETS!

 **Ultimate Trade Analyzer**

 **Broker Evaluation Checklist**

 **Trade Chart Visualization Tool**

 **HTChop Histogram Indicator**

TWO WAYS TO ACCESS YOUR FREE DIGITAL ASSETS

Use the camera app on your mobile phone to scan the QR code
or visit the link below and instantly access your digital assets.

or

go.quickstartguides.com/forex

📱 SCAN ME　　**🖥 VISIT URL**

Appendix

A Guide to the Currencies and Pairs

CURRENCY SYMBOL KEY			
Symbol	**Currency**	**Symbol**	**Currency**
AUD	Australian dollar	**MXN**	Mexican peso
CAD	Canadian dollar	**NOK**	Norwegian krone
CHF	Swiss franc	**NZD**	New Zealand dollar
CZK	Czech koruna	**PLN**	Polish zloty
DKK	Danish krone	**SEK**	Swedish krona
EUR	European Union euro	**SGD**	Singapore dollar
GBP	Great British pound	**TRY**	Turkish lira
HUF	Hungarian forint	**THB**	Thai baht
HKD	Hong Kong dollar	**USD**	US dollar
JPY	Japanese yen	**ZAR**	South African rand

fig. 120

PAIRS	
MAJOR PAIRS	**MINOR PAIRS**
EUR/USD	EUR/AUD
USD/JPY	EUR/GBP
GBP/USD	EUR/JPY
USD/CHF	GBP/AUD
USD/CAD	GBP/CAD
AUD/USD	JPY/AUD
NZD/USD	JPY/CHF
	JPY/NZD

fig. 121

PAIRS

EXOTIC PAIRS

AUD/CAD	EUR/CZK	GBP/SGD	USD/DKK
AUD/CHF	EUR/DKK	GBP/ZAR	USD/HKD
AUD/HKD	EUR/HKD		USD/HUF
AUD/JPY	EUR/HUF	HKD/JPY	USD/MXN
AUD/NZD	EUR/NOK		USD/NOK
AUD/SGD	EUR/NZD	NZD/CAD	USD/PLN
	EUR/PLN	NZD/CHF	USD/SEK
CAD/CHF	EUR/SEK	NZD/HKD	USD/SGD
CAD/HKD	EUR/SGD	NZD/SGD	USD/THB
CAD/JPY	EUR/TRY		USD/TRY
CAD/SGD	EUR/ZAR	SGD/CHF	USD/ZAR
		SGD/HKD	
CHF/HKD	GBP/AUD	SGD/JPY	ZAR/JPY
CHF/ZAR	GBP/CHF		
	GBP/HKD	TRY/JPY	
EUR/AUD	GBP/JPY		
EUR/CAD	GBP/NZD	USD/CNH	
EUR/CHF	GBP/PLN	USD/CZK	

About the Author

TROY NOONAN

Troy Noonan is the author of the best-selling *Day Trading QuickStart Guide*, full-time professional day trader, trade system developer, and trading coach with decades of experience in the study of markets and their behavior. The original Backpack Trader, Noonan cut his teeth executing trades in internet cafés while backpacking through Europe and traveling in South America in the late nineties. Using the freedom that trading provides, he continues to travel the globe and execute trades from the road.

As a teacher and mentor, Noonan has helped thousands of students in more than one hundred countries take the plunge and find day trading success on their own terms. He has single-handedly developed and refined numerous effective trading strategies, including the wildly popular Counter Punch Trader and Spotlight Master Suite methods, to name a couple of his most recent.

His signature strategies are simple, accessible, and highly effective for new and veteran traders alike. The durable and robust nature of Noonan's creations has been tested and proven time and time again—they are just as effective today as the day they were released.

With a professional trading career that spans decades, Noonan has extensive experience in successfully applying and teaching others the art and science of forex, futures, options contracts, and day trading.

About QuickStart Guides

QuickStart Guides are books for beginners, written by experts.

QuickStart Guides® are comprehensive learning companions tailored for the beginner experience. Our books are written by experts, subject matter authorities, and thought leaders within their respective areas of study.

For nearly a decade more than 850,000 readers have trusted QuickStart Guides® to help them get a handle on their finances, start their own business, invest in the stock market, find a new hobby, get a new job—the list is virtually endless.

The QuickStart Guides® series of books is published by ClydeBank Media, an independent publisher based in Albany, NY.

Connect with QuickStart Guides online at www.quickstartguides.com or follow us on Facebook, Instagram, and LinkedIn.

Follow us @quickstartguides

Glossary

52-week range
The highest and lowest prices over a period of 52 weeks (one year).

A-book broker
Also called *dealing desk broker* or *market maker*, the intermediary between customers and the interbank market.

Ask
The price at which a broker sells currency to a trader.

Auction market
Market in which buyers and sellers determine the highest price to pay/lowest price to accept.

Baby pip
Smallest unit of measurement used to show the change in value between two currencies. Also called *pipette* or *tick*.

Backtesting
A process by which traders test a strategy by using past market prices to see how the strategy would have performed.

Balance of payments
The system of accounting used for international transactions.

Bank for International Settlements
Global organization owned by 62 of the world's central banks; manages the clearing of transactions on a global level to simplify international trade.

B-book broker
Broker that takes the other side of its clients' orders. Also called *no dealing desk broker*.

Bid
The price that a broker pays to buy an asset.

Bid-ask spread
The difference between the bid price and the ask price on a price quote. The broker buys at the bid price and sells at the ask, so the difference is equal to the dealer's profit on a sale. The wider the spread, the harder it is to make a profitable trade.

Blockchain
A system used to record transactions made in cryptocurrencies through a digital key that is shared among computers linked together in a peer-to-peer network.

Bond market
A marketplace on which investors can buy debt securities.

Bracket order
A special type of trade order where the entry is "bracketed" between a target and a stop.

Broad-based index
An index that represents the performance of the entire market.

Broker
An agent that brings buyers and sellers together and makes a profit for doing so.

Call option
A contract with an expiration date that gives someone the right to buy an asset on a date sometime in the future at a price determined now.

Capital
Money or assets available for trading.

Capital account
Part of the balance of payments, recording transfers of capital such as patents, trademarks, and funds that migrants send back home.

Central bank
Government agency that supports a nation's financial system, such as the US Federal Reserve or the Bank of Japan.

Collectibles market
Market for things like antiques, stamps, jewelry, coins, etc.

Commission
A small percentage of the price of a sale, given to a broker for arranging the sale.

Commodities
Basic tangible assets such as agricultural products, metals, oil, gold, beef, etc.

Commodities market
Marketplace where commodities are traded.

Commodity Futures Trading Commission
Organization that oversees trading in agricultural and financial contracts in the United States.

Common stock
Type of stock that gives the owner a share in the profits and the right to vote on matters of corporate policy of a publicly traded company.

Consolidation
When price action fails to break in one direction or another, but instead remains "sideways," choppy, or stagnant.

Counterparty
The entity that takes the other side of a trade.

Cryptocurrency
Digital currency earned by solving a series of computer problems, and whose ownership is tracked through a decentralized system using a cryptographic key.

Currency
A measure of value. Must be universally accepted, not change value quickly, and be reasonably scarce.

Currency strength meters
Analytics that show which currencies are tending to be stronger and which are tending to be weaker.

Current account
Part of the balance of payments that shows imports and exports of goods and services.

Day trading
Trading method that involves placing short-term trades, watching the market in real time, and closing out all trades by the end of the day.

Day's open
Price of an asset at the opening of the market.

Day's range
Highest and lowest prices of an asset over one day.

Dealer
Legally different from a broker; buys and sells securities for their own account.

Dealing desk broker
Intermediary between customers and the interbank market. Also called *market maker* or *A-book broker*.

Debt securities
Securities that represent borrowed funds that must be repaid.

Deflation
A steady decrease in price levels.

Demo account
Also known as a *simulated* (sim) trading account. Used to build experience with trading strategies and platforms.

Derivative
Financial asset whose value is derived from the performance of some other entity. Options, futures, and warrants are examples of derivatives.

Derivatives market
Market on which derivatives are traded.

Dirty float
Government intervention in the market by nudging the exchange rate to support particular economic policies. Also called *managed float*.

Dividend
A payment made by a company on a regular basis to owners of its stock.

Dollarization
The process of a country abandoning its currency in favor of the US dollar.

Downtrend
Market trend with lower highs and lower lows.

Drawdown
A loss that reduces one's amount of trading capital.

Efficient market hypothesis
Also called the *efficient market theory*, purports that assets bought and sold on exchanges always trade at their fair value.

Electronic communication network (ECN)
Trading network that completes securities transactions outside of traditional exchanges.

Exchange-traded funds
Also called ETFs, collections of stocks and bonds that trade as a single share. Exchange-traded notes are related securities.

Exchange-traded note
A debt security issued by a financial institution.

Exotic pairs
Free-floating developing nation currencies that tend to have wider spreads and are traded less often than major pairs.

Extrinsic value
Value that comes from the eye of the beholder, such as the artistic merit of a picture or the condition of a coin.

Federal Deposit Insurance Corporation
A government entity that provides insurance to depositors in US banks.

Federal discount rate
The rate charged by the Federal Reserve Bank for overnight loans to banks.

Federal funds rate
Banks with balances over the required amount can deposit the extra money with the central bank to earn interest; the Fed funds rate is the rate paid by the central bank.

Fiat currency
Currency not backed by anything of value yet perceived to have value by its government and its users.

Financial market
Any type of marketplace at which buyers and sellers can exchange assets, such as stocks, bonds, currencies, equities, and derivatives.

Fixed exchange rate
Also called a pegged exchange rate, currency that is legally defined in terms of another currency.

Floating rate system
System in which the value of a currency is determined via supply and demand (the free market) instead of being tied to an underlying asset or set by the government.

Foreign exchange
Also known as *forex*. The process by which people trade one currency for another.

Forex market
A global market for the trading of currencies from different countries.

Forward contract
Contract that locks in a future price on an asset. Unlike futures contracts, forward contracts are negotiated.

Forward testing
Reviewing and tracking the ongoing results of your trades.

Fundamental analysis
The process of researching markets and economies to form a long-range forecast and determine an asset's intrinsic value.

Futures contract
Contract that comes with the obligation to buy or sell an asset in the future at a price agreed upon today.

Gold standard
System in which a country's currency was redeemable for a fixed quantity of gold.

Hyperinflation
A steady and dramatic increase in price levels, usually considered to be an inflation rate higher than 20%.

Indicators
Calculations, based on price and volume activity that are used alongside or overlayed on top of price charts, that can give traders powerful signals about when to buy and sell currency pairs.

Industry index
Index that concentrates on one segment of the stock market, such as technology stocks.

Inflation rate
The rate by which price levels are increasing.

International Monetary Fund
Organization created to manage the world's monetary system; provides loans to nations that need help managing their balance of payments.

Intrinsic value
The value of the materials that make up an object, like the metals that make up a coin.

Investment account
Part of the balance of payments that includes investments in stocks, bonds, and real estate by private investors, corporations, and governments.

Key level
A technical level indicating probable support or resistance, often attributed simply to a round number that should be cleared (overtaken) by the price action prior to one's entering or exiting a trade.

Know Your Customer
Screening process done by brokers before a new account is opened to ensure that someone is who they say they are.

Lagging indicator
Indicator confirming that a change in trend is taking place. It shows how past decisions are playing out in the current markets.

Law of supply and demand
Economic theory asserting that when prices increase, the quantity demanded will decrease.

Leading indicator
Indicator offering predictive information and signaling that a change in price trends will soon occur.

Lending investment
Type of investment in which one lends money with the understanding that they will get back the principal, along with interest, in a specified period of time.

Leverage
Investment strategy in which one uses borrowed money to increase the potential return of an investment, allowing them to trade a large position with a small amount of trading capital.

Liquidity
The ease with which an asset can be bought or sold in the market at a price that reflects its real value.

Long
Buying ("going long") or owning an asset.

Long-term trading
Trading strategy that focuses on trends in the long term. This is closer to investing than to trading.

Major pairs
Currency pairs that involve the largest economies with free-floating currencies, such as the US dollar and the Japanese yen.

Managed float
Market intervention by central banks of countries with free-floating currencies, to manage the exchange rate. Also called a *dirty float*.

Margin
Also called *margin requirement*. Minimum amount of money that must be in a trader's account when using leverage.

Market maker
Financial institution that commits to creating order activity in certain securities or currency pairs.

Market price
Most recent price at which a good or service can be bought or sold.

Minor pairs
Major non-US dollar currencies whose values are compared with one another or with the free-floating currency of smaller developed nations, such as Canada or Australia.

Mobilization of funds
The process of money getting to where it needs to be so that the economy can function.

Momentum
An acceleration in the rate of a price increase of a currency pair.

Money market
Lending and borrowing of cash and very short-term investments, particularly for corporate finance.

Money market account
An account similar to a bank savings account. The money is invested in money market securities and may or may not have federal insurance.

Money market funds
Mutual funds that are invested in money market securities and treasury bills.

Mortgage-backed securities
Securities in which mortgages are pooled together and investors buy a share of the pool, receiving a portion of the principal and interest in the pool until all mortgages are either paid off or defaulted on.

Moving average
Average of prices over a rolling time period, such as 5 days, 10 days, or 20 days.

National Credit Union Administration (NCUA)
An agency that insures accounts based in credit unions. A counterpart to the FDIC.

National Futures Association
Self-regulatory organization for derivatives exchanges.

Net asset value
Value of a fund when its liabilities are deducted from its assets.

No dealing desk broker
Also called *B-book broker*. Broker who works with several interbank traders to collect the best prices on the market, giving traders the best rates on the market.

Nominal rate of interest
The actual rate of interest quoted on loans and bonds. Unlike the "real interest rate," the nominal rate does not take inflation into account.

Numeraire
The essential unit of value by which prices in a market may be measured. In the global commodity market, for example, the US dollar often serves as the numeraire currency.

Option
Derivative that gives someone the right (but not the obligation) to buy or sell an asset in the future at a price determined today.

Over-the-counter market
Market made up of banks and trading companies rather than organized exchanges.

Pegged exchange rate
See *fixed exchange rate*.

Pip
Unit of measurement used to show the change in value between two currencies, generally a thousandth of a percent (.0001).

Pipette
Also called *baby pip* or *tick*; the smallest increment of change that can be recorded in currencies that are frequently traded.

Position trading
Trading strategy in which one's trades are held anywhere from five days to one month.

Preferred stock
Type of stock that pays owners a fixed dividend.

Previous close
The price of a currency pair at the end of the last (most recent) price bar.

Price chart
Chart that lets someone trace the price of an asset over time.

Primary market
The first time a security comes to be sold, such as through an initial public offering of common stock by a corporation.

Put option
An option that gives one the right (but not the obligation) to sell an asset in the future at a price agreed upon today.

Range-bound
Also called *sidewise*, markets with no clear uptrend or downtrend.

Real estate investment trust
A traded investment company that owns different types of real estate.

Real rate of interest
An interest rate that has been adjusted to remove the effects of inflation.

Reserve requirement
The percentage of total customer account balances that a bank is required to keep in cash in their vault.

Resistance
Price level at which an asset looks expensive, so sellers are willing to get out while the price is high.

Retail foreign exchange dealer
Firm that handles currency trading outside of business contracts as well as options and futures on currencies.

Reversal
Significant and lasting change in a trend.

Scalping
Trading strategy that involves fast, repeated buying and selling of currency pairs throughout the day.

Secondary market
Market where trading takes place after a primary transaction.

Short
Sale of an asset that one doesn't own, betting that the price will drop.

Sidewise
Also called *range-bound*, a market with no clear uptrend or downtrend.

Slippage
Instances where all a market trader receives a lower trade execution price than intended.

Sovereign issuer
Term used by bond rating agencies to refer to governments.

Specie
Money in the form of metal coins, especially gold and silver.

Spot market
The market to buy or sell financial instruments or commodities right now, in contrast to a futures market in which delivery is due at a later date.

Spot price
Price quoted in the market at a given moment.

Spread
The difference between the bid and ask prices of an asset. It is the dealer's profit.

Spread-beating
A process in which European traders bet on price changes in Forex.

Standard deviation
A measure of how much any one item in a series is likely to deviate from the mean.

Stock
A share of a publicly held company.

Stock exchange
An entity that hosts markets within which stocks and other securities can be traded.

Stock market
A group of organized markets and exchanges where traders buy and sell stock.

Stock market index
A measure used to determine the performance of a stock market on any given day.

Stock portfolio
A collection of stocks owned by a single entity.

Stop loss
Also called a *stop*, an order to a broker to close out a position automatically when it hits a specified price.

Straight-through processing
A method by which B-book brokers place trades to get them worked quickly.

Support
The price level where buyers recognize that a pair of currencies is a good value, causing them to step into the market and begin buying.

Swap
A trade that allows one party to change the form of a payment due.

Swing high
A bar that has a higher high than the bar to its left and the bar to its right.

Swing low
A bar that has a lower low than the bar to its left and the bar to its right.

Swing trading
A trading strategy that requires holding positions longer than in day trading or scalping, usually a few days.

Technical analysis
The act of studying patterns of supply and demand that show up in price trends to make forecasts of short-term directional moves.

Tick
See *pipette*.

Trading on margin
Trading using leverage (borrowing).

Trading platform
An electronic system that allows individuals to participate in the market.

Treasury bill
Also called a T-bill, a short-term money market instrument issued by a central bank.

Uptrend
A trend characterized by higher highs and higher lows.

Volatility
How much the price of an asset changes in a given period of time.

Whale
Trader lingo used to refer to the largest participants in a market.

World Bank
An entity that provides economic development assistance and loans to help countries expand their infrastructure and create more opportunities for economic activity.

Zero-sum game

An activity that has a loser for every winner.

References

INTRODUCTION

Beattie, Andrew. 2020. "How Did George Soros Break the Bank of England?" March 20. https://www.investopedia.com/ask/answers/08/george-soros-bank-of-england.asp.

CHAPTER 1

Ambrose, Jillian. 2020. "Oil prices dip below zero as producers forced to pay to dispose of excess." *The Guardian*. April 20. https://www.theguardian.com/world/2020/apr/20/oil-prices-sink-to-20-year-low-as-un-sounds-alarm-on-to-covid-19-relief-fund.

Bank for International Settlements. n.d. https://www.bis.org/statistics/rpfx19_fx.htm.

Chen, James. 2020. "Money Market." *Investopedia*. May 31. https://www.investopedia.com/terms/m/moneymarket.asp#:~:text=The%20money%20market%20refers%20to,accounts%20opened%20by%20bank%20customers.

DeCambre, Mark, and Sunny Oh. 2020. *MarketWatch*. June 1. Accessed June 1, 2020. https://www.marketwatch.com/story/stock-market-futures-knocked-around-as-us-cities-rocked-by-protests-amid-pandemic-2020-06-01

Maverick, J. B. 2020. "How Big Is the Derivatives Market?" *Investopedia*. April 28. https://www.investopedia.com/ask/answers/052715/how-big-derivatives-market.asp.

Jones, Charles M., and Sirri, Erik R. 2010. "Examining the Main Street Benefits of Our Modern Financial Markets."PDF. *CenterforCapitalMarkets.com*. March 12. https://www.centerforcapitalmarkets.com/wp-content/uploads/2018/03/Center-for-Capital-Markets-Competitiveness-Examining-the-Main-Street-Benefits-of-our-Modern-Financial-Markets.pdf.

CHAPTER 2

n.d. https://www.bitcoin.com/get-started/.

n.d. https://www.imf.org/en/About.

n.d. https://www.worldbank.org/en/about/history.

Soros, George. 1995. *Soros on Soros: Staying Ahead of the Curve*. Hoboken: Wiley.

CHAPTER 12

Lindsay, Charles. 1991. *Trident: A Trading Strategy*. Brightwaters: Windsor Books.

CHAPTER 13

Tharp, Van. 2006. *Trade Your Way to Financial Freedom*. New York: McGraw-Hill Education.

Index

WHAT DID YOU THINK?

We rely on reviews and reader feedback to help our authors reach more people, improve our books, and grow our business. We would really appreciate it if you took the time to help us out by providing feedback on your recent purchase.

It's really easy, it only takes a second, and it's a tremendous help!

—— NOT SURE WHAT TO SHARE? ——
Here are some ideas to get your review started…

- *What did you learn?*
- *Have you been able to put anything you learned into action?*
- *Would you recommend the book to other readers?*
- *Is the author clear and easy to understand?*

TWO WAYS TO LEAVE AN AMAZON REVIEW

Use the camera app on your mobile phone to scan the QR code or visit the link below to record your testimonial and get your free book.

or

www.quickstartguides.review/forex

SCAN ME   VISIT URL

GET YOUR NEXT
QuickStart Guide®
FOR FREE

Leave us a quick video testimonial on our website and we will give you a **FREE *QuickStart Guide*** of your choice!

RECORD TESTIMONIAL   **SUBMIT TO OUR WEBSITE**   **GET A FREE BOOK**

SAVE 10% ON YOUR NEXT
QuickStart Guide®

USE CODE: QSG10

www.quickstartguides.shop/real-estate

www.quickstartguides.shop/trading

www.quickstartguides.shop/investing

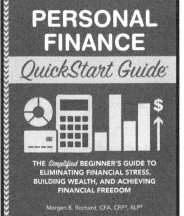

www.quickstartguides.shop/finance

Use the camera app on your mobile phone to scan the QR code or visit the link below the cover to shop.
Get 10% off your entire order when you use code 'QSG10' at checkout at www.clydebankmedia.com

LISTEN TO *QuickStart Guides* ON THE GO

NEW AUDIBLE MEMBERS GET THEIR FIRST AUDIOBOOK

FREE!

DIGITAL MARKETING *QuickStart Guide*

FOREX TRADING *QuickStart Guide*

FLIPPING HOUSES *QuickStart Guide*

REAL ESTATE INVESTING *QuickStart Guide*

INVESTING *QuickStart Guide*

TWO WAYS TO SELECT A FREE AUDIOBOOK

Use the camera app on your mobile phone to scan the QR code or visit the link below to select your free audiobook from Audible.

📱 **SCAN ME** or www.quickstartguides.com/free-audiobook 🖥 **VISIT URL**

Terms: Your free Audible membership will rebill at up to $14.99 after the end of the 30-day trial period and is subject to Audible's terms and conditions. There are no commitments, and you can cancel your Audible membership at any time, including before the end of the trial period. Free monthly credits can be redeemed for audiobooks from the Audible catalog and are yours to keep. This promotion is provided by Audible and is restricted to US and UK customers only. ClydeBank Media QuickStart Guides are not affiliated with Audible. Any devices depicted on this page are for illustrative purposes only and are not included in this promotion. ClydeBank Media QuickStart Guides may receive affiliate compensation should you choose to start a paid Audible membership using any of the links we provide.

CLYDEBANK MEDIA

QuickStart Guides®

PROUDLY SUPPORT ONE TREE PLANTED

One Tree Planted is a 501(c)(3) nonprofit organization focused on global reforestation, with millions of trees planted every year. ClydeBank Media is proud to support One Tree Planted as a reforestation partner.

Every dollar donated plants one tree and every tree makes a difference!

Learn more at www.clydebankmedia.com/charitable-giving or make a contribution at onetreeplanted.org.

Made in the USA
Las Vegas, NV
10 September 2023

77363588R00188